James Samuelson

Bulgaria Past and Present

Historical, Political, and Descriptive

James Samuelson

Bulgaria Past and Present
Historical, Political, and Descriptive

ISBN/EAN: 9783337080457

Printed in Europe, USA, Canada, Australia, Japan

Cover: Foto ©ninafisch / pixelio.de

More available books at **www.hansebooks.com**

BULGARIA

PAST AND PRESENT

Historical, Political, and Descriptive

BY

JAMES SAMUELSON

Of the Middle Temple, Barrister-at-Law
AUTHOR OF "ROUMANIA PAST AND PRESENT," ETC.

ILLUSTRATED WITH A MAP OF UNITED BULGARIA,
COLLOTYPE VIEWS AND PORTRAITS FROM SEVENTEEN PHOTOGRAPHS BY
KARASTOJANOFF OF SOFIA, CAVRA OF PHILIPPOPOLIS,
AND O. MARCOLESCO OF TIRNOVA,

And Numerous Woodcuts and Vignettes Engraved from
Original Sketches by the Author

Post Tenebras Lux

LONDON
TRÜBNER & CO., LUDGATE HILL
1888

[All rights reserved]

VOLUNTEERS IN THE SERVIAN WAR

PREFACE.

THIS treatise is intended as a companion and complementary to my former work on Roumania. Whilst, however, very little has been written in our language on that country, the reader will find in one of the Appendices attached hereto a list which includes no less than twenty-four original and translated works on Bulgaria in English alone. He may be disposed to ask, then, on what grounds I have added another to the number; and whilst such an inquiry would be quite pertinent, and I shall no doubt feel the consequences should my treatise be found to contain nothing new worth recording, it must be admitted that the employment of so many pens affords at least a convincing proof of the absorbing interest of the subject.

Many of the works which I have catalogued have, however, been quite fugitive; some purely controversial, and others so completely partisan as to be robbed of much of their value for purposes of information. It has been my endeavour to put the reader in possession of a few of the most important historical events in Bulgaria from the earliest period, and by means of illustrations as much as by verbal description to enable him to judge of its condition at the present time. If he wishes to study the past history and the present state of the country in greater detail, I would recommend him (without prejudice to any of the other valuable works on the subject) to read Jireček's "Geschichte der Bulgaren," warning him, however, that in the history of this country, as in that of Roumania, dates, genealogies, and precise historical names must not be accepted with implicit confidence. He will also find in Krek's learned treatise, referred to in the text, a valuable guide to the knowledge of Sclavonic customs and literature. Following upon these works, he may have in those of Von Huhn (translated into English) interesting details of recent events in Bulgaria; whilst Holland's " European Concert on the Eastern Question" will place him in possession of the text of every treaty bearing upon the subject under consideration. And, finally, if he have the patience to wade through a voluminous blue-book, the dispatches of our representatives at foreign courts relating to Bulgaria and Eastern Roumelia (in "Turkey, No. 1, 1887") will give him much original matter for reflection upon the events which occurred in the Balkan Peninsula during the year 1886, a year that was fraught with danger to the liberties of Bulgaria. As regards the geographical and social state of North Bulgaria, there are many useful and interesting works extant; but if the reader desires to traverse every mountain-pass and to study every important locality in that part of the country, to learn how many huts each little hamlet contains, and what is or was the nationality of its occupants, if he would delight his eyes with numerous xylographic illustrations of places and recent events, and, above all, if he desires to preserve a somewhat idealistic in preference to a realistic remembrance of the interesting country, I would recommend for his perusal Kanitz's well-known work, " Donau-Bulgarien und der Balkan."

So far as my own sketch of Bulgarian history is concerned, I have laboured under some disadvantage in having already written that of Roumania; for at various periods the two histories overlap one another, and I have hesitated to repeat here what has already been said elsewhere. The reader will, therefore, I hope, not attribute to egotism occasional references to my earlier work. Whether he will be disposed to deal so leniently with other instances in which my own personality has been obtruded into these pages, I greatly question; but even for those trespasses on my part there is some justification. Some of my generous critics expressed disappointment that I should not have communicated more freely my own views and experiences in Roumania; and in seeking to remedy what they considered a defect, I shall probably have laid myself open to the charge of egotism—it may be of levity. It was said, too, by the same authorities, that I had been blind to the faults of the Roumanians; that my book contained nothing but praise, and no blame. Well, I have endeavoured to remedy that defect also in the present volume, and I hope that, in seeking to avoid Scylla, I may not be engulphed by Charybdis! However much I may have rallied the Bulgarians, good-naturedly, I trust, upon some of their weaknesses, I have not forgotten, nor must the reader forget, that their national imperfections are largely due to the fact that they have but recently begun to breathe the atmosphere of freedom; that Mussulman rule weighed upon the country for centuries like a nightmare, and that when the Russians tendered them their liberty with one hand, with the other they dealt out humiliation and corruption.

In my former work I spoke of the folly of prophesying on the Eastern Question; and although I have not attempted here to predict what will be the combination revealed by the next turn of the political kaleidoscope, I have considered it safe and consistent with the objects of the present treatise to scan cursorily the present aspect of the question, and to afford such of my readers as are precluded by their occupations from making it a special study some assistance in following the future course of events in the East. As regards our own policy, I have nothing to add to what I have already said elsewhere, and repeat in the present chapter on the subject. If it be considered undesirable that the Turk should remain in Europe (and I do not by any means assert that to be the case), surely no person who has studied history, or who knows anything about the present condition of Russia, will venture to affirm that his place should be filled by the Muscovite!

Whether the rampart of freedom in South-Eastern Europe is to be a Danubian Confederation, or a Garibaldi or a Bismarck is to arise and unite the scattered and incoherent territories as they now exist there, or, finally, whether each individual State is to grow in strength and influence as a counterpoise to the overbearing military empires of our Continent, no one can prognosticate; and yet our course is, under any circumstances, sufficiently plain. That should not be guided by selfishness nor by timidity (I will not use a stronger expression), nor should it be governed by considerations of expediency alone; but in the future, as in the past, our policy should be to further the cause of justice, of liberty, and of civilisation.

JAMES SAMUELSON.

CLAUGHTON, BIRKENHEAD,
December 6 1887.

NOTE TO PREFACE.

WHILST the following pages have been passing through the Press, I have had the advantage of reading the work just published on "The Present Position of European Politics," by the author of "Greater Britain," and its important bearing upon the subjects here treated must serve as my excuse for making a very brief reference to some of the views of the talented statesman from whose pen it emanates, with which I am not in complete agreement. As to Russia, he seems to me greatly to over-estimate the power of numbers. Hitherto she has fought on her own soil; or with an unbroken line of communication in friendly states supported by the population; or against poorly-equipped Turkoman hordes. And yet in the Crimea, fighting in her own territory and in her own defence, her numbers availed her little. More recently, at Plevna, although she took the credit of the final victory, it was the Roumanians who made the breach and held the fort, whilst time after time her vast masses of troops served only to fill the trenches with tens of thousands of her slain, and to satiate the thirst for blood of her Skobeleffs! As regards Roumania, the author rates her, in such a short war as he believes wars will be in future, as the sixth military power in Europe (p. 208), placing this country below her in the scale. Here too I think his estimate ranks her too highly, and I hope his undoubtedly authoritative opinion may not inspire the Roumanians with too great confidence. At the same time I am rejoiced to find the reasons given in my last chapter, "Why Russia does not occupy Bulgaria," receiving such valuable support; and if the recent semi-official utterances of Russia are worth anything, the cause of her present "moderation" is not far to seek. My further views, which must be taken for what they are worth, will be found in the last chapter. As to the work above referred to, I should like to add that, although recent events on the Continent must necessarily modify some of the author's conclusions, I think that in throwing over the traditions of diplomacy and giving the world the benefit of his experience in foreign affairs, he has rendered great service to his country (and to others also if they would but see their true interests), and he has produced the most valuable contribution to contemporary history that has yet appeared.

January 2, 1888.

CONTENTS.

PART I.
HISTORICAL.

CHAPTER		PAGE
I.	A Brief Preliminary Survey of Bulgarian History	3
II.	The Slaves or Sclavonians	14
III.	The Bulgari and their Early Rule	22
IV.	The Two Bulgarian Empires	34
V.	John Asen II. (1218-1241) and his Times—The Fall of the Second Empire	47
VI.	The Turkish Rule in Bulgaria	54
VII.	The Liberation of Bulgaria	65
VIII.	Alexander, the First Prince of Bulgaria—The Union, and the Servian War	75
IX.	The Abduction and Retirement of Prince Alexander—The Regency—Prince Ferdinand—Conclusion of Part I.	91

PART II.
BULGARIA, TO-DAY.

X.	Geographical and Physical	111
XI.	Bulgarian Cities—Sofia, the Capital—National and Official Life	116
XII.	Sofia—Social and Economical Matters—A Political Meeting—The Press	129

CHAPTER		PAGE
XIII.	Travelling in Bulgaria—Philippopolis	136
XIV.	An Excursion to the Monastery of St. Kyriak	149
XV.	The Rose-Fields of Kezanlik—Over the Shipka Pass—Gabrovo and its Gymnasium	155
XVI.	From Gabrovo to Tirnova—Land-Customs and Agriculture	165
XVII.	Tirnova and its Antiquities	172
XVIII.	Tirnova—Innkeeper's Politics—To Rustchuk—Farewell, Bulgaria!	183
XIX.	Bulgarian Trade—Agricultural Resources—Game and the Chase	188
XX.	The Budget and the National Services	198
XXI.	The Two Princes, Ferdinand and Alexander	202
XXII.	The Eastern Question and Bulgaria	210

APPENDICES.

APPENDIX		
I.	Estimated Budget of United Bulgaria for 1887	225
II.	The Most Important Decrees of the Constitution of Bulgaria	226
III.	Bibliography of Bulgaria	227
IV.	Abstract from Consular Report No. 237, just issued, from Mr. O'Connor (Mr. Harding), Sofia	230
	INDEX	235

LIST OF ILLUSTRATIONS

COLLOTYPE PLATES.

Macedonian Volunteers in the Servian War	*Frontispiece*
Alexander, the First Prince of Bulgaria	*To face page* 76
The Russian Agency, Sofia, with British Agency on the Right	103
The New Part of Sofia, showing Palace	117
Mutkouroff, Stambouloff, Natchevitch, Stoiloff	,, 125
Karaveloff, Zivkoff, Radoslavoff, Gavril Pasha	,, 127
View of Jambasz-Tepé, and of Boys' Lycée, Church of St. Alexander, River Maritza and Bridge, Philippopolis	142
Old Gate in Philippopolis	144
The New Palace, Sofia	,, 203
Prince Ferdinand	,, 206

WOODCUTS IN TEXT.

	PAGE
Baldwin's Tower, Tirnova (*vignette*)	34
The Black Mosque Prison in Sofia	119
Bulgarian Billiards	131
Ruins of Turkish Etape, or Resting-Place for Troops, at Novichan	141
The Monastery of St. Kyriak, near Philippopolis, from the ascending Road	150
Russian Memorial Obelisk on the Shipka Summit	158

	PAGE
The First Glimpse of Tirnova (*vignette*)	172
Part of Tirnova, from the Promenade	173
The Rocher-Coupé, or Cleft Rock, and Bridge at Tirnova	176
Diagram showing respective Positions of Hissar and Trapezitz	178
Roman Column, with Inscription of John Asen II., in the Church of the Forty Martyrs, Tirnova	179
Copper Doors of the Metropolitan Church, Tirnova	180
Discs and Crosses in the Arches of the Church of St. Demeter, Tirnova	182

Map of United Bulgaria *To face page* 111

PART I.
HISTORICAL.

CHAPTER I.

A BRIEF PRELIMINARY SURVEY OF BULGARIAN HISTORY.

The Greeks and Romans in the Balkan Peninsula—The Barbarians—The Sclavonians or Slaves—The Bulgari and the First Bulgarian Empire—The Northmen or Russians—The Byzantine conquest—The Asen rising and the Second or Wallacho-Bulgarian Empire—The Servian conquest of Bulgaria—The Turkish occupation—Bulgaria after the Crimean War—"The Bulgarian Atrocities"—The Russo-Turkish war of liberation—The Treaty of Berlin—Alexander, the first Prince of Bulgaria—Aleko Pasha, Governor of Eastern Roumelia—The union of Bulgaria and Eastern Roumelia under Prince Alexander—Russian intrigues in Bulgaria—The withdrawal of Russian officers—The Servian invasion—Temporary successes—Defeat at Slivnitza—Servian evacuation—Pursuit by Prince Alexander—Treaty of peace—Further Russian intrigues in Bulgaria—Abduction of Prince Alexander to Reni, in Russian Bessarabia—His release from captivity—Return to Sofia and abdication—The Regency—Continued Russian intrigues—Election of Prince Ferdinand—His position—Explanatory paragraph—Conclusion.

THE earliest ages of that part of the Balkan Peninsula which is now known as Bulgaria are buried in obscurity. Before the time of Philip of Macedon both sides of the Balkans (Hæmus of the Romans) were peopled by a number of savage tribes of Thraco-Illyrian race, and the name of *Thrace* was generally applied to the whole district from the Danube to the frontier of Macedonia. Philip and his successor, Alexander, brought those tribes under subjection, and incorporated the country with their possessions. It is not known at what particular time the Romans began their conquests in Thrace, but the country was definitively annexed by Vespasian, and about A.D. 75 it became a Roman province. The district north of the Balkans was called *Mœsia*, and long before the Romans crossed the Danube they had founded colonies on the southern bank of that river, which were periodically attacked and ravaged by the Dacians of the northern bank.

The conquest of Dacia by Trajan [1] (A.D. 106) was followed by its evacuation by Aurelian about 270 to 275 A.D., and the tract north of the Balkans and south of the Danube then received the name of *Dacia Aureliani*. For some time first the Roman and then the Greek rule prevailed in Dacia Aureliani, the chief Roman colonies on the Danube being Œscus at the mouth of the Isker, Novae (Sistova), Nicopolis, &c.; and down to the present day numerous remains (some of which will be referred to later on) are to be found either *in situ* or removed by the Bulgarian Czars to other parts of the country. Constantine the Great included Dacia Aureliani in the subdivision of his empire into provinces; but in his time already (about A.D. 328) the tide of Eastern barbarism was sweeping along the plains on both banks of the Danube. The Goths under Hermanrich were actually in possession; but Constantine overran their territory, which he succeeded for a time in holding. The Goths were driven out by the Huns, and other tribes followed, including one who had already for centuries before the Christian era been moving slowly westward from their original Asiatic habitat, namely, the *Sclavonians* or *Slaves*. This tribe is said to have gradually settled itself in the country now known as North Bulgaria between the third and seventh century A.D., and from thence it carried its nationality, its customs, and its language over a considerable part of South-Eastern and Eastern Europe. Their descendants, influenced by, and commingled with the subsequent dominant races of the Balkan Peninsula, constitute the present population of Bulgaria as well as of some of the neighbouring States, and from their advent and settlement begins the interesting phase of Bulgarian history.

Amongst those dominant races, the earliest were the *Bulgari*, a horde of Asiatics, of Turkish strain,[2] who about the third half of the seventh century overran the country, and subjected it to their rule; but whilst they gave it their name in permanence, their identity as a race was completely absorbed in the Slavonic

---

[1] "Roumania," Part II. cap. ix. Philip, Son & Nephew, London and Liverpool.
[2] *Türkischem Blute entsprossenen Bulgaren.* Krek, *Einleitung in die Slavische Literaturgeschichte*, p. 395. Graz: Leuschner & Lubensky, 1887.

population. They founded the "*first Bulgarian Empire*," which attained its zenith under Czar Simeon (893–927 A.D.), but waned and fell under Byzantine rule about a century later, the whole country having been conquered and annexed by the Emperor Basilius II., 1018 A.D.

In the interim, however, events had occurred in Bulgaria which, although of little importance at the time, have since exercised great influence over the destinies of Eastern Europe. About the year 965 the Greek Emperor, Nikephoros Phokas, in his attempts to conquer Bulgaria, called in the aid of a tribe of Northmen (? Russians), under their chief Sviatoslav. At first this leader entered the country as an ally of the Greeks, it is said, with 10,000 followers, and overran the southern banks of the Danube, capturing Silistria and other strongholds. His victories and rapid advance, however, soon terrified even the Greek Emperor, who thereupon formed an alliance with Boris II., the Bulgarian Czar, and for a time succeeded in getting rid of his savage ally. Shortly afterwards, Nikephoros having meanwhile died, and being succeeded by Zimisces, it occurred to Sviatoslav that he might with advantage revisit Bulgaria on his own account, and once more taste those delights of a southern clime, which have even now such attractions for the men of the north; and about the year 969 he entered Bulgarian territory, defeated and captured Boris the Czar, and pushed his victories across the Balkans, taking Philippopolis, and carrying his arms as far as the Greek frontier. Here, however, his fortunes deserted him. The Greek Emperor, with the aid of Bulgarian and other allies, succeeded in driving him back across the Balkans, and compelled him to take refuge in Drster (Silistria). There he was besieged, and, after an obstinate resistance of three months, was obliged to capitulate. Although he was liberated and permitted with his remaining followers to return to his native land, he encountered a tribe of Petschenegues[1] on the banks of the Dnieper, by whom he was defeated, captured, and slain. The result of this first "Russian" invasion of Bulgaria is said by some writers to have led to that fusion of race

---

[1] "Roumania," p. 151.

between the Northern and the Southern Slaves which has long been used by Russia as a pretext for interference and aggression in South-Eastern Europe.[1]

Bulgaria now constituted part of the Greek Empire, but in the course of the eleventh and twelfth centuries the power of the latter declined, and at the close of the twelfth century (about 1186) the Bulgarians rose in revolt under the brothers Asen, and succeeded, with little difficulty, in shaking off the Byzantine, or perhaps it would be more correct to say the Greek rule. There is some confusion and doubt about the names and number of the brothers Asen, but one of them, known as Asen I., was chosen "Czar," and founded the so-called Asenide dynasty. By many writers a portion of this epoch in Bulgarian history is known as the "*Wallacho-Bulgarian Empire*" (for nearly the whole of Wallachia was for a time incorporated with Bulgaria, and Wallachians abounded south of the Danube), and that dynasty reached its zenith under Asen II. (1218–1241), and maintained itself with tolerable steadfastness altogether about two centuries, although during that period wars were waged, with varying success, between the Bulgarians and the Greeks, Franks, and other neighbours.

About a century after the reign of Asen II., Bulgaria fell for a time under Servian rule; and although she was still permitted to retain her "Czars," yet for nearly forty years, not that country alone, but a great part of the Balkan Peninsula was under Servian influence, and one Servian monarch, Dushan (1331–1355), raised his country to an eminence which it has never, either before or since, enjoyed.

It was to this Dushan that reference was made in the shouts of the populace of Belgrade before King Milan commenced his expedition against Bulgaria in 1885. The French raised the cry of "*A Berlin!*" previous to their campaign against Germany, but the Servians invoked the name of their great ruler of old before commencing their unjustifiable attack upon their neigh-

---

[1] Krek, p. 336–341, where the whole question is fully discussed, with the aid of numerous authorities.

bour, and in both instances the aggressors met with the same well-merited failure.

After the death of Dushan the northern part of the Balkan Peninsula began to feel the effects of the Turkish invasion. For some years, during which time Philippopolis fell to the Turkish arms, the Bulgarians defended their country with great bravery and determination; but at length the Czar, John Shishman III., deserted by his allies, Greeks, Wallachs, and Serbs, was compelled to succumb, and about 1365 he paid tribute and acknowledged himself a vassal of Sultan Murad I. The country was, however, not brought completely under Ottoman rule until after the battle of Kossovo pole in 1389.

The records of Bulgarian history during *the Ottoman occupation*, which virtually lasted until the close of the last Russo-Turkish war (for there have been many), are scanty in the extreme, and not alone are the memorials of that period almost entirely wanting, but, thanks to the fanaticism of the Phanariote clerics, many of those of an earlier age have also been destroyed, the object of the "vandals" being to blot out from the memory of the Bulgarians all remembrance of their former greatness. Of this more hereafter.

The Crimean War of 1854–56, which resulted in the liberation of Roumania from Ottoman rule, brought no relief to Bulgaria. On the contrary, the Turks being victorious, used their advantage to oppress the Bulgarian Christians more harshly than ever, and it was not until 1876, when Mr. Gladstone raised his voice in their favour, and exposed to the civilised world the so-called "Bulgarian atrocities" practised by the Turks, that the great Northern Power was permitted to strike a blow for the emancipation of the Southern Slaves. Whatever may have been the ulterior object of Russia, there can be no doubt that the war of 1877–78 was undertaken and successfully carried out by her, with the indispensable aid of Roumania, for the relief of one of the most grievously oppressed peoples in Europe. The blood which was spilled by the allies, Russia, Roumania, and Bulgaria, in the siege of Plevna, the defence of the Shipka Pass, and elsewhere, was not shed in vain, and the subsequent Treaty of San Stefano between Russia and Turkey, modified by that of

Berlin between the Great Powers (including the one just named), gave a second birth to a nation which is destined to play an important part in the world's history. By the Treaty of Berlin (July 13, 1878[1]) *Bulgaria* was constituted an "autonomous and tributary principality," under the suzerainty of the Sultan; and *Eastern Roumelia* was also made to a large extent autonomous, but still under his "direct political and military authority." Bulgaria was to be governed by a Prince, to be "freely elected by the population, and confirmed by the Porte with the assent of the Powers," whilst Eastern Roumelia was to be ruled by a "Christian Governor-General," to be "nominated by the Sublime Porte, with the assent of the Powers, for a term of five years."

After a permitted temporary occupation of the Principality by the Russians, with a provisional Governor-General in the person of Prince Dondukoff-Korsakoff, that Power recommended, and the Bulgarian nation accepted, Alexander of Battenberg as their first hereditary prince. On the 9th July 1879 he took the oath of fidelity to the Constitution, which had been meanwhile framed and adopted by an Assembly of Notables, prompted by the Russians. The first Governor-General of Eastern Roumelia nominated by the Sultan was Prince Vogorides, a Bulgarian Christian, known as Aleko Pasha, and he was succeeded in May 1884 by Gavril Pasha Krestovich, during whose term of office the union of the two States was accomplished.

Soon after the arrangements referred to were completed, it became apparent that the objects of the parties to them were not identical. On the one hand, Prince Alexander refused to be a mere agent for furthering the ambitious designs of Russia, and manifested an independent spirit which was highly displeasing to his patrons, whilst, on the other hand, the people of Eastern Roumelia were not at all disposed to be left out in the cold under the benign influence of the Porte, whilst their compatriots and co-religionists on the northern side of the Balkans were enjoying the sweets of liberty. So by a bloodless revolu-

---

[1] Holland's "The European Concert on the Eastern Question" (which contains the text of every important treaty relating to Greece, Samos and Crete, Egypt, the Balkan Peninsula, Russia, Great Britain, Austria, and the Porte from 1828.) Oxford: Clarendon Press, 1885.

tion they broke the last actual bonds which allied them to Turkey, and united themselves as "*South Bulgaria*" to the northern province under the rule of Prince Alexander (1885).

As already stated, long before this act was accomplished, Prince Alexander had fallen into disfavour with the Russians, who were straining every nerve and employing every device, lawful or otherwise, to rid themselves of his hated presence. For although their Governor-General had been withdrawn from North Bulgaria, the army in that country had been trained and was officered by Russians, and Russian influence predominated everywhere. This determination was manifested not only in their dealings with the Prince, but in their attitude after the union of the two countries. By the Treaty of San Stefano, Russia had endeavoured, for her own ends, to create a "Great Bulgaria," by the fusion of North Bulgaria and Eastern Roumelia; but the Powers had objected. As soon, however, as the union had taken place without her aid, she did all in her power to prevent its accomplishment, and obstinately refused to allow the name of Prince Alexander (who had been nominated as Governor-General by the Porte) from being associated with the appointment. But this was nothing compared with a step which the Emperor of Russia, Alexander III. (the successor of Alexander the Liberator) took shortly afterwards, and one which has for ever alienated the affections of the Bulgarian people, and turned their undoubted gratitude into open and violent dislike.

Whilst it was still doubtful whether the union of the two States would be permitted by the Powers (and their severance was probably only prevented by the mutual jealousies of the latter), Prince Alexander and his advisers had concentrated the national forces for defence upon the Turkish frontier. The Emperor Alexander III. showed his ill-will towards Bulgaria by withdrawing all Russian officers from the Bulgarian army, hoping thereby to cast her prostrate at the feet of her enemies. At the same time, the Servians, it is presumed at the instigation of Austria (although that is a matter of controversy), taking advantage of the perplexity of their neighbour, declared war against Bulgaria and hastily marched an army across her western frontier (November 1885). Prince Alexander and his advisers overcame all these difficulties. The Conference of the Powers came to nought, largely through the generous moral support of the representatives of Great Britain, Sir William White at Constantinople, and Mr. Lascelles, our agent in Bulgaria, who did not hesitate to accompany Prince Alexander on some of his journeys whilst he was, as his successor now is, boycotted by the Powers of Europe. The Prince reorganised his army, advanced his younger officers (whose skill and courage afterwards justified his confidence) to the higher posts which had been vacated by the Russians, and hastily marched an army towards the western frontier, where the Servians had, in the absence of serious opposition, obtained some temporary successes. He met the enemy at Slivnitza, and after three days' hard fighting (November 17th to 20th) drove him from all his positions and followed him across the frontier, entering in triumph the Servian town of Pirot.[1] Here he found himself confronted by Austrian influence, and was compelled by the force of circumstances to make peace with the aggressors. To their credit, however, be it said, that the Servians have since lived in amity and good-will towards their neighbours, and so far as can be judged from the public and private utterances of some of the leading statesmen, they are now anxious to enter into alliance with Bulgaria for purposes of general defence against the aggression of neighbouring Powers.

Then followed a crisis in Bulgarian history which is not yet terminated. Finding all her schemes of open violence to fail, Russia instigated a conspiracy (not the first) against Prince Alexander, which ultimately led to his abdication. By means of bribery and promises of promotion, her agents corrupted a number of Bulgarian officers, two of whom, Benderoff and Gruell, were leaders of the plot, and who in their turn influenced parts of two regiments and the cadets of the Military College at Sofia to turn traitors to their Prince and country. By these ruffians, many of whom were intoxicated, the palace

---

[1] Rendered infamous by the recent murders and plunder of unoffending travellers by the gens-d'armes.

of the Prince was invaded on the night of the 21st August of
last year (1886), and after they had compelled him, by placing
a revolver at his head, to append his signature to an illegible
document purporting to be his abdication, they carried him off
to Rahova, on the Danube, and placing him on board his own
yacht, they conveyed him down the river and delivered him up
to the Russian authorities at Reni in Bessarabia. Here he was
for a short time held a prisoner, but the outburst of indignation all over Europe against this infamous international crime
soon compelled the Emperor of Russia to set him at liberty.
Whilst he was at Lemberg, on his way to Darmstadt, Alexander
received the intelligence that the loyal portion of his army, led
by Lieutenant-Colonel Mutkuroff (now Minister of War), had
marched upon Sofia and disarmed the traitorous soldiers; that
a self-constituted " Provisional Government" of conspirators,
including, besides those already named, Dragan Zankoff (now
an exile in Constantinople) and Bishop Clement (who still
remains in office in Bulgaria), was dissolved, and that his
return was anxiously desired by his loyal subjects, or it would
be more correct to say, by his subjects who had remained
faithful to him.

With great reluctance the Prince retraced his steps, making
a triumphal tour through Austria and Roumania, and landing
amidst great rejoicing at Rustchuk. Here he was met not
only by his own Ministers, led by M. Stambouloff (the present
Premier), but by the Consuls, including the Russian Consul, in
uniform; and in a weak moment he sent a conciliatory, but
unfortunately a submissive telegram to the Emperor of Russia,
which the latter treated with disdain. Continuing his triumphal
progress, the Prince re-entered Sofia on the 3d September, and
for a brief period resumed the reins of power.

Under ordinary circumstances, Benderoff and Grueff, the
military traitors, who had been arrested and tried by court-
martial, would have been shot; but whilst the question of
dealing with them was being considered, the Prince received
peremptory communications from the Austrian, German, and
Russian capitals that those men must not be injured. At the
same time the Russian agent Nekludoff informed the Prince, in

the presence of his friends and councillors, that if *he* withdrew from Bulgaria the enmity of Russia would terminate, as the feeling of the Emperor was inimical to him personally, but that he was a well-wisher of Bulgaria. Upon this the Prince's determination was taken. He asked that assurances should be given by the Russian Government that there would be no further interference in the internal affairs of Bulgaria, in which case he would abdicate and leave the country. That assurance was conveyed from the Government of the Emperor to the Prince in the presence of his ministers, and on the 7th September the Prince issued a manifesto in which he announced the formal promise made by the Russian Government, nominated three Regents—MM. Stambouloff, Karaveloff, and Mutkuroff, and abdicated the throne. He at once left Sofia, and, embarking at Widdin, quitted the country, probably for ever!

How the Russians have fulfilled their promise has been shown by the candidature of the "Prince of Mingrelia;" the futile expedition and stumping tour through Bulgaria of General Kaulbars; the intrigues against and refusal to acknowledge Prince Ferdinand; the attempted mission of General Ehrnroth; and every act, overt and secret, which has been committed by that Power since the abdication of the Prince. The events which followed the departure of Prince Alexander are contemporary history. A great Sobranje or parliament was elected according to the Constitution, and formally opened by the Regents. After performing its routine duties, the Sobranje proceeded to choose Prince Ferdinand of Saxe-Coburg second Prince of Bulgaria, and after his arrival and accession to the throne the Regents resigned. Through the intrigues of Russia the Porte has been induced to withhold her assent to the new Prince's election, and consequently the Powers have been unable to ratify the choice of the people. That the Prince *is* their choice has been clearly proved by the recent elections to the National Assembly. So for the present the "great" Powers of Europe are boycotting, and some are harassing, the "little" Balkan State; but it is to be hoped that before these sentences are published a diminished fear of Russia and a higher sense of justice than at present prevails in the councils of Europe will have removed the last obstacles to the complete emancipation of Bulgaria.

But having concluded this very dry, superficial, and perfunctory history of Bulgaria, it may with justice be asked why in this first chapter I have adopted so unusual a method of proceeding. The answer is, that I have done so for the convenience of my readers. In the first place, there are many who do not care for the details of the past history of a little-known country, and who will probably be content to learn something of the actual condition of Bulgaria, and her fitness for self-government. For those readers the foregoing brief summary will have sufficed, and they will find such information as I can give them on the present state of the country in the Second Part. Furthermore, many of the published details of Bulgarian history are untrustworthy—more especially dates—and historical writers have not seldom endeavoured to fill up gaps by drafts on the imagination. Again, the history of Bulgaria overlaps that of Roumania, or *vice versâ*, and many portions of my work on the latter country deal with events and periods which need not be referred to again at any considerable length. The plan which I consider to be the most convenient, therefore, in this treatise will be to select from consecutive periods in Bulgarian history such incidents as have a special bearing upon her condition to-day, and for the sake of continuity I propose sometimes to conduct the reader at once from the consideration of past ages to the contemplation of phases of Bulgarian life in the present day. For example, there is not only a direct association between the customs of land-tenure now and of old, but many traces remain for those who care to visit and search for them which recall to memory the past greatness and barbaric splendour of the old Bulgarian Czars; and amidst scenes which captivate the sense and charm the imagination will be found visible records that give unwonted freshness and interest to the study of past events in history.

CHAPTER II.

THE SLAVES OR SCLAVONIANS.

Reputed origin of the Slave races—Resources and customs of the early settlers in Bulgaria—Patriarchal government and communistic land-tenure—The "Grad"—The "Zupa"—The Council of Elders—Hidden treasures—Hospitality—Industry of the women; of their descendants—Method of warfare—Modern Sclavonic names of places—Sclavonic religious rites.

THE hand of man has been far more destructive than it has been constructive in some parts of Bulgaria. In order to form some idea of the scene which the Balkans must have presented in pre-historic times, the reader should see them as they are to-day. Formerly the mountain slopes were clothed with vast forests of oak, frequented by the bear, the wolf, and other animals of prey, whilst the aurochs roamed at large over the plains. To-day the oak of ages is seldom seen; and although even in autumn the mountain-sides are still covered with a carpet of bright green, this is found on a closer inspection to consist of self-sown oak scrub, on which goats and cattle browse, the ancient woods having been ruthlessly destroyed to supply the needs of successive generations of barbarians—even of those who still remain, in the shape of wandering gipsies and ignorant herdsmen—to whom nothing consumable for firewood (not even the new kilometre posts on the wayside) comes amiss. But with the plains it is different; Nature had there supplied no such objects of utility, and they must have presented much the same appearance as at present, resembling as they do great inland seas drained of their aqueous contents, and covered with grasses and wild herbage. It was on these rich alluvial plains that the Slave immigrants settled, and it is here that their descendants still follow their pastoral and agricultural pursuits with primitive implements, differing but little from those of their early ancestors. The ancient Slaves who settled in Bulgaria are believed to have been a portion of what is known as the "Slavo-Lithuanian" branch of the Aryan race; to have occupied first the plains between the Don and the Dnieper during the Iron Age, and then to have wandered westward about the fifth century before Christ. So far much is conjecture. They were in all probability originally a pastoral people; but when they gradually settled down on the plains of the Danube, from about the third to the seventh century of the Christian era, their lives were more largely devoted to agricultural pursuits. Our information regarding their customs and condition at that period is by no means speculative, and is derived from various sources, principally from Greek (or Byzantine) writers, such as Procopios (born about 500 A.D.) and others. Our conclusions may also be safely based upon the researches of modern philologists, who have carefully compared the appellations of objects, customs, and localities, chiefly in the districts inhabited by Slave descendants, so as to arrive at their common origin. Some striking examples of this will be given presently.

From these sources of information, then, we learn that the Slaves were acquainted with agriculture, and probably also with bee-culture. They had ploughs, which can hardly have been more primitive than those now in use, but were probably well adapted for turning over the soil, which is in many places still choked with "cobbles." They sowed wheat, barley, oats, rye, and millet; ground corn in handmills and watermills. From the flour they made some kind of bread, on which they subsisted, along with meat, fruits, and vegetables. Of the latter, they had turnips, lentils, and beans; of fruits, they possessed the grape, from which they made wine, and upon that (and mead made from honey) they got drunk, as their descendants do to-day upon a spirit made from the husks and dregs. They also had the apple, plum, sour cherry, and pear; but they need certainly not have cultivated the last-named, for they most probably had the little wild pear which one now sees with its bright golden and crimson fruit growing in such plenty by the roadside, and as their palates would not be very sensitive, its acrid taste would be no bar to its enjoyment. Besides the ordinary plants here named, they probably cultivated hemp, flax, and hops, made cheese from milk, cooked their meat, and were acquainted with some primitive forms of scythe, spade, and flail to aid them in their agricultural employments. The trees which grew in their forests were the oak, which still preponderates, lime, maple, beech, birch, elm, willow, alder, and pine.

Their domestic animals were the ox, cow, buffalo (still largely used as draught animals), calf, goat, dog, and goose; and at the same early period of their national life they already knew how to apply the products of those animals in a variety of ways, not only as food, but for purposes of clothing and ornament. From furs and rude textile fabrics they made garments, such as mantles, and rough underclothing;[1] and they also ornamented themselves with gold, silver, and the inferior metals.

With agricultural pursuits came the appropriation of land, and therewith a primitive form of society, and finally the "state." At first, naturally, the members of the tribe, as it wandered over the plains, settled in families, often at considerable distances apart, and a patriarchal government prevailed; but it was a peculiar communistic system, which still obtains amongst many Slave peoples, and, in a somewhat modified form, in Bulgaria down to the present day. In fact, there is a peasant proprietary, to which is superadded the "Mera,"[2] or communism in the tenure of land, to be described hereafter.

At first the respective families were governed by a patriarch, the oldest and most experienced member; but when the country became less sparsely settled, they formed themselves into clans or communities (Zupa), and each elected a chief. In some central part of the Zupa, a fortified house or "Grad" was built, around which the families of the clan congregated, living either in semi-subterranean abodes, such as still exist plentifully on

---

[1] "Linen kerchiefs, over-garment (shirt)." Jireček, *Geschichte der Bulgaren*, note, pp. 99–100. Von Tempsky, Prag, 1876. Much additional information concerning the customs of the early Sclavonic races will be found in Krek and Jireček, with the names of authorities.

[2] Another form of the old Sclavonic tenure of land, as it exists, modified, to-day, will be found described and criticised at length by the late Julius Faucher, Berlin, in "Systems of Land Tenure in Various Countries," cap. vi., "Russia," published for the Cobden Club by Cassell, Petter, & Galpin.

the plains on both sides of the Danube, and perhaps also in rude wooden huts. The "Grad" was a place of refuge, and the appellation has descended to our time in Belgrad, Razgrad, Gradiste, Tr-nov-grad (Tirnovo), said to be derived from *Tr* (three), *nov* (new), *grad* (fort),[1] and was also formerly applied to Czarigrad (Constantinople), because the Greek emperors resided there. The "Grad" was usually built in some place that was difficult of access, in a marsh or on an acclivity, where it was protected by a stream, precipices, or a natural wall of rock. Kanitz describes and beautifully illustrates many such localities, especially the one at Belogradčik;[2] but perhaps the grandest and most perfect development (by the Bulgarian Czars) of this system of fortification is to be seen at Tirnova, where the Jantra river forms a broad fosse, and the remarkable escarpments of rock running round the hills and the great wall of rock approaching the "Hissar" were supplemented by the addition of strong artificial works (to be described hereafter), and made to constitute a range of almost impregnable hill-fortresses. The chiefs of the Zupa were hereditary, and the families from whom they were chosen subsequently constituted, such as it was, the Slave aristocracy. All affairs of public interest were debated and settled by an assembly of elders, who decided on matters relating to war, defensive or offensive. If an expedition was to be undertaken or an invasion to be resisted, the clans united temporarily, but as soon as the common danger was averted or the occasion for union past, they again separated and returned to their respective Zupas. Thus it was that the Slaves never acknowledged a head or ruler, but they were in consequence disunited, and easily fell under the domination of powerful and aggressive foes. Is it the consciousness that they have inherited this ancestral weakness and an instinctive sense of the attendant danger that has caused their descendants to-day to prefer a young German prince to a republic?

---

[1] Joreček derives the word Tirnovgrad from Trnov-Grad, Thorn-Fort. I believe the other derivation, which was given to me at Tirnova, is the correct one.

[2] *Donau Bulgarien und der Balkan*, vol. i. p. 16; woodcut and plate. Leipzig: Renger'sche Buchhandlung, 1882.

It is said that the Slaves hid their treasures underground—a very necessary precaution when hordes of wandering barbarians poured through the land and they were never safe from surprise; and unfortunately the political conditions in Bulgaria have been such as to necessitate a continuance of the practice down to this day. First the barbarians, including their own rulers, then the neighbouring peoples, who held the country for a time, and finally the Turks were constantly draining the life-blood of the peasantry; and yet it is said that there is hardly a peasant of any note even now who has not his store of coins of various periods hidden somewhere about his rude dwelling! The Slaves are described as a peace-loving but still courageous people; that is precisely the character of their descendants in our time. Their men were fine and powerfully built, as they are now. They were hospitable to a fault, and are said even to have committed theft in order to be enabled to fulfil the rites of hospitality. To-day they do not carry this excellent quality to the same extreme lengths. If you enter the cottage of a peasant or small tradesman in a Bulgarian village, you are cordially welcomed. You may take a look round, and the storeroom, with its heaps of fruit and "paprika" (red pepper), is shown to you with pride. You are invited into the best room, with its couch along one or two of the walls, its little bookcase with a few books in the Bulgarian, and even in the French or English language. You may watch the baby swinging in its hammock suspended from the ceiling, and Madame, in her picturesque many-hued costume, will place before you a little table, and set upon it a plate with a large bunch of luscious grapes and a goblet of clear water. Yes, the peasantry are hospitable; so too are the people of Philippopolis, exceedingly so; of Tirnova and the smaller towns; but whether or not an increase of petty larceny is one of the results of this hospitality, I am unable to say. In Sofia I should certainly imagine that the volume of crime suffers no accession from that source.

As one of the results of the common tenure of land, every industrious member of a Zupa was enabled to work for the general welfare, and with the exception of the idle and vicious, there were no poor, and poverty was always regarded as a disgrace. There are still hardly any mendicants in Bulgaria. I only recollect meeting with three or four. One was what the Americans call a "beat"—evidently a broken-down *roué*—in Philippopolis, and two or three gipsies, who are the scourge of all those Eastern countries, at Tirnova and elsewhere. The women are said to have been treated with consideration, and in the absence of the house-father his wife ruled the household. It is very improbable that they were exempted from the labour of the field, but it was the duty of the men to attend to the herding and care of the cattle. The women were very brave, as many examples prove in the history of the country, and they were also very industrious. This quality has indeed descended to their posterity, for one of the most remarkable sights in Bulgaria is to see the women plying their spindle and distaff. If you drive through a village or meet them on the roadside, it is spin, spin, spin. They spin standing, and walking, and sitting down, and making their purchases—at all times and everywhere.

Monogamy is said to have been the rule, but the authority is doubtful. The men, I have said, were brave. They fought on foot, often almost without any clothing, with swords, spears, bows and poisoned arrows, and clubs, and protected themselves with shields. They resembled all the barbarians in their mode of warfare, seldom appearing in the open field, and often feigning retreat to decoy the enemy into ambushes. They never allowed the enemy to rest, and attacked him in morasses, woods, and mountain passes. A strange device in warfare was attributed to them. It is said that when they were hotly pursued they plunged into the water, and sinking to the bottom, stayed there, and breathed through a long reed which reached just above the surface. In the case of fresh enemies unacquainted with this ruse, they were perfectly safe in their subaqueous retreat; but when their pursuers had learned the trick, they looked for those tubes, and either closed them up, and so compelled the warrior to rise to the surface (where he was slain), or they forced the tube down the throat of the unfortunate man and choked him. In time the Slaves learned the use of more dangerous and complicated weapons of offence and defence from the Byzantines with whom they came in contact, and they were even able to besiege the strongholds of their enemies. They are said to have treated their captives with lenity, and not to have put them to death, nor kept them long in captivity, nor even unnecessarily to have murdered them when prostrate on the field of battle.

The names of many modern towns and localities must have been handed down from Sclavonic times, just as we have such names even in connection with our own towns and districts to remind us of the Anglo-Saxon and Danish periods. Some of those places are called after the natural products which were found there in plenty, as Slivovo, Sliven, Slivnitza, from the plum; Jablanica, the apple; Bucovica, the beech; Vishnica, wild cherry; Vinica, grape; also Bebbrovo, the beaver; Turovo, the aurochs, and many others. Some of the names of places were corruptions of the Roman appellations (just as with us), as Nisch, from Naïssus; Lom, from Almus; Drster (Silistria), from Durostorum, &c.; and in other cases the name of the prevailing industry has come down to our time incorporated with that of the locality.

When they had attained a certain degree of civilisation and barter commenced, the circulating medium of exchange was cattle (Krek says the cow was probably the unit), and in cattle, too, fines were levied.

Of the religion of the Slaves little appears to be known that is authentic. They were heathens, and probably worshipped a supreme deity, the author of lightning, to whom they offered oxen and other animals as sacrifices. They, moreover, believed in good spirits (*bogy*) favourable to mankind, and in evil and malevolent spirits (*besy*). They honoured nymphs, nixies, rivers, dancing fairies, and a good many of the supernatural beings of mediæval and modern times. They worshipped in the open air and held festivals, some of which from being heathen rites became Christian celebrations. They are said to have believed in a soul distinct from the body, in a future state, a heaven or paradise, and a place of torment. Their superstitions were (and in some places are still) numerous, and that of the vampyre. which held possession of human bodies, was widespread, and is still to be found amongst the more ignorant peasantry in Slave countries.

Such was the character and those the customs of the ancient people who migrated from the east and settled in Bulgaria from the third to the seventh century of our era ; and although their possession of the country has been at various times disputed by (Byzantine) Greeks, by Wallachs, Turks, and Russians, they still constitute by far the largest proportion of the present inhabitants, and maintain the distinguishing characteristics of the race.

CHAPTER III.

THE BULGARI AND THEIR EARLY RULE.

Divergent views of their origin—Kuvrat and Asparich—Krum and his victories over the Byzantines—His death, 815 or 820 A.D.—Omortag—His persecution of the Christians—The warlike Bulgari—Their appearance and customs—Their cruelty—Their advance towards civilisation—The Khan and his surroundings—Czar Boris—The monks Constantine and Methodios—Their missionary labours—Constantine assumes the name of Kyrill—The Kyrillic alphabet—His sacred writings—His death about 889 A.D.—The conversion of Boris to Christianity by the Greeks about 864 A.D.—Legendary accounts—A business transaction—The first fruits of Christianity in Bulgaria—Negotiations with Pope Nicholas—The 106 questions concerning the Christian faith, and the replies—Oscillating between Greece and Rome—The heretic sects—The Bogomiles—Their origin, their faith, and doctrines—Dualism of their belief—God and Satanael—Their powers and attributes—Their acts in sacred history—Christ "an appearance only"—Mary an angel—Religious professions and teachings of the Bogomiles—Their contempt for orthodoxy and Church ritual—Their initiatory ceremonies—Proselytism—The "Perfecti"—Their asceticism—Persecution of the Bogomiles—Charged with hypocrisy and immorality—Their political influence—Martyrdom of Basilius (about 1119 A.D.)—Duration of the heretical sects—Abdication of Boris—His death about 907 A.D.

OF the customs and career of this race, who dominated in the country to which they have given their name, I have already published elsewhere a tolerably complete outline,[1] but the importance of the subject in this place necessitates a repetition of the main facts and the addition of some further details. Like that of the Slaves, and indeed of most of the so-called barbarians, the origin of the race Bulgari and their early history are largely matters of doubt and conjecture. By some writers they are said to have been of Scythian origin, others speak of them as a Finnish, others again as a Turkish tribe. Gibbon, along with some other historians, believes that, in company with the

---

[1] "Roumania," cap. x. secs. iv. vii. viii.

Slaves, they wandered over the plains of Russia, Lithuania, and Poland. Many are of opinion that they crossed the Danube, or at least migrated southward, along with the Slaves; others, that they followed and conquered the Slave settlers. Be that as it may, it will be seen that they were a distinct race from the one which they held in subjection for centuries. To give some idea of the mythical character of our information concerning them before their advent into Bulgaria, it may be mentioned that they are said to have had in the course of 515 years (from 164 to 679 A.D.) only five princes, giving an average reign of 103 years to each. One chief, *Kurrat*, who is mentioned in Byzantine chronicles, is said to have formed an alliance with the Emperor Heraclius, and to have aided in defeating and breaking up the tribe of Avari. He then settled with his followers somewhere north of the Danube, probably in Bessarabia, and his successor, *Asparich*, having crossed that river and carried his arms as far as Varna, subsequently (about 680) occupied the whole of what is now North Bulgaria, bounded by the Danube, the Black Sea, and the Balkans. After this time the history of the Bulgari is better defined. About 802 A.D. or 807 another notorious character appears upon the scene. This was *Krum* or *Kremus*, a savage chief, who carried on a continued warfare with the Greek Emperor Nicephoros, who about 811 invaded and ravaged Bulgaria and destroyed Krum's fortress-residence. The latter then closed the passes of the Balkans, attacked and utterly routed the Greek army, captured and killed the Emperor, and converted his skull into a goblet—a very common method of utilising the remains of one's enemies in those days. Michael, the Greek Emperor who succeeded, fared little better than his predecessor at the hands of Krum. The latter devastated Thrace and Macedonia, defeated the Emperor about the year 813 near Adrianople, and pressed forward to the gates of Constantinople. Unable to capture that city, he committed unheard-of atrocities in the surrounding country, slaughtering men and cattle before the gates. In order to make peace, the Emperor was compelled to agree to pay him an annual tribute, including a number of virgins, and to release many captive Bulgarians who had been detained as prisoners from former wars.

Whilst the negotiations were proceeding, however, Krum nearly fell into an ambush with a few of his followers, whereupon he renewed his barbarities, and retreating across the Balkans, he carried fire and sword in his track, and returned home laden with every kind of plunder. About 814 the Greek Emperor, Leo, invaded Bulgaria, and nearly captured Krum, who thereupon recommenced his advance upon Constantinople with a mighty army, but died suddenly of apoplexy, according to some writers in 815, by other accounts in 820, in which year he was followed on the throne by *Omortag*.

The rule of that chief was not characterised by any stirring events in Bulgarian history. Renouncing the designs of his predecessor upon Constantinople, he concluded a thirty years' peace with the Emperor Leo, and devoted himself to the development of the peaceful resources of the country. He persecuted the Christians, who were already beginning to make converts in Bulgaria, martyred Manuel, Bishop of Adrianople, along with three other bishops and 374 captive Christians. According to a tablet, which is said to have been found in 1858 in a mosque in Tirnova, he built what were then considered fine palaces, both on the Danube and at Tirnova; but the said tablet gave no clue to his nationality or religion, and bore no date. The date of his death is unknown, and nothing of note occurs in Bulgarian history until the conversion to Christianity of one of his successors, *Boris*, of which more will be said presently; meanwhile a brief account of the Bulgarian conquering race may not be uninteresting.

From whatever quarter the Bulgari came—and the opinions in that respect are as numerous and divergent as the origin of the Roumanians—they were a warlike tribe of nomads, in many respects the very opposite of the Slaves whom they conquered. They lived by and for war, and before they settled down in Bulgaria and became the ruling caste, they wandered from place to place with their herds of cattle and horses in search of pasture. Their chief food was milk and the flesh of certain animals which were reckoned clean, and from which (as in the case of the Jews) the blood flowed in killing. They are said in many respects to have resembled the Avari, to have shorn the hair off their heads, excepting a tuft, and to have worn turbans. (The wearing of turbans and of long robes probably belonged to a later period.) They fought chiefly on horseback; their standards were horses' tails. Their frontiers were guarded by many outposts, beyond which no one was allowed to pass, and any one who, either by accident or design, strayed beyond these posts was killed by the guard, or, if the latter failed to prevent his passage, he was himself put to death. The time of combat was fixed by soothsayers, who sought propitious signs, and only permitted an attack to take place on certain days. Before a battle songs were chanted, and beasts and even human beings were offered as sacrifices. All arms were carefully inspected before the departure of the warriors, and it is said that any one having an imperfect weapon was put to death. Treaties were made with an oath taken upon a naked sword, and were ratified by cutting a dog in two parts. In time of peace their customs were cruel in the extreme. Executions, including quartering alive, were of daily occurrence; thefts of horses and cattle were capital offences; if a "noble" of rank revolted against the prince, not only were his life and possessions forfeited, but his children were put to death and his family exterminated. Blinding by piercing the eyes with a red-hot needle or by exposure to a glowing piece of metal was regarded as a commutation of the capital sentence. Noses and ears were slit for small crimes. Accused persons were clubbed on the head or stabbed in some non-vital part of the body if they refused to confess. At the death of a chief his wives and slaves were sacrificed, the latter being buried alive with the corpse. These were probably the chief characteristics of the Bulgari before and on their settlement in the Balkan Peninsula, and even subsequently; and the records of the two Bulgarian empires and their communications with the Papacy show that cruelty and superstition pervaded all their customs in peace and war. Afterwards, although much time was spent in war and warlike pursuits, they made considerable advance in civilisation, more especially after their conversion to Christianity. Whilst they continued to live in tents made of the skins of animals in summer, they built wooden houses for winter, and some kind of courtesy and etiquette became apparent in their demeanour towards their chiefs and towards one another. Still they fed largely on horse-flesh, drank mead to excess,—a sure sign of advancing civilisation, some of my readers may think. The chief or Khan had absolute power over life and death. He and his nobles, six of whom formed a council of state, practised polygamy, and their harems were guarded by eunuchs. The Khan is said to have eaten his meals alone at a small table, whilst his wives and court squatted around upon the floor and satisfied their appetites in that posture. If an ambassador visited the court, it was customary for him to inquire first after the health of the Khan and his family, next after the six great Boyards, then after the nobles within and without the court, and finally after the inhabitants generally. In the course of our historical inquiry, and when we come to visit those places where many remains of the ancient and mediæval Bulgarians are still to be found, other features of interest in their political and social life will be presented to our notice.

About thirty years after Omortag, in the reign of *Boris* (probably about 852–888), there lived two brothers, *Constantine* and *Methodios*, whose literary labours and ministrations led to the introduction of Christianity into Bulgaria. They were probably born in Thessalonica, their father being military governor of that place, but soon left the locality, and at first adopted different professions. Constantine removed to Constantinople, and prepared himself for a literary and religious career, whilst to Methodios was confided the governorship of a minor Greek province. When the former had become acquainted with Eastern languages, he was sent by the Emperor as a missionary to certain tribes on the Don or Dnieper, whom he is said to have converted to Christianity. On his return the two brothers met, and united in following the lives of recluses, and subsequently missionaries of Christianity in the Sclavonic States of South-Eastern Europe. Their lives, as they moved about from place to place, were very eventful, and their literary and proselytising labours were highly appreciated by both sections of the Catholic Church. Constantine adopted the name of Kyrill, and invented part of the alphabet which has been named after him. He translated the Gospels, the Acts of the Apostles, and the Psalms from the Byzantine text into the Slave language, and published treatises on the "true faith," &c. His works were publicly read in Rome, where he was received with great honour, and died at the early age of forty-two, about February 869. Methodios translated into Sclavonic part of the Old Testament and many other sacred writings, and died about fifteen years after his brother, somewhere on the Danube. The works of both were largely circulated, and were instrumental in making converts of men of all ranks, not only in the settled Slave countries of Eastern Europe, but also amongst the still savage tribes of South-Eastern Russia.

The accounts of the mode in which Boris and his people were converted to Christianity vary, some of them being miraculous. It was long believed that Methodios the monk had painted a picture of the Last Supper for him, which exercised such an influence over his mind as to induce him to renounce heathenism and embrace Christianity. The story is very pretty, but it is probably erroneous in nearly every particular. The Methodios who executed the picture is said to have been a painter of the same name as the missionary, and Boris probably became a Christian from motives of policy rather than from conviction. Another story is that his sister, having been taken prisoner and conveyed to Constantinople, was there converted, and being subsequently allowed to return to her brother, that she persuaded him to adopt the new faith. The real facts are probably these: Boris had need of allies from time to time to help him to maintain his independent position, but as the missionary efforts of the two brothers, Constantine and Methodios, had already caused the conversion of the rulers of some of the States bordering on Bulgaria, Boris found himself at a great disadvantage as a heathen. Whilst he was engaged in a war with the Greek Emperor, Michael III., a famine broke out in his own land, and Boris found it necessary to make peace with the Emperor. It was then that he considered it politic to become a convert, which he did on the field of negotiations. He was baptized, along with many of his followers, and took the Christian name of Michael, the Emperor himself acting as his godfather. This happened about the year 864, and one of the fruits of Boris's conversion was the acquisition by Bulgaria of a considerable tract of country up to that time in Greek possession. Boris is not the only man either, before or since, who has adopted a new or a reformed faith—for a valuable consideration. On his return home he manifested the zeal of a convert by endeavouring to introduce the new faith amongst his subjects. This led to an insurrection of the Boyards as well as of the common people, who still remained heathens. The revolt was suppressed; the Boyards and their wives and children were put to death, but the people were spared. Endeavouring to turn his conversion to the best account, Boris also sought the alliance of the Pope, Nicholas I. This he did chiefly because the Greeks would not grant ecclesiastical superiors to the newly-converted people, and thereupon Boris sent a mission to Rome in order to secure, if possible, a Patriarch.[1] Of his success in this respect it is only necessary to say, that although the Pope bid rather higher for the adhesion of the Bulgarians than the Greek ecclesiastics, he at first promised only to send bishops, but no higher dignitary of the Church. It is true his successor, Adrian, sent an archbishop, but by that time Boris was again coquetting with Constantinople, and he refused to receive him.[2] What has imparted such interest to this mission, however, is that it gives us a further insight into the social life of the Bulgarians at that time, for by a series of 106 questions formulated for the Pope's replies, the envoys sought to become acquainted with the faith and doctrines of Christianity and to follow the Christian life, but at the same time to retain as many as possible of their pleasant heathen practices. Those questions were answered by Pope Nicholas through two bishops whom he sent to Bulgaria

---

[1] Much valuable information concerning the conversion of Boris and his negotiations with the Eastern and Western Churches will be found in Neander's "Church History" (Bohn's Standard Library), vol. v.; also in the pages of Jireček and Krek.

[2] Later on, under the second empire, a much more interesting negotiation took place between one of the successors of Boris, namely the Czar Joannitz, and Pope Innocent III., which I have already described at some length elsewhere ("Roumania," cap. x. sec. viii.), but to which further reference will be made hereafter.

with a letter in the year 865, and although some of them were very amusing, on the whole they showed an earnest desire on the part of the questioners to lead an improved life.[1] Here is the substance of a few of them. What should be done with persons unwilling to renounce idolatry? The answer was that exhortation and rational persuasion should be used rather than force, and if those means failed, they should be "severely let alone." God required only a voluntary obedience; had it been His pleasure to use force, none could have resisted His almighty power, &c., &c. The Pope also remonstrated with them for their cruelty towards Greek priests who had visited them, denounced their modes of torturing accused persons, and the infliction of the penalty of death for minor offences. On what festival days should they refrain from work? (It has been said by some writers that this question was put rather with a desire to avoid keeping those days, as they were then forced to refrain from eating flesh-meat.) The answer not only named the days, but pointed out that their object was to leave more leisure for attendance upon divine worship. What must they do if they were surprised by the attacks of an enemy whilst in church engaged in prayer? The answer was that they might finish their prayers elsewhere. Many other questions concerning festivals and war were answered in a similar strain. Should they have recourse to sorcery and divinations? No. They must prepare for war by prayer and fasting, by freeing prisoners and giving alms to the needy. How should they treat freemen attempting to flee from their country? With greater leniency, as a man who cannot be allowed to leave his country is not a free man.[2]

But some of the questions concerning social life were amusing as well as instructive. Might they receive dowries of gold, silver, oxen, &c., with their wives? Yes, of course. Must they alter their mode of dress, and might they in future wear trousers? The answer was that no alteration was necessitated

---

[1] Neander, vol. xxv. pp. 426-432, who deals with the subject at considerable length.

[2] Let me commend this injunction to the powers that be to-day in Bulgaria.

in their outward garb, but only reform of the inner man. Was it proper for the king to sit alone at table and compel not only his courtiers, but his wife (? wives) to sit on separate stools at a distance? (There must already have been an improvement in the social life of the court, for even stools were at one time denied to them.) The answer was that although the practice was decidedly bad form, *contra bonos mores*, it was in no way at variance with Christian doctrine, and they might do as they pleased in that respect.

Bibles and other sacred books were sent to them, books on civil law promised, but a "Patriarch" was politely refused. The oscillations of Boris between Greece and Rome, although they eventually secured for him from Constantinople such ecclesiastics as he desired, had the ill effect of throwing his country open to the strife and influences of many differing sects, all of whom called themselves Christians. The tenets of those sects, the Paulicians, the Catharists, the Bogomiles, &c., had much in common, and they have been described at considerable length by various historians, especially by the learned Neander; but as one of them, the Bogomilians or *Bogomiles*, for a long period exercised considerable influence not only in the religious life of Bulgaria, but over her political history, a brief notice of them may not be deemed inappropriate. Their origin is doubtful. According to some authors, they took their name from a priest, Bogomil, whilst others derive their appellations from the Sclavonic *Bogomil*, "Beloved of God," or from *Bog milui*, "Lord, have mercy."[1] The peculiar character of their faith and doctrine consisted in its being a compound of Christianity and heathenism, for they interwove with Christian story and teachings many of the old heathen legends, and so addressed themselves to the intelligence or want of intelligence of the uneducated masses, amongst whom they readily made converts. It may be said generally, that for a long time after the introduction of the Bogomilian "heresy" the nobles were of the orthodox Greek faith, but the masses Bogomilians. It is

---

[1] See Neander, cap. viii.; Jireček, cap. ix.; Krek, p. 781. All three contain, along with voluminous authorities, much information concerning the Bogomiles.

difficult to define their faith with precision. They believed in God and in *Satanaël*, his first-born, fallen away. The former was a spiritual being, from whom nothing imperfect or temporal proceeded; the wicked one created everything visible and corporeal,—the physical universe, in fact. This leading tenet, this dualism with modifications, appears to have pervaded the beliefs of most of the so-called heretical sects. The earth, according to the views of the Bogomiles, being the work of Satan, was doomed to destruction. The soul of man is an imprisoned fallen angel, which after death returns to God and heaven. Satan made Adam of earth, but being unable to vivify him, sought the help of God, who breathed of His own life into him. Cain, according to them, was the son of Satan and Eve, Abel of Adam and Eve, Cain representing the evil, and Abel the good principle in humanity. Satan was held responsible for all the evils which fell upon mankind—the flood, the dispersal at Babel, the destruction of Sodom. The presence of the Saviour and His death upon the cross were only appearances. Christ disgraced Satan, and bound him with a heavy chain. Mary was an angel, not the mother of Christ; and only the moral and religious teachings of Christ were credited to Him. Forms, ceremonies, and sacraments being material, were the works of Satan in the eyes of the Bogomiles, and consequently they rejected them as Satanic symbols. When it suited them they professed to believe in the Trinity, but they called themselves simply "Christians." They held the orthodox bishops in contempt, and called them vipers and the monks foxes, whilst they proclaimed themselves to be the "heavenly life," the "salt of the earth," the "light of the world," the "lilies of the field," the "holy ones, without sin or blemish." Only grown-up persons were admitted into the community, and these were obliged to spend a considerable time before their initiation in fasting and prayer. The ceremony of initiation was performed by the presiding officer placing his hands upon the neophyte, calling upon the Holy Ghost, and then laying the Gospel of St. John upon his head. After this he returned to his fasting and prayer, and the same ceremony was repeated at a later period, when he was formally admitted. Every "accepted" man and woman might preach, but the Church elders were chosen by the popular vote. Amongst themselves they professed to despise temples and religious edifices of every kind, for they said that Satan had first lived in the Temple of Jerusalem, then in the Church of St. Sophia in Constantinople. In order to make converts, however, they frequented places of worship and joined in the ceremonies there practised, and in some districts they afterwards built plain and undecorated church houses. There were various degrees of sanctity, the highest being the " Perfecti," or perfect ones. All the initiated adopted a grave, silent demeanour, but the " perfect," who were few in number, were rigid ascetics, and wherever they went they were received with marked reverence. They practised celibacy, denied themselves animal food, eschewed all worldly enjoyments, and spent their time in the perusal of sacred works. " Perfect " women followed a like existence, devoting themselves to works of charity, tending the sick and educating the young. The lay members of the community lived as other people, took part in all the ordinary pursuits of peace and war, and amassed property. On their deathbeds they were admitted into the ranks of the " perfect " by a religious ceremony. Being schismatics, they naturally incurred great hatred and suffered much persecution. They were charged with hypocrisy and with self-indulgence and immorality, notwithstanding their professions of asceticism; and at a later period of their history there is said to have been truth in those accusations. They exercised great political influence amongst the masses, and that perhaps as much as their heresy caused them to be fiercely persecuted. Councils were held to denounce their doctrines, and one of the Greek Emperors more especially, Alexius Comnenos, resorted to the most despicable devices to discover and punish them. He succeeded in arresting and casting into prison a large number of the heretics, including one of their leaders, Basilius; compelled some to recant, kept others imprisoned, and burned Basilius at the stake (A.D. 1119). The Bogomilian schism or " heresy " lasted through both Bulgarian empires down to the Turkish occupation, which it is said to have facilitated through the division which it caused between classes. After the Turkish occupation there were only two faiths, that of Mahomet, professed by the conquerors, and that of the Eastern Church of Christ. But the heresies of the Bogomilians and of the various sects were met by other means than violence, namely, by controversy and preaching, and to these reference will be made in treating of a later reign. At present we must return for a moment to that of Boris. That prince abdicated the throne about the year 888, and entered a monastery with the intention of spending his remaining years in religious exercises. About four years afterwards, however, he was compelled to leave his retreat on account of the misgovernment of his eldest son, whom he deposed, and having placed the crown on the head of his younger son, *Simeon*, he once more withdrew into his monastery, and died there about the year 907.

Under Simeon the first Bulgarian monarchy reached its zenith.

CHAPTER IV.

THE TWO BULGARIAN EMPIRES.

Czar Simeon—His wars with the Greeks—His successes—His death about 927 A.D.—Condition of Bulgaria—John of Ryl—Simeon's palaces—Mediæval account of them—Decline of the first Bulgarian Empire—Boris II. and Zimisces—The Sismans—Samuel—Basilius the Second, the "Bulgar-Slayer"—His wars against Bulgaria—His cruelty—Death of Samuel (1014 A.D.)—Complete conquest of Bulgaria—The Greek occupation—Wallachs and Slaves—The controversies concerning their origin and early history—The "Strategus" or Greek governor of provinces—Greek oppression—Barbarian invasions—Decline of the Greek power—The revolt under the brothers Asen (1185 A.D.)—The second Bulgarian Empire—Asen I.—His wars with the Eastern Emperor Isaac—Victories of Asen—His assassination—Czar Johannitz or Kalojan—His invasion of Greek territory—Penetrates to the walls of Constantinople—His negotiations for a crown with Pope Innocent III.—The correspondence—Occupation of Constantinople by the Crusaders—Count Baldwin of Flanders, the first Frank Emperor—Baldwin and Kalojan—Reception of a crown from the Pope (1204 A.D.)—"Kalojan's Alliance"—Battle of Adrianople between Kalojan and Baldwin—Defeat of the Greeks—Capture and fate of Baldwin—Assassination of Kalojan about 1207.

BALDWIN'S TOWER AT TIRNOVA.

SIMEON is one of the heroes of Bulgarian history. If you go into a Bulgarian school and ask the children to name some of the greatest rulers of their country, he will probably be the first mentioned.

He reigned from about 893 to 927, and was as celebrated in peace as in war. Of his military exploits I shall say but little, although their results were of considerable importance in history. During the greater part of his reign he was at war either with the Greek Empire or with the neighbouring States; probably he was the first aggressor. On account of some commercial misunderstanding, he invaded Byzantine territory, defeated the Greeks, and sent his prisoners back to Constantinople with their noses slit. Enraged at such treatment of his subjects, the Greek Emperor Leo called to his aid the Magyars,[1] the fiercest of all the Eastern hordes, who laid waste Bulgarian territory and defeated Simeon's army. On their return to their steppes, however, they were followed by the latter, who attacked them and decimated their tribe. After this Simeon again assumed the offensive, and pursued Leo as far as Adrianople, where a peace was concluded which lasted until Leo's death (about 911).

Under his successors, Alexander and Constantine Porphyrogenetos, the wars with Bulgaria were renewed, and the very existence of the Greek Empire was threatened. Simeon twice captured Adrianople, besieged Constantinople several times, defeated the Greeks and their barbarous allies more than once, and nearly exterminated the latter. Through these and other campaigns and victories he succeeded in extending the Bulgarian Empire far beyond its former limits; indeed, he reigned over a great portion of the Balkan Peninsula, exercised a quasi-sovereignty over Wallachia, and assumed the title of "Czar of the Bulgarians and Autocrat of the Greeks." Setting the ecclesiastical authorities of Constantinople at defiance, he refused to recognise the headship of the Greek Church, but elevated a man of his own selection to the rank of Patriarch of Bulgaria—an example which, I venture to think, will soon be followed by one of his modern successors; for at present an "Exarch" is the highest Bulgarian ecclesiastic, granted by favour of the Sublime Porte!

It was during one of his campaigns against Constantinople

---

[1] "Roumania," pp. 148-150.

that "Czar" Simeon died, probably in 927. Although his military achievements have here been summed up in a few sentences (for their recital would afford little interest to English readers), an account of them would fill pages, and, as already stated, he ranks as one of Bulgaria's greatest heroes of antiquity. During his reign and that of his successor Peter, notwithstanding the creation of a Patriarch, the power of the Orthodox clergy declined, and the heretical sects were wide-spread and influential. Sclavonic literature began to extend, and generally the arts of civilisation flourished.

Of the heretical sects I have already spoken. Their chief legitimate orthodox opponents were, like themselves, monks and ascetics; indeed, it was they who kept the spirit of religion alive in Bulgaria. The most famous of the anchorites was John of Ryl, who became the patron-saint of Bulgaria. Originally a shepherd, he adopted the life of a recluse, and is said to have passed twenty years in a dark cave, and subsequently in the hollow of an oak tree on the Ryl Planina (Ryl Mountains). He then removed to an inaccessible rock, under which was subsequently built the still existing Ryl Monastery.[1] John of Ryl ended his days about 976 A.D.

And now a word concerning Art at that period. The residence of Simeon was at Great Preslava (Rom. *Marcianopolis*, Turk. *Eski-Stambul*), and accounts of its magnificence have been handed down to us which show that it must at least have been a marvel in the eyes of the barbarous people of that age. It is thus described by a writer of the period:—"When a stranger arrives at the forecourt of the princely residence, he is astonished, and entering at the gates, he makes many curious inquiries. When he comes into the inner courts, he sees on both sides buildings beautifully constructed of stone and decorated with parti-coloured woods; and as he penetrates farther into the residence, he observes high palaces and churches with innumer-

---

[1] A visit to this monastery and the beautiful mountain scenery of Rilo is still a favourite excursion with the few tourists who visit Bulgaria. It is situated from one to two days' journey south of Sofia, and it was here that the Member for one of the divisions of Lancashire had recently his celebrated encounter with invisible "political brigands."

able examples of carved masonry and woods and paintings, the interior being so ornamented with marble, copper, silver, and gold, that he knows not wherewith to compare them; for in his own country he has seen only miserable straw huts. He is almost beside himself and faint with surprise. But if haply he should catch a glimpse of the Prince (Knez) himself as he sits there in his robe trimmed with pearls with a chain of coins round his neck, with bracelets on his wrists, girdled with a purple belt, and a golden sword at his side, whilst on both sides of him are seated his Boyards wearing golden chains, girdles, and bracelets; then, if some one asks him on his return home, 'What did you see there?' his answer will be, 'I do not know how to narrate all that to you; your own senses only could enable you to comprehend such magnificence.'" This was the impression made upon an ecclesiastic of the period by the ancient Bulgarian capital. The seat of Government was afterwards removed to Tirnova, and on the site of Preslav now stands a miserable village, which has been graphically described along with the ruins of the ancient residence by that persevering traveller and archæologist Kanitz.[1] I fear, however, that the startled imagination of the old chronicler has imparted a somewhat idealistic character to his description of the ancient capital. It shows plainly that whilst Prince and nobles dwelt in barbaric splendour in extensive palaces, the mass of the people burrowed (as indeed many of them do to-day) in subterranean dwellings, whose "straw-thatched roofs" just peered above the ground. But when we come to visit the ruins of the ancient palaces of the Czars of the Second Empire at Tirnova, we shall find that the walls decorated with gold were really inlaid with mosaics of gilt glass (copied no doubt from Byzantine models), and that what in the chronicler's eyes appeared to be carved stone, was most likely painted plaster. That ancient Roman pillars of polished marble and Roman tablets and tiles entered largely into the construction of the residences of the Czars, there can be little doubt; for they are not only found amongst the ruins, but, as we shall see, they still serve as supports to the interiors of existing edifices.

---

[1] Vol. iii. pp. 73–77.

After the death of Simeon the first Bulgarian monarchy rapidly declined. Of the appearance of the Northmen (Russians) during the reign of Peter his successor, and of their subsequent retreat and dispersal, mention was made in the first chapter, and it is unnecessary to add anything here concerning them. It will be remembered that during his incursion into the country, the chief Sviatoslav took the Czar Boris II. prisoner, and that he was liberated by the Greek Emperor Zimisces. The latter, however, had no intention to restore the Bulgarian ruler to his throne, but on his return in triumph to Constantinople he compelled him to abdicate, to put off all the emblems of royalty, and to content himself with the position of a magnate at the Byzantine court. In order effectually to exterminate the dynasty, he also caused Roman, the brother of Boris, to be emasculated, and these proceedings broke up the first Bulgarian Empire, after an existence of nearly three centuries. The annexation of Bulgaria to the Greek Empire was, however, far from being complete; for in the western portion a Boyard family, the Sismans (pronounced Shishmans) had been rapidly growing in strength and influence, and for a considerable time they maintained their supremacy as rulers of Macedonia, Albania, Servia, and part of what is now Bulgaria; but eventually they too succumbed to the power of the Greek Empire. During the reign of Samuel, one of the dynasty, the Bulgarians came into collision with Basilius II., the successor of Zimisces. Basilius was at that time a youth of twenty-five years of age; but from his advent to the throne he had made up his mind to conquer and annex the remaining Bulgarian territory. He was a celibate and an ascetic, tasting neither wine nor flesh-meat, was heartless and cruel, and for more than forty years carried on a series of wars against Samuel and his successors, until he had accomplished his design. Those wars were, however, not always successful, and the courage displayed by Samuel has also secured for him a place amongst Bulgarian heroes; indeed, at a later period he was even referred to as a great monarch in the correspondence which took place between Pope Innocent III. and one of the Bulgarian Czars of the Second Empire. The first attempted inroad of Basilius into the territories of Samuel resulted in the humiliating defeat of the former and a narrow escape from capture. After this Basilius was glad to conclude a peace, which lasted for fifteen years. A second and a third war followed, during which the Greek Emperor gradually gained ground in Samuel's territories. Unheard-of cruelties were practised by Basilius during these conflicts. In one case he is said to have blinded fifteen thousand Bulgarian captives, leaving to one in every hundred the sight of a single eye to enable them to lead their companions back to Samuel's headquarters. This barbarous practice was, as already stated, quite common in those days, but it must in this instance have been carried to a terrible excess; for it is said that when Samuel saw the long procession of blinded captives enter his camp, he was so horrified that he sank insensible to the ground, and died shortly afterwards (1014) of a broken heart. The West Bulgarian realm survived his death only a few years, and although he had two or three nominal successors, the Emperor Basilius was able in (1019) to celebrate the complete conquest of the country in Constantinople, dragging the daughter of Samuel and a number of Bulgarian Boyards in his train. His determined cruelty secured for him the well-earned title of the "Bulgar-Slayer."

Little is known to us of the history and condition of Bulgaria during the Greek occupation, which lasted through the eleventh and twelfth centuries: indeed, even the limits of the country were ill-defined, for whilst the power of the Greek Empire was rapidly declining, various races of barbarians were invading and temporarily holding possession of districts on both banks of the Danube. There can be no doubt that during the first Bulgarian monarchy some of the princes who ruled on the southern bank of that river also extended their sway far northward towards the Carpathians, and in like manner there was a fusion of the populations. A controversy has been carried on, and still continues, concerning the origin of the inhabitants of Roumania and Bulgaria; and so far as the former people are concerned, I have already dealt with the matter at length elsewhere.[1] A few

---

[1] "Roumania," cap. x. sect. vi., and elsewhere. Besides the numerous authorities referred to in that work, the reader will find a copious list in Krek, p. 286-290 and notes, and in Jireček, pp. 220-221, and elsewhere.

words on the subject must, however, be added in this place. One of the disputed questions is whether the Roumanians are of Daco-Roman origin, or whether they are only descendants of the pastoral tribe of Wallachs who migrated northwards from Thrace and Bulgaria; and I have accepted the view that they are of Daco-Roman origin, but that there has been a large admixture of the Hungarian and nomad races—the barbarians, as they are called. That view is quite confirmed by a consideration of the contradictory evidence and opinions on the matter as it affects the origin of the inhabitants of the South Danubian plains. During the tenth, eleventh, and twelfth centuries, and later, the Wallachs dwelt in great numbers on both sides of the Danube, but at first chiefly on the southern bank. There (on the south) were districts known to the Greek writers as Great Wallachia, Little Wallachia, and White Wallachia, whilst on the north, Moldavia, or part of it, was known as Black Wallachia. Judging from the past history of the two countries and of the surrounding states, coupled with the results of archæological and philological research, the probabilities, simply and roughly stated, are that originally the Latin or Roman element entered largely into the constitution of the nationalities on both sides of the Danube; that on the south the Slave element prevailed, whilst on the north the old Latin strain has secured the strongest foothold. One thing is certain, namely, that each successive wave of barbarian incursion exercised a perceptible influence upon the population, the more active of whom on the south side took refuge in the Balkans, on the north in the Carpathians. When more peaceable times supervened, the hardy mountaineers again ventured into the plains, often in a hostile attitude. Added to this fusion of races, it must be remembered that the Hungarians crossed the Carpathians from the north, and the Greeks traversed the Balkans from the south, and for a time occupied the respective countries as conquerors; and that circumstance, along with the Turkish occupation of both banks, must have led to very mixed populations to-day, whose precise origin will probably always remain a debated question.

Under the Greek rule Bulgaria was professedly, or it would be more correct to say nominally, autonomous, but was really misgoverned by a considerable number of delegates from Constantinople. It was divided into provinces, over each of which was placed a "Strategus" or governor, who united in his person the civil and military functions, whilst a governor-general exercised authority over the whole. Just as in the case of the Turkish pachas of later days and the Phanariote voivodes in the Principalities, those governors and deputy-governors seldom remained long in office; and whilst they possessed the power they ground down and bled the people to their heart's content. During the Greek occupation inroads of barbarians, especially of the Kumani, were frequent; but they were always eventually repulsed; so also were internal risings, which were more or less successful for the time being; but it was not until the close of the twelfth century that the spirit of the people was fully aroused by the long course of oppression to which they had been subjected, and that they were able to shake off the Greek yoke and once more assert their independence.

About the year 1185, during the reign of the Greek Emperor Isaac Angelos, there dwelt in Tirnova two wealthy brothers, Peter and John Asen, it is said of ancient and noble descent, but who lived as simple citizens. One of them, probably Peter (if not both), had founded the Church of St. Demetrius, whose ruins still remain in good preservation in Tirnova; and that and other works of charity and religion caused him to rank high in the estimation of his fellow-citizens. It is probable that about this time another revolt against the declining Greek rule was contemplated, and, according to some accounts, the two brothers visited Constantinople in search of a pretext for precipitating the revolution. Be that as it may, they are reported to have visited the capital, and to have preferred some request to which the Emperor gave an evasive reply, whilst the "Sevastokrater," a court official of high rank, inflicted a blow in the face upon John Asen, the more high-spirited of the brothers. On their return home, they narrated the occurrences to their fellow-citizens, and a public meeting of the inhabitants was called in the Church of St. Demetrius.[1] The accounts of the meeting

---

[1] It will be seen hereafter that political meetings are still held in churches in Bulgaria.

vary, and some miraculous or legendary circumstances are connected with it; but the facts seem to have been that the people became excited and angry when they were told what had occurred, and cries were raised for the independence of Bulgaria. It is said that some one asked a leading priest, probably the bishop, who had been taking part in the proceedings, "How can our ancient greatness be restored to us without a Czar? Who is there to lead us?" and that the bishop, pointing to Peter Asen, replied, "There stands your leader." Thereupon the cries for independence were renewed, Peter was chosen leader, was crowned, and publicly proclaimed "Czar of the Bulgarians and Greeks."[1] At the same time an independent Patriarch was elected. At first the Bulgarians had great difficulty in securing their independence. Asen and his army were attacked by the Emperor and driven across the Danube, whereupon the latter returned in triumph to Constantinople. Aided by the Kumani, Asen rallied, and crossing the Balkans, invaded Thrace, but was again defeated by the Sevastokrator, John, who was, however, shortly afterwards recalled to the capital, and from that time forward success attended the Bulgarian arms. In 1190 the Emperor Isaac attempted to cross the Balkans, but found the passes strongly fortified, and his troops were harassed and attacked at every available point. Showers of rocks and flights of arrows decimated the troops, and eventually, when the whole army was nearly destroyed, the Emperor beat a retreat, glad to escape with his life, and get back in safety to his capital. On this the Bulgarians assumed the offensive. Sofia was taken, and Asen with his army marched southward; but in the midst of his triumphant career he was assassinated by Ivanko, one of

---

[1] Great confusion exists as to the number and names of the brothers Asen, as I mentioned in my former work. To give a further instance, Jireček, who professes to be very accurate, and gives a genealogical table, says at p. 226, "*Peter* was crowned Czar," &c.; at page 229, "Thus fell *John* Asen;" and on p. 230, "*Peter* undertook the government along with his brother Kalojan." Kalojan really is Kalo-Johann or *John* again. The first ruler was in all probability *John* Asen. Whilst I was at Tirnova, I found on inquiry from men conversant with the history of the country, that only a very general knowledge exists on the subject, and that details are untrustworthy.

his Boyards, whom he had suspected of an intrigue with the sister of the Czarina, and had intended to kill.

Another brother of the Asenidæ now appears upon the scene, namely, Kalojan or Johannitz, and the two surviving brothers prevented Ivanko from mounting the throne, compelling him to take refuge amongst the Kumani. Peter (or John) was soon murdered, and then *Johannitz* reigned alone.[1] This Prince had married a Kumanian, and, with that people as allies, he waged a successful war against the Eastern Emperor, Alexius III., and more than once appeared with his army before the walls of Constantinople.

The two events of the greatest importance in the reign of Kalojan (about 1197 to 1207) were his alliance with Rome and his victories over and capture of the Eastern (Frank) Emperor, Baldwin. His arms had been so successful that he had once more extended the Bulgarian realm over a considerable part of the Balkan Peninsula, for it reached from Belgrade to the Black Sea, and from the Danube (indeed, in all probability, from the northern plains of that river) to the River Vardar. But one thing was needed to give security to his throne, and that was the sanction of the Church, which everywhere exercised great influence over the State. From Constantinople he could not expect such a favour, for the Greeks were his bitterest enemies; indeed, they regarded him and his race as usurpers of their territory, and he therefore appealed to Rome. More than once his emissaries tried to reach the Eternal City, but were intercepted by the Greeks and Hungarians, until at length Innocent III., hearing of the attempted missions, sent an envoy to him in the person of a Greek priest of Brindisi, who appealed to him as the descendant of an old Roman line (he addressed Johannitz as a Roumanian) to submit himself and his people to the Apostolic Chair.[2] After attributing the victories of Kalojan to the protection which God had afforded to him, the Pope goes on to say:—" We, when we heard that thy forefathers sprang

---

[1] See preceding note.

[2] In another place I have already given a full account of the correspondence, published *in extenso* by Lauriani, but, as it forms part of Bulgarian rather than Roumanian history, a further reference to it must be made here.

from the noble city of Rome, and that thou didst not only inherit the nobility of their race, but also true humility towards the Apostolic Chair, had contemplated ere this to address thee in writing as well as by word of mouth through our Nuncios, but the cares of the Church have prevented us hitherto from carrying out our design, . . . and we have now sent to thee our beloved son Dominicus, Archpriest of Brundus," whom he required Johannitz to protect, and through him to send his complete submission to the Church. Whether on account of his nationality (he was a Greek), or from some other cause, the Bulgarian prince received the Nuncio with suspicion, but at length he sent the Pope a letter in which he styles himself "Calojohannes, Imperator Blacorum" (of the Wallachs) "et Bulgarorum," acknowledges the Pope's letter, and, after complacently reciting and accepting all the flattering things which the latter had said about him, he goes on in a roundabout way to profess his desire and that of his subjects to become children in the bosom of the mother Church, and winds up with a request that a crown may be sent to him with an acknowledgment of his sovereignty. He also asks him to send a higher Nuncio, for he was not quite satisfied with the *bonâ fide* character of the bearer of the Pope's first letter.

A further correspondence ensued, beginning with a letter from the Pope, in which he said he had searched the registers, and found that Michael (*i.e.*, Boris), an ancestor of Kalojan, had indeed embraced Christianity, and that he had received from Pope Adrian a sub-deacon and some priests, but that, seduced by the bribes and promises of the Greeks, the Bulgarians had driven them away and had taken Greek priests in their place. In consequence of this, he (Innocent) did not see his way to send a cardinal, but he sent his chaplain John with full power to "improve everything of a *spiritual* nature in the realm." He also sent by him a *pallium* for the Archbishop, and a Bull, which was to be promulgated by Kalojan, announcing the investiture; indeed, the new Nuncio was empowered to ordain ecclesiastics of all ranks, and to substitute the Roman for the Greek faith throughout the realm. The crown was, however, not sent at that time, as the Pope "had to institute inquiries as to the exact position of the ancestors of Kalojan." Just as in the case of the first Christian Prince Boris or Michael, Kalojan found it politic, on secular grounds, to comply with the request of Innocent, and submit himself to the Apostolic Chair, and the Bull was accordingly published.

The circumstances which expedited his decision were these: In the year 1203, the army of the Fourth Crusade, led by Dandolo, the Venetian Doge, appeared before the walls of Constantinople, and in the following year captured that city, and temporarily broke up the Greek Empire, Count Baldwin of Flanders having been crowned as the first Emperor of the Franks.[1] Terrified by their approach, Kalojan sought the alliance of the Crusaders, and offered to aid them before Constantinople with a large army, if they would acknowledge him as sovereign of Bulgaria. His offer was rejected, and when at a later period the Emperor Baldwin entered Thrace, and Kalojan again made friendly advances, he was told that he ought to approach the Emperor not as a prince, but as a slave who had usurped the territory of his master. Just about that time, however, the Pope sent another envoy to Tirnova in the person of Cardinal Leo, this time the bearer of a crown and sceptre for Kalojan, who was crowned amidst great rejoicings about November 1204. He received along with his diadem a standard bearing the picture of St. Peter, and the right to coin money with his own likeness.[2] At the same time an Archbishop or Primate and several bishops and minor ecclesiastics were installed in Bulgaria. These proceedings are known as "Kalojan's Alliance."

It would have been better for the Frank Emperor if he had treated Kalojan with a little more respect and consideration, for in the following year the scattered Greeks solicited the aid of

---

[1] Hallam's "Middle Ages," vol. ii. p. 130-132, 12th edition, Murray, contains a graphic description of the city of Constantinople, and an account of the political events of the period.

[2] Jireček, p. 237, and Kaintz, vol. i. p. 160. Many of the coins of the Bulgarian Czars are preserved in the museums of Belgrade, Philippopolis, &c. They bear rude images of the Czar, and usually of his wife. Reference will be made to them hereafter.

the latter against the Franks, and he joyfully responded to their call. An encounter took place near Adrianople between the Greeks, Bulgarians, and Kumani (Kalojan had, as stated, married a Kumanian woman, and was in close alliance with the people), led by Kalojan and a brave Kumanian chief, and the Franks under Baldwin, the Emperor, when a portion of the Frank army, headed by the Count of Blois, was drawn into an ambuscade, and a complete rout of the Latins was the result. The Count of Blois and many knights were killed, and Baldwin himself was taken prisoner. The fate of the latter is buried in mystery. According to some historians he was well treated by Kalojan, whilst others say he caused him to be mutilated and buried alive. One thing is certain, he was kept a prisoner, probably in a castle, of which the ruins still remain, on the walls of Tirnova, and known as Baldwin's Tower;[1] and almost equally certain it is that he died a violent death not long after his defeat before Adrianople. Shortly afterwards, when he had carried through one or two more successful military adventures, Kalojan was himself killed, it is said by his own general, a Kumanian, at the instigation of the Czarina. This man is said to have entered the Czar's tent at night, to have stabbed him whilst he was asleep, disappeared, and returned from an adjoining tent in answer to the cries of the wounded Czar. The wound was, however, fatal only on the following day, and not until the Czar had accused his general of his murder, which the latter strenuously denied.

From the death of Kalojan until the year 1218 the throne of Bulgaria was occupied by a usurper, Boril, and nothing occurred during his reign to call for notice. In that year he in his turn was defeated and dethroned by *John Asen II.*, the son of one of the founders of the dynasty, who reigned from 1218 to 1241, and is regarded as the greatest of the Bulgarian Czars of the Second Empire.

---

[1] See initial letter and also the chapter on Tirnova in Part II.

CHAPTER V.

JOHN ASEN II. (1218-1241) AND HIS TIMES—THE FALL OF THE SECOND EMPIRE.

The victories of John Asen II. over the Greeks—Capture of the Emperor—Eulogies of Asen's greatness—Zenith of the Bulgarian Empire—Return to the Greek Church—Election of a Patriarch—Tirnova, the capital—Its grandeur—The condition of society—The Bulgarians, Wallachs, Saxons, Greeks, &c.—Traders and trade with Ragusa, Venice, and Genoa—Rise of towns—Serfdom—Agriculture—The ruling classes—Court officials—Czarinas—Court extravagance—The alliances of John Asen II.—The extent of his realm—His death, 1241 A.D.—His immediate successors—Dissolution of his empire—The Tartar invasion—Ivajlo—Conquest of Bulgaria by Stephen Uros of Servia—King Dushan—His government of the Balkan Peninsula—His death (1355)—First appearance of the Turks in Bulgaria.

THE long reign of John Asen II. is remarkable not so much for his victories over his enemies and the extension of his realm, although those were great, and he carried his arms successfully to the very gates of Constantinople,[1] where the surrounding districts acknowledged his sway, but because during his reign his country took equal rank with other European powers of more ancient date. His own voice reaches us through the ages, for in a tablet or inscription, which will be found fully translated farther on, and which may still be seen in the Church of the Forty Martyrs at Tirnova, he himself tells us how he went forth in the twelfth year of his reign against the Greeks (who

---

[1] "The Latin Emperors of Constantinople were more contemptible and unfortunate, not so much from personal character as from political weakness, than their predecessors; their vassals rebelled against sovereigns not more powerful than themselves; the Bulgarians, a nation who, after being long formidable, had been subdued by the imperial arms, and only recovered independence on the eve of the Latin conquest, insulted their capital."—*Hallam*, "*Middle Ages*," vol. ii. p. 130-131.

still maintained their hold on part of the Peninsula), conquering them and all their allies and neighbours, and how he took the Greek Emperor, Theodor Komnenos, prisoner, with all his nobles, and overran and subjected all lands held by the Greeks in Albania and Servia, and appeared before Constantinople, which was almost the sole remaining stronghold of the Franks in Europe, and that, although he did not capture the city, even the Franks acknowledged his sway. And his contemporaries of many nations have also sung his praises, including the chroniclers of his own realm. An anonymous Bulgarian monk says concerning him :—" Johannes Asen, the great and pious Czar, son of the old Czar Asen, exalted the Bulgarian Empire with great devotion to the Almighty more highly than all his predecessors. He built monasteries, and adorned them with gold, pearls, and precious stones; endowed all sacred and divine churches with many presents, and displayed towards them great generosity; every rank of the hierarchy were the recipients of his benefits and honours, and he re-established the Patriarchate of the Bulgarian Empire."

In connection with this eulogium, it should be mentioned that when Kalojan, his predecessor, had succeeded in obtaining his crown from Pope Innocent, and in conquering and capturing the Frank Emperor Baldwin, he gave himself little further trouble about the Papacy or the Church of Rome; and John Asen II., as it appears, reintroduced the Greek faith, which prevailed in Bulgaria amongst the Christian population down to the recent establishment of the National Church.

But the benefits of his (John Asen's) reign extended to all ranks and classes, secular as well as sacred. His capital, Tirnova, was greatly beautified, and was the admiration of all by whom it was visited, and who pronounced it to be second only in grandeur to Constantinople. In the second part of this treatise we shall inspect some of the relics which bear witness to the mediaeval grandeur of the old Bulgarian capital; but meanwhile we can only gather from the divergent and fragmentary notices of writers of various dates that two high and extensive hills which constitute part of the city, and between which the River Jantra flows, were surrounded by fortified walls, composed partly of natural escarpments of limestone rock and partly of artificial stonework; that upon those hills stood the palaces of the Czars and of the Primate or Patriarch, which are described much in the same strain as was the residence of Simeon at Preslava. Hammer, the historian of Turkey, quoting Hadji Chalfa (died 1658), says that in the sixteenth century " in the centre of the town there rises a hexagonal castle with six towers, built of hewn stone; the Jantra flows round the castle like a crescent, and two of the towers communicate with the river." One of these is no doubt Baldwin's Tower. Upon those two hills there are said to have been also beautiful gardens containing fruit-trees and flowers. Of the trees some traces remain, but generally speaking they are as bare as the summit of a Welsh or Derbyshire hill. The town surrounding those eminences is believed to have been founded by John Asen II., who also either beautified existing churches or built new ones in various parts of the city. But as a matter of fact, a ramble over the ruins of modern Tirnova, and an inspection of its existing buildings which have remained intact from the time of the Czars, will enable us to form a better idea of the vastness and grandeur of the ancient capital than even the most high-flown accounts of mediæval chroniclers or of their modern successors, into whose descriptions the play of the imagination has freely entered. Compared with the surrounding States, and indeed with most European countries, Bulgaria must have attained at that time a much higher stage of civilisation than it enjoys in the present day. For its greatness and prosperity were not confined to the court and capital. Under John Asen and his immediate successors, agriculture, trade, and handicrafts flourished. The population consisted of Bulgarians and Wallachs, the latter in such numbers that, as we have seen, the monarchs styled themselves Czars of the Wallachians and Bulgarians; of Greeks, who chiefly dwelt in the seaports; Saxons, who had crossed the Danube from Transylvania, where they had established colonies (and where they still constitute the most industrious and thrifty members of the community), and had entered Bulgaria proper through Servia; and Jews, who were spread over the whole country. The inland trade was carried on by and with the

D

Ragusans, Venetians, and Genoese, chiefly, however, by the first-named, who enjoyed and granted the Bulgarians special trading privileges. In a treaty made with them by Michael Asen, 1253, it was decreed that the Bulgarian traders should be permitted, without paying toll or tax at gate, ford, or bridge, to enter the city of Ragusa and dispose of whatever they had for sale, and to purchase and bring away gold, silver, drapery, gold-embroidered stuffs, or any other manufacture or product except grain, for which special permission was requisite; and in like manner the merchants of Ragusa and the other towns named were permitted to establish guilds throughout Bulgaria, where they settled in the towns, built churches, and dwelt unmolested with their wives, concubines, and children. They then already had Consuls, and the Venetian Consul lived in Varna.

Towns sprang up or were enlarged, and a free burgher class existed; but the mass of the population consisted of serfs, who were attached to the soil. Then, as now, great herds of cattle, sheep, and horses (the latter bred chiefly for warlike purposes) pastured upon the plains, and agriculture was largely followed.

I have said that the serfs were attached to the soil, but in time they became chattels, the property of the princes and Boyards, and the free peasants, of whom many existed, became debtors from inability to pay taxes, and afterwards also serfs. These were sold and given away with estates, including even the lower order of priests, who were often vassals not only of the landed proprietors, but of monastic corporations. Slaves there were also, namely, barbarians captured in war. It is needless further to describe the system of vassalage, which, in its customs of forced labour, &c., closely resembled that which prevailed throughout Europe. In like manner, the ruling classes there, as elsewhere, existed in different degrees. There were greater and lesser Boyards, as in Wallachia (and as we had greater and lesser barons), who constituted the Imperial Council, presided over by the Czar, and who acted as a check upon his absolute rule. Many of these were semi-independent, and exercised unrestricted authority on their estates and in their own neighbourhood, where they resided part of the year; the remaining portion was spent in Tirnova, the capital. Besides the last-named, important towns were Vidin, Sofia, Preslava, Sliven, Sredec, Great Nicopolis (at the junction of the Rusica and Jantra rivers), Silistria, Varna, &c.

Monasteries were numerous and richly endowed, that of Ryl, already referred to, being the chief, and the monastic orders, like the merchants of the three cities named, enjoyed special trading privileges.

The officials of the court bore a close resemblance to those of Wallachia, and their titles were chiefly borrowed from Constantinople, indicating the duties which appertained to the office; as Protovestiar, Master of the Robes; Protocomus, Master of the Horse; Logothet, Minister of Justice, &c.[1] The highest court official was the "Despot" (his wife, "Despotica"), the next the "Sevastocrator,"[2] both these being usually (as in Constantinople), members of the royal house.

The Czarinas were of all nationalities, and there appears to have been only one legitimate wife. Amongst them were eight Greeks, five Bulgarians, three Servians, two Wallachians, one Kumanian (the wife of Kalojan), one Hungarian, and one beautiful Jewess, for whom the Czar Alexander (1331–1365) divorced his wife Theodora, daughter of the Prince of Wallachia, who retired into a convent. The Jewish Czarina embraced Christianity.

The customs of the court were ostentatious and extravagant, and its hospitality unbounded. Especially were the marriage ceremonies gorgeous. One royal bride brought sixty horse-loads of gold, silver, silk, and other adornments as dowry, and each beast of burden was decked in red velvet, which trailed many feet behind. During his negotiations with the Papacy, Kalojan sent the Pope presents of great value. One mission (which did not reach him) was accompanied with gifts of gold, silver, silk, wax, horses, mules, and other valuables; and we read of carousals on great state occasions lasting over several weeks.

In this brief account of the condition of Bulgaria during the

---

[1] The Wallachian court officials have been described in "Roumania," p. 179.
[2] It will be remembered that the Sevastocrator struck one of the brothers Asen before the declaration of independence.

time of John Asen II., I have included some details which belong more properly to the reigns of his immediate successors, Kaliman and Michael; the reason being, that from the time of his death down to the Turkish conquest, the influence and prosperity of Bulgaria declined, and its territories diminished in extent, as rapidly as they had grown under him and his predecessors, and there is very little in the course of events during that period to interest English readers.

Like many other Eastern rulers of his day in Hungary, Wallachia, Constantinople, and elsewhere, John Asen was constantly making and breaking alliances; now with Bela, the great king of Hungary, then with Vatatz, ruler of Nice, who occupied one of the fast-dissolving territories of the Eastern Empire; and again when it suited his views, with the Pope, in order if possible to secure the possession of Constantinople; but the only important outcome of these alliances was that they contributed to the fall of the Frankish rule in the last-named city, and facilitated the restoration of the Greek dynasty, which took place in 1261, when Michael Palæologus resumed the sway at Constantinople.[1]

In 1241 died John Asen II. His youth, says Jireček, was passed in exile, and his advent to the throne was surrounded with great difficulties, but after Simeon he was the greatest ruler Bulgaria ever had. His realm was washed by three seas, his alliances were made with all the surrounding great Powers, the State Church of his country was re-established, all sects were tolerated, edifices sprang up, trade flourished, and prosperity reigned throughout the whole land.[2]

With the death of John Asen II. (1241 A.D.), the rule of the Asenide dynasty (and with it the second Bulgarian Empire) was practically at an end. His sons, Kaliman and Michael, followed in the course of sixteen years, and then their cousin, Kaliman II., a usurper, seized the throne, after murdering the

---

[1] Hallam, "Middle Ages," ii. 191.
[2] An excellent account of the condition of Bulgaria during the twelfth to the fifteenth centuries will be found in Jireček, chap. xxv., where the mode of levying taxes, the names and value of coins, and other information is given in detail.

second named; but he reigned only a few months, the last of
the Asenidæ, and was killed like his predecessor. During this
brief period all the possessions of John II. had melted away,
reverting to the Greek, Macedonian, and Servian rulers. Other
Bulgarian chiefs followed, some of whom took the name of
Asen; and amidst the decline of the native power Tartar hordes
invaded the countries north and south of the Danube. These
were manfully resisted, not by the rulers of the country, but in
the south by independent warlike adventurers. One of them,
Ivajlo, is said to have been originally a shepherd, who gathered
an army of free-lances about him and repelled the invaders.
Growing in power, he attacked, routed, and killed the reigning
prince, married his widow, and for a short time established his
throne at Tirnova (about 1278). He was, however, soon dislodged in his turn, and took refuge with some tribal chief in
the south of Russia, by whom he is said to have been assassinated. Ruler followed ruler, if the succession of pretenders
can be so called, until one of these, Michael of Bydn (Vidin),
waged an unsuccessful war against Servia. He met the king,
Stephen Uros, at Köstendil (1330), where (the battle being
known as that of Velbuzd), although the Bulgarians are said to
have performed prodigies of valour, they were defeated. Michael
was slain, and the Servian king marching to Tirnova, received
the homage of the Bulgarian nobility. Although a nominal
king was permitted to Bulgaria, the country practically fell
under Servian rule, and the successor of Stephen Uros, King
Dushan, extended his realm almost as widely as John Asen II.,
assuming the title of " Czar and Autocrat of the Servians, Greeks,
Bulgarians, and Albanians." Trade recovered throughout the
land, order prevailed, a code of laws was instituted based upon
the edicts of the older rulers; but during the reign of Dushan,
and in all for a quarter of a century, Bulgaria was a mere
dependency of Servia.

About the year 1353 a new Power, the Ottomans, made their
appearance in Bulgaria, and after the death of Stephen Dushan
(1355), that people gradually overran and took possession of
the country.

CHAPTER VI.

THE TURKISH RULE IN BULGARIA.

Advent of the Turks in Europe—Extension of their power into Bulgaria—Defeat of the Christians at Kosovo pole by Bajazet I.—Fall of Tirnova—Fate of the inhabitants—The Patriarch Euthemius—His exile—Capture and death of Sisman—Complete subjection of Bulgaria—The great battle of Nicopolis—Destruction of the Frank army, 1396—Fall of Constantinople, 1453—Absence of records during Turkish rule in Bulgaria—Name changed to Rumelia—The Government—Oppressive taxes—Conscriptions for the army—Forced contributions and rape of girls—Tyranny of the military and of the Begs—Continuance of oppression down to the Russo-Turkish War—Anecdotes of Turkish arrogance and debauchery of the young Begs—Extortion of officials—The Phanariote priests and ecclesiastics—Their extortion and corruption—The Phanar—Sale of offices—Immorality of the priesthood—Bulgarian priests to-day—Charges against them—Semi-independence of the mountaineers—Their raids into the plains—Brigandage—Revenge upon the Turks for Christian wrongs—Fate of a young Turkish nobleman—"Robin Hood" in the Balkans—Osman of Vidin and his history—His raids and conflicts with the Porte—Takes service under the Government—Death, 1807—Condition of Bulgaria after the Crimean War—Increased cruelty and oppression by the Turks—Revival of national education and literature—The first Bulgarian school at Gabrovo—Aprilov and Neofyt—The struggle for religious freedom—Foundation of the Bulgarian National Church—The Greeks and the "Schismatics"—The Mohammedans and the Bulgarians—Their amicable relations.

ABOUT the middle of the fourteenth century a section of the Greeks, who still retained power in the Balkan Peninsula, invited as allies a Turkish tribe, who had settled in Bithynia, to cross over into Europe. Of this invitation they eagerly availed themselves, and, either under Amurath [1] or under Suleiman the son of Orchan,[2] a band of Ottomans first set foot on the European mainland, and planted themselves in the neighbourhood of Constantinople. Thence they carried their arms throughout the peninsula, captured Adrianople, in which city the Sultan

---

[1] Hallam, ii. 132.   [2] Jireček, p. 308.

Murad took up his residence about 1365; and in the course of about twenty-five years they reduced the greater part of Bulgaria, Albania, and Thrace under subjection. Rallying themselves for a supreme effort, the remaining Danubian peoples formed an alliance, and in the year 1389 the battle of Amsel (Kosovo pole) was fought between the Turks under Bajazet I. (his father having been assassinated before the fight) and a Christian army consisting of Servians, Bosnians, Bulgarians, and Wallachians from beyond the Danube. The Christians were completely defeated, and after the battle Bajazet returned in triumph to Adrianople, where he is said to have indulged in every kind of excess. Shortly afterwards Bajazet made an incursion across the Danube into Wallachia, aided, it is said, by a Bulgarian renegade leader, a "Shishman;" but the brave Voivode Mircea repelled the invasion, and drove the Turks back into Bulgaria.[1] Meanwhile the whole of that country was being rapidly subdued. In 1393 Tirnova was besieged, and occupied after a three months' investment. The priests were driven from the churches, the sacred elements cast to the dogs; churches were converted into mosques, stables, and baths (just as mosques have recently been converted into churches, printing-offices, and gaols!). The forts and palaces of the "Hissar" and "Trapezitz" (the two hills already referred to) were set in flames and destroyed, and plunder and outrage followed the capture of the city. The Patriarch Euthemius for a time succeeded in mollifying the fury of the conquerors, and he was treated with respect by the commander-in-chief (probably Bajazet's son). As soon, however, as the latter had retired, and the city was left in the hands of a governor, this one renewed the slaughter and excesses. Euthemius himself was imprisoned, and at first condemned to death, but afterwards (putting aside legendary accounts of his escape from death) he was driven out of the city and became a wanderer in Macedonia. Priests and laymen who possessed wealth or rank were exiled to the East, and the Mussulman faith and rule permanently established.

---

[1] "Roumania," p. 165. Mircea was, however, obliged to become a Turkish vassal after the battle of Nicopolis, referred to in the text.

After the fall of Tirnova, in the pithy sentence of an Eastern chronicler, "Bajazid caught Sišman, the ruler of the Bulgarians, and killed him in the year 6903, and at that time the Turks took the whole land of the Bulgarians."

It is necessary now to say a few words concerning the battle of Nicopolis (1396), which decided the fate not alone of Bulgaria, but of all the Christian States of South-Eastern Europe. After the defeat of the Christians at Kosovo pole, alarm at the Turkish advance spread throughout Europe, and hundreds of emissaries were sent from all the Eastern Christian States to solicit Western aid. A powerful army was organised under the command of King Sigismund of Hungary, and after capturing some of the fortresses on the Danube, it was met at Nicopolis by a superior force under Bajazet.[1] The Christian army comprised the flower of the nobility of Europe, embracing knights with their following from Burgundy, France, Nuremberg, Bavaria, Suabia, and Styria; also Knights of St. John and other Christian orders, with contingents from Servia, Transylvania, and Wallachia, the last under Voivode Mirçea, who is said to have deserted to the Turks when he found the tide of victory setting in favour of their arms. The first onslaught by the Christian army, which was divided into a centre and two wings, was completely successful, and about 15,000 Janissaries and Spahis are said to have been slain. Flushed with victory, the Christian knights descended from their horses to mount an eminence in pursuit of the fleeing Turks, but when they arrived on the summit, they found themselves confronted by the flower of Bajazet's army, which he had kept in reserve under his own command, and which numbered, according to some chroniclers, upwards of 40,000 men. From that moment the fate of the Christians was decided. The Turks assumed the offensive, and although the Christian knights fought with their accustomed valour, their ranks were soon thrown into confusion, and a rout followed. Many of the leaders, along with the bulk of their followers, fell upon the

---

[1] There has long been a controversy as to the place at which this battle was fought. Some writers say it was at Nicopolis on the Danube, others at "Great Nicopolis," now a wretched village, near the junction of the Jantra and Rusica rivers.

field of battle; others, with many prisoners, were heartlessly murdered on the following day; the more wealthy and influential nobles were ransomed for large sums of money, and Sigismund escaped with difficulty back into his own kingdom. The fall of Constantinople in 1453 completed the Turkish victories, and firmly established the Ottoman rule in Europe.

For more than three and a half centuries Bulgaria had no history, or at least no historical records worthy of the name, and the fanaticism of her rulers during that period destroyed many documents which would have thrown light upon her earlier history. We shall find traces of this Vandalism when we come to visit the churches of Tirnova. The very name of the country was changed; it was Rumelia, a Turkish province, divided into sanjaks, which were governed by Begs, and who in their turn were supposed to be under the authority of a Begler-Beg, resident in Sofia. As a matter of fact, however, the petty governors were in many cases semi-independent, and were often Bulgarian Christians who had become converts to Islamism. The soil of the country became to a large extent the property of Turkish lords, who levied a tax of one-third of the produce. The taxes and imposts were otherwise onerous—the haratsch, a poll-tax of a ducat per head per annum; a tenth of the products of the soil; forced labour; and, above all, "free-will gifts" to Pashas and Begs. But these were not the worst phases of Turkish rule. Whilst the corps of Janissaries existed, every fifth male child was forced into the Turkish military service, and young girls were carried off by thousands to fill the harems of the conquerors, or otherwise minister to their lusts. The Mohammedans were the privileged governing class, and the haughty bearing of their troops, which marched to and fro in the country, their tyranny and extortions, so cowed the Christian population, that in the course of time they became timid serfs, just as in Wallachia. Many escaped death or the loss of property by embracing Islam, and in later years it was not uncommon for parents voluntarily to send their daughters into the harems of the Begs, so that they might themselves be able to appeal to them for protection against the tyranny of minor officials. Without reference to the periods of revolt and insurrection, which justified still greater lust and cruelty in the eyes of the conquerors, it is a fact that this was the state of affairs even down to a very recent period. Whilst I was at Philippopolis, I met on several occasions a gentleman, still comparatively young, who described what he knew personally of the relations between the two races before the Russo-Turkish war. He was a gentleman who had risen from a comparatively humble station, and during his earlier life he had seen instances without number of the arrogant bearing of the Turks towards the poorer rayahs. It was not at all an unusual thing, he said, for a number of young Begs, or men of station, to make an excursion into some neighbouring village, order the girls to be brought out to dance for their amusement, and afterwards to compel them to spend the night with them in debauchery. Respectable girls fled in terror when a Turk entered a Christian village or house; they blackened their faces and resorted to various devices to make themselves repulsive. As the hour of liberation approached, the relatives or friends of maltreated girls retaliated, and, as in Ireland, seducers and tyrants were often assassinated. He told me of one circumstance which appeared to me so ludicrous and incredible, that I doubted it until another Eastern friend, who is well acquainted with the Turks and their ways, assured me that it was a common occurrence. A Beg, or Turkish official of some kind, walked into the house of a relative, I believe the father of my acquaintance, and requested him to prepare a meal for him. This was done at once, and an excellent repast was placed before the intruder, who, however, waited for something farther and did not begin eating. The host, if his enforced entertainer could be so called, said, "Will not my lord partake of the good things which I have prepared for him?" "Certainly not," said the Turk; "first I must have my tooth-money" (I forget the technical name for it); "do you suppose I am going to wear out my teeth for nothing?" As I said, this was not long before the vision of independence, and the host was disinclined to bleed any farther; so he said, "I don't understand you, my lord; but I will fetch the Kmet (Mayor), who will explain." He hastily departed, and shortly returned with the Kmet, having no doubt told him whilst he was absent what had occurred. The Turk was still waiting for his "tooth-money," and had not begun his meal. "What is it my lord desires?" asked the Kmet; "is not the food to your liking?" "Yes," said the Turk, "I daresay it is all right; but tell that fellow to pay me my tooth-money." "Your tooth-money!" said the Kmet, coming close up to him, and putting his fist in the face of the Turk; "if you are not satisfied with what is put before you, you will have this for tooth-money." The Turk rose without tasting the food, and left the house, saying to the two men, "You shall suffer for this insolence." But they neither heard nor saw anything more of him.

Nor was it from their Moslem conquerors alone that the people of Bulgaria had to suffer exactions and oppression. The Greek Phanariotes, who in Wallachia secured the highest civil posts by bribery and corruption, succeeded by the same means in obtaining clerical or ecclesiastical offices in Bulgaria.

I have given elsewhere at considerable length a history of the Phanariotes and their doings north of the Danube,[1] but a few words concerning them must be added in this place. It is well known that they occupied a quarter of Constantinople called the Phanar; that they were enterprising and learned as compared with the Mohammedan rulers and chiefs, and that many of them from being menials rose to the highest offices in the State. What their moral character was in after years may be gathered from an account which is given of them by the Prussian Ambassador in Constantinople in 1779; and as it would lose by translation, I prefer to transcribe the original: "Le quartier est la demeure de ce qu'on appelle la noblesse grecque, qui vivent tous aux dépenses des princes de Moldavie et de Valachie. C'est une université de toutes les scélératesses, et il n'existe pas encore de langue assez riche pour donner des noms à toutes celles qui s'y committent. Le fils y apprend de bonne heure à assassiner si adroitement son père pour quelque argent, qu'il ne saurait être poursuivi. Les intrigues, les cabales, l'hypocrisie,

---

[1] "Roumania," p. 208 et seq.

la trahison, la perfidie, surtout l'art d'extorquer de l'argent de toutes mains y sont enseignés methodiquement."[1] It is not to be wondered at, if youths learned at an early age to assassinate their fathers for money without fear of detection, and were instructed in all the arts of extortion, that they should become adepts in those arts when they attained manhood and found a field for enterprise in a conquered State. The high places in the Church in Bulgaria were openly sold to them by the Porte, and the purchase-money *with interest* was recovered from the unfortunate flocks to whose spiritual welfare they ministered. Cooks and barbers, and Kafedzis (coffee-makers) and Chibukdzis, (pipe-fillers) became bishops; and it is said that the cost of the Patriarchate varied at different times from 5000 to 150,000 ducats. Practically all the clerical posts were sold to the highest bidder. In about 400 years there were 140 Patriarchs, which means that before one had time to recover his "purchase-money" and line his purse, intrigues in Constantinople (just as in the case of the Phanariote princes in Wallachia and Moldavia) led to his deposition, and the office was sold to his successor. The clergy, even the highest of them, are charged not only with extortion and tyranny, but with every species of immorality, and some of the bishops are said to have led lives of drunkenness and debauchery. They treated their priests as menial servants, compelled them to fetch firewood, draw water, and groom their horses; and it was no uncommon occurrence for a bishop to strike one of his priests at the altar.

The Bulgarian clergy are still accused of drunkenness and dissolute living, but I think the charge, like all such accusations against an entire class, is too general. In moving through the country I had frequent opportunities of noticing the priests, especially in the smaller towns, and I made a point not only of looking at them, but of inquiring into their habits. The faces of some of the older ones as they trudge along the road sufficiently justify a portion of the charge, but there are many energetic priests, both young and old, who perform their duties

---

[1] Zinkeisen, *Geschichte des Osmanischen Reiches*, vi. 252. The reader should peruse Marc Zallony, "Essai sur les Phanariotes," Marseilles, Ricard, 1824, for a full account of the Phanariotes.

well, and lead as exemplary lives as the clergy of any denomination in any land.

Although the spirit of the nation was broken by the Turkish conquest and subsequent rule, it was not entirely extinguished, and in the mountainous districts the people managed to retain a kind of semi-independence. The taxes were lighter, and in return for accorded privileges, auxiliaries were voluntarily sent to support the Turkish arms in their foreign wars. But this semi-independence was of doubtful advantage to the inhabitants of the plains, into which the mountaineers descended for purposes of plunder. A curious state of affairs, however, often resulted from this anarchy. When the peasantry and the inoffensive populace generally were maltreated by the Turkish Begs or other officials, they appealed to the brigands, Haiduts, Kirdjalis, or by whatever name they were known, for protection or revenge. We read in one place of a young Turkish nobleman who had been guilty of the greatest cruelty and excesses—had committed rapes on the wives and daughters of the peasantry, captured and sold children—entering a village on horseback surrounded by his retinue all decked in silk and gold. He had not proceeded far when a band of Haiduts, led by a well-known chief, sprang from places of concealment, pulled the Beg from his horse, broke his arms and legs, and struck off his head, which was fixed on a spear and carried in triumph in front of the band as it retired from the village. Many similar instances are recorded of brigand chiefs with their followers leading a kind of Robin Hood life in the mountains. Some of them became so formidable that the Porte was obliged to take them into its service and recognise their authority. One illustration must suffice, namely, that of Osman Pasvanoglu, the independent Pasha of Vidin, who lived during the latter half of the last century. He was born about the middle of the century, and his first experience as a young man was the murder of his father by a Turkish official at Vidin; whereupon he left the town and adopted a brigand life in the mountains of Albania. Tired of that life, he took service under the Porte at the head of a troop of volunteers; but his power grew so rapidly that he exercised an almost independent rule, and the formidable forces which he had at his command roamed about the country fighting and plundering to their hearts' content, so that it was unsafe for travellers, even ecclesiastics, to move about from place to place. Many vain attempts were made by the Porte to reduce him to submission; large armies were sent against him, but they were driven back discomfited, and it was not until he felt his power beginning to wane that he again offered his services to the Sultan in his war with Servia. They were accepted, and he was confirmed in the possession of his Pashalik at Vidin. He died in 1807; and about that time a small army of Turkish regular troops succeeded in breaking up and dispersing the formidable bands of brigands which infested various parts of Bulgaria and the neighbouring States. About brigands and brigandage I shall have a few words to say in the Second Part of this treatise.

The political position of Bulgaria as it was affected by the struggles between Russia and Turkey (which I have described elsewhere[1]), differed in some respects from that of the Principalities north of the Danube. In what is now Roumania the Turkish rule had never been so fully established as in Bulgaria; in fact, the Hospodars who ruled in the former country for some time after the treaty of Adrianople (1829) were under Russian protection, and Russian influence was predominant in Roumania until after the Crimean War. On the other hand, in Bulgaria, which was farther from the Russian centre of operations, the tyrannical power of the Porte still prevailed, and the temporary relief afforded during a war in which the Russian forces pressed down towards Constantinople, the aid and countenance given to their fellow-Slaves by the Bulgarians, the hopes of liberation that were raised at the conclusion of a peace, and the risings which resulted after the desertion—or it would be more correct to say the retirement—of the Russians, only led to a more vindictive retaliation and the infliction of greater cruelties and excesses by the dominant race when they had no longer any cause to apprehend interference from their formidable Northern enemy. Thus it was that, after the conclusion of the Crimean

---

[1] "Roumania," p. 215 et seq.

War, which brought with it emancipation from Ottoman rule for the Principalities north of the Danube, the condition of Bulgaria was worse than before, and that for nearly twenty years she continued to languish in Turkish fetters, and when she revolted was scourged with whips of scorpions.

But throughout this period of trial a new force was silently at work in the country, which did more to animate the spirit of patriotism than foreign aid or the hope which it engendered in the minds of the people—I mean the revival of national education. As far back as the middle of the eighteenth century a monk of Athos, Païsius, published a "Slaveno-Bulgarian History of the Bulgarian Nation, Czars, and Saints," and this, with kindred productions, fostered a strong spirit of animosity against the Turkish rule. The pupils of Païsius continued to disseminate Sclavonic literature, and the result was a desire for native schools. When we visit Gabrovo, we shall have an opportunity to judge of the importance of that movement, for it was there that the first Bulgarian school was opened, through the generosity and patriotism of a wealthy trader, Aprilov, in the year 1835. It was there, too, that a young monk, Neophytus, gathered round him, as its first director, over a hundred scholars, most of whom afterwards became missionaries to foster education throughout Bulgaria, and, as we shall find, it is there that some of the leading youth of Bulgaria are still prepared for active life and public service. With the revival of literature and a knowledge of the past history of the country came the determination to be rid of the Phanariote priesthood and a desire to found a National Church. An account of the struggle for religious freedom between the Bulgarians and the Greek hierarchy, although very important to those whom it nearly affected, would have little interest for English readers, and it must suffice to say that the Greek Patriarch and hierarchy at Constantinople for a long time opposed the appointment of high Bulgarian ecclesiastics, in which they were aided by the Porte; but that at length, by a firman given in 1870, the Bulgarians were allowed to have an Exarch or Metropolitan of their own choosing, whose appointment has to be confirmed by the Sultan. The Greeks still regard the Bulgarians as schismatics, and this religious difference, as well as the idea that they (the Bulgarians) stand in the way of the Greek extension of territory, may serve to account for a regrettable feeling of animosity which still animates the Greek community in Bulgaria against their fellow-citizens. Regrettable indeed it is, for the Mohammedans (the Bulgarian Mohammedans, I should say, for they are not Turks in national sentiment), who have far greater cause for harbouring ill-will, are now living on terms of cordiality with their Christian fellow-subjects; and one or two instances of delicacy and consideration shown by the latter towards the Mussulman population which occurred whilst I was on my tour of observation have left a very pleasant impression upon my mind. But we must return to a less pacific period in the intercourse of the two nations.

CHAPTER VII.

THE LIBERATION OF BULGARIA.

Events which preceded the Russo-Turkish War—Revolt in Bulgaria—The "Bulgarian Atrocities"—Mr. Gladstone's pamphlet—The Czar Alexander the Liberator—Action of the Tory Government—Mr. Gladstone's views—Tergiversation of the Porte—Russian declaration of war against Turkey (April 1877)—The alliance between Russia and Roumania—Russian ingratitude to Roumania the salvation of Bulgaria—Devotion of the Bulgarians—Incidents of the campaign—A brave Bulgarian boy—Condition of the country during the war—The defence of the Shipka Pass—The Bulgarian contingent—The events of the war and its results for Bulgaria—The Treaties of San Stefano and Berlin—Stipulations of the last-named as regarded Bulgaria—Limits of the Principality—Action of the Russians subsequent to the ratification—The Russianising of Bulgaria—The stipulations concerning Eastern Roumelia—Limits of the province—Turkish indifference regarding its government—The political rank of the two States.

PEN of Mr. Gladstone and the sword of the Emperor Alexander—not the present one—his father, the liberator of the Russian serfs—severed the chain which for more than four centuries had fettered the liberties of Bulgaria. The causes which led to the Russo-Turkish War of the last decade, and the chief events which preceded it, must still be fresh in the minds of most of my readers. During the year 1875, when a rising took place in Bosnia and Herzegovina, followed by one in Bulgaria in 1876 and in the early part of 1877, the Powers of Europe were occupied with pourparlers, conferences, and protocols, the objects of which were, so far as Turkey was concerned, to compel her to grant religious freedom and relief from excessive taxation to her Christian subjects in the Balkan Peninsula;

on the part of Russia, to give her an opportunity to regain her military prestige, damaged by the Crimean War; to enable her to lend a helping hand to the oppressed Slave races; but before all, to justify another step in the direction of Constantinople; and as it regarded ourselves, or rather the Tory Government of the day, to maintain the integrity of the Ottoman Empire and keep open our road to India, without a breach of the peace of Europe, but also without due regard to the terrible sufferings which were being inflicted upon the subject races of Turkey; whilst Mr. Gladstone availed himself of the course of events to demand autonomy for Bulgaria, as he had helped to secure freedom for Roumania, and to overthrow his own political opponents and occupy their place.

The chief events which occurred during the period above referred to were, besides the risings in the Turkish dependencies, to which Servia lent her assistance; a war between the latter country and Turkey, wherein a large number of Russian volunteers took part; the fanatical murder by the Turks of the German and French Consuls at Salonica; the mission of the British fleet to Besika Bay, intended for the protection of the Christians, but which the Porte adroitly construed into a movement on the part of Great Britain (as it probably was to some extent) to keep Russia in check; and finally, the well-known "Bulgarian Atrocities." The last-named event, of which the representatives of foreign courts in Constantinople, including our own, either were or professed to be ignorant, consisted in the massacre by the irregular troops of the Porte of over 15,000 Christian men, women, and children, under the most revolting conditions of lust and cruelty, for the purpose of striking terror into the population and suppressing the revolt. Those massacres, which were revealed to a horrified world by the correspondents of the English press and by Mr. Schuyler, the American Consul in Constantinople, were fully avenged (notwithstanding all that has been said to the contrary) by the equally irregular forces of Bulgaria on the advent of the Russians; but our chief affair with them here is their bearing upon the subsequent war and the liberation of the country from the Ottoman rule.

A careful study of the events of the time, of the declarations of Governments and individuals in high places, and of printed documents, not the least Mr. Gladstone's famous pamphlet on the "Bulgarian Horrors,"[1] will, if I mistake not, lead to certain well-defined conclusions on the part of future historians. First, that the desire of the great Emperor Alexander II. was to extend to the Sclavonic races of Turkey the same freedom as he had, at great risk to himself, conferred on the serfs of his own country, but that, personally, he was very loth to draw the sword even with that object; and let me here add, that until his deplorable assassination by his own subjects, that seems to have been the mainspring of his subsequent actions. Secondly, that the Tory Government was faithfully carrying out the policy of this country, for which many thousand lives and a hundred millions of money had been sacrificed in the Crimea, and that, so far as it concerned the designs of the Russian war-party, which, through Turkish obduracy, ultimately prevailed, they fairly appreciated, and are certainly not to be blamed for seeking to counteract them; and lastly, that whilst Mr. Gladstone's love of liberty, his trust in the promises and declarations of the great and good Czar, and the actual position of affairs in the East at that time quite justified his denunciations of Turkey, his trusting disposition and impetuosity led him to propound a policy which appeared to favour Russian aggression. Persons who then read his pamphlet, under the influence of the feelings of horror engendered by the accounts of "the wholesale murders, rapes, tortures, burnings, and the whole devilish enginery of crime," were likely to be guided by sentiment rather than reason, and would probably overlook his advice "to emulate Russia by sharing her good deeds, and to *reserve our opposition until she shall visibly endeavour to turn them to evil account.*"[2]

Unfortunately, the misdeeds and endeavours of the great aggressive Northern Power are not always "visible;" but I hope that in this instance they have been sufficiently so for Mr. Gladstone's keen perception, and that he, too, is of the same opinion as the world in general, that "Russia likes Bulgaria, but not the Bulgarians!"

---

[1] Published by John Murray, 1876. [2] Pamphlet, p. 30.

The policy of the Porte, which finally justified the separate action of Russia, was to deny or minimise the injustice and cruelty which were charged against her impotent rule in her Christian dependencies, and to avail herself of the jealousies and differences between the European Powers, to evade all reforms and every serious proceeding for ameliorating the condition of her subject races. When the Powers appeared to be unanimous and in any way determined, she made promises which she had no intention to perform; when they showed signs of weakness, she openly set them at defiance. At length, under a feeble protest from the British Government, but with the tacit consent of the other Powers, the Czar declared war against the Porte on the 24th April 1877, and marching his armies into her territory, he was shortly afterwards joined by Roumania, acting very reluctantly for the preservation of her own liberties. As I have already described at considerable length elsewhere the part which Roumania took in the war, indeed the events of the war generally,[1] and as it is not my intention to make any further reference to that Power, I beg the reader to excuse a short digression on this part of the subject.

It has always appeared to me that it is to Roumania quite as much as to Russia that the Bulgarians owe their enfranchisement from Ottoman rule. Possibly if the Roumanians had not acted as their allies, if they had not led them to victory at Plevna, and if Prince Charles of Roumania had not been the commander-in-chief of the allied armies, the Russians might, notwithstanding the numerous defeats which they sustained from the Turkish arms, eventually have proved the victors; but it is more than questionable whether they would have been able to enforce such favourable conditions for Bulgaria and the other Balkan States as they afterwards did at San Stefano. And whether or not Roumanian aid was instrumental in snatching Bulgaria from the grasp of Turkey, Roumanian sacrifices have certainly since helped to save her from the clutches of Russia. Of course, the reader is well

---

[1] "Roumania," p. 235-255.

aware that after the war was over the Russians requited Roumania for her services by demanding the cession of Bessarabia north of the Danube, and tendering in exchange the Dobrudscha on the south. For some time the courageous little State resisted the Russian demand, until a *corps-d'armée* under General Ehrnroth (the person who was recently designated as a Russian envoy to "restore order" in Bulgaria!) was instructed to commence offensive operations against Bucharest. Roumania then yielded to superior force, and the exchange was made. Now, if the reader will kindly look at the map, he will find that, in committing this act of injustice against a people who had saved her honour, Russia placed a barrier between herself and Bulgaria which has presented a formidable obstacle to the accomplishment of her aggressive designs upon that State. Had the Dobrudscha remained Russian territory, it would have been an excellent gathering-ground for "emigrants,"—traitors who have accepted Russian gold, but have been driven out of Bulgaria,—and her troops would have occupied a position favourable for an entrance into that country. But whilst Russia proposes a Higher Power disposes.

In a military sense, the help afforded by Bulgaria in the war was comparatively unimportant. Her army was not yet organised, and it was only in her subsequent campaign against Servia that she won her spurs. Indirectly, however, her aid to the allies was invaluable. Everywhere they were received as friends and liberators: Bulgarian men, women, and children furthered their progress, serving as guides, keeping their presence secret from the enemy, and misleading the latter as to their movements. On one occasion, says an eye-witness, two hundred Cossacks were working for three days on a road over which the Russian troops were to pass, "the Bulgarian peasantry coming and going all the time freely, but the Turks never got a whisper of their presence."[1] In the fighting in the Shipka Pass, another war-correspondent tells us, the Bulgarian peasant boys displayed great gallantry " by going

---

[1] "War-Correspondence of the *Daily News*," vol. i. p. 264. Macmillan.

down into the actual fight, into the first line, with stone crocks full of water for the fighting men" (Russian). "This water was fetched from far in the rear, along a bullet-swept road, for there is no water on the position itself. One lad had his crock smashed by a bullet as he passed me, and he wept, not for joy at his fortunate escape, but for sorrow at the loss of the article which enabled him to be of service."[1]

As I have already said, the retaliatory acts of the Bulgarians, which I was told were committed chiefly by the mountaineers, who had escaped the Turkish massacres, were as savage as those of the Turks had been before the war; but all eye-witnesses agree in absolving the peaceful inhabitants from any charge of cruelty after the war had commenced. They plundered deserted houses, and it may be houses that were *not* deserted, but there are few records of homicide. On the other hand, the Turks continued to treat the Bulgarians as rebels, and numbers of them were executed to strike terror into the people, and prevent them from siding with the Russians. The whole country suffered under the curse of the war. The roads were crowded with Turks fleeing from their homes; Bulgarians escaping from the Turkish legions, or following those of the allies for protection, and the Russian soldiers are said to have behaved with great humanity and tenderness to the wretched fugitives.

I have said that the aid rendered by the Bulgarians in this war was unimportant, but it must not be supposed that their co-operation was wanting, or that they behaved otherwise than bravely. It is true they appeared to disadvantage by the side of the trained forces of Russia and Roumania, but their services were considerably enhanced by their knowledge of the localities. During General Gourko's operations in the Balkans he was accompanied by a Bulgarian legion (seven battalions, numbering about 5000), who rendered great service in securing and retaining the passes; and in an encounter near Eski Zagra they lost 1200 out of a force of 1600 men. In the defence of the Shipka Pass they played an important part, holding their ground with great pertinacity, and it was there chiefly that they dis-

---

[1] "War-Correspondence of the *Daily News*," vol. i. p. 415. Macmillan.

played that courage and *élan* whereby they subsequently won their laurels at Slivnitza.

The general course of events during the war, so far as it affected Bulgarian territory, is well known. The passage of the Danube by the Russians (June 1877); their occupation of Tirnova, and the passage of the Balkans (July); the occupation of Kezanlik, Yeni Zagra, and Eski Zagra, and the subsequent retreat of the Russians under Gourko into the Shipka Pass (August); the determined attempts and repulses of Suleiman Pasha to recover the fortified pass; Osman Pasha's brave defence of Plevna; the great slaughter and frequent discomfiture of the Russians before that stronghold; the capture of the first redoubt—the Grivitza—by the Roumanians, and the final capitulation of Osman Pasha in December 1877, which practically terminated the war, have been too frequently described by far abler pens than mine to justify repetition, and we will now inquire what was the nett result of the war to Bulgaria, as it was determined by the subsequent treaties and negotiations.

The Treaty of San Stefano,[1] made after the close of the war between Russia and the Porte, is interesting to us in one particular only, namely, that it stipulated for the union under one prince of Bulgaria proper and Eastern Roumelia—a union which was vetoed by the Great Powers, although it was proposed on account of the nationality of the two provinces, and which Russia did her best to prevent when it subsequently took place without her intervention. As regards the Treaty of Berlin,[2] it constituted Bulgaria an "autonomous and tributary principality, under the suzerainty of his Imperial Majesty the Sultan; it will have a Christian government and a national militia." The limits of the new Principality followed the River Danube on the north, the Balkans on the south, whilst on the east it was bounded by the Black Sea, and on the west by Servia. The Prince was to be "freely elected by the population, and confirmed by the Sublime Porte, with the assent of the Powers;"

---

[1] Holland, p. 339.
[2] Parliamentary Paper. London: Harrison & Sons, and Holland, p. 279 *et seq.*

but no member of the reigning dynasties of the Great European Powers was (or is) eligible. "In case of a vacancy in the princely dignity, the election of the new Prince is to take place under the same conditions and with the same forms." Nothing is said in the Treaty of Berlin as to whether or not the title should be hereditary, but the second chapter of the Constitution declares the "Principality to be a hereditary and constitutional monarchy."

An assembly of notables to be called at Tirnova was to frame a Constitution prior to the election of a Prince; and in draughting this, the rights and interests of the various nationalities—Bulgarian, Turkish, Roumanian, Greek, &c.—were to be taken into consideration as regards the elections as well as in the Constitution itself. There was to be complete religious equality and perfect freedom of worship, and no difference of creed should present a barrier to the election of citizens to any public office or employment. The customs tariff of Bulgaria was to be (as it is still) identical with that of the Porte, and no transit dues to be charged on goods passing through the Principality.

For the purpose of carrying out the stipulations of the treaty, the provisional administration which was formed "shall be under the direction of an Imperial Russian Commissary," aided by a Turkish Commissary, and "the Consuls delegated by the other Powers," &c.; but the provisional *régime* was not to be prolonged beyond a period of nine months from the exchange of ratifications.

The treaty further stipulated for the payment of an annual tribute and part of the national debt of the Ottoman Empire, and contained conditions affecting the control of the Rustchuk-Varna Railway. It declared that as soon as the organic law (Constitution) was completed and the Prince elected, "the Principality shall enter into the full enjoyment of its autonomy."

Finally, it bound the Sultan at once to withdraw his army from Bulgaria; and by a stipulation regarding Eastern Roumelia, a Russian corps of occupation, which was to remain temporarily in both States, and was not to exceed 50,000 men, must also be withdrawn within nine months from the ratification of the treaty.

THE LIBERATION OF BULGARIA.

It is hardly necessary to say that the Ottoman army was withdrawn, and so too was the Russian force, according to the letter of the treaty; but during the nine months of Russian rule—for that is what it amounted to—the chief permanent military appointments were given to Russian officers; the Bulgarian army was organised under Russian control; "the entire Russian army rules and regulations had been simply taken over, and the words of command were given, as well as the service generally carried out in Russian. Broadly speaking, one can say that the Bulgarian military forces were organised in such a manner that they could be looked upon as forming an integral portion of the Russian army, ready at any moment to act as an advanced guard of the Russian main body."[1]

The liberties of Eastern Roumelia were, by the Treaty of Berlin,[2] more restricted than those of Bulgaria. It was designated "a province," and was to "remain under the direct political and military authority of his Imperial Majesty the Sultan. It shall have a Christian Governor-General." The boundaries of the province were fixed by the treaty and by a European Delimitation Commission; and, broadly speaking, they were, on the north, the Balkans; on the south, a frontier line fixed by the Commission, which passed south of Philippopolis and north of Adrianople; on the east, the Black Sea; and on the west, parts of Servia and Turkey. The Sultan was to have the right (which he did not exercise) to erect fortifications on the frontiers, and of sending *regular* troops (Bashi-Bazouks and Circassians being specially excluded) into the province in case of necessity, for its protection; but generally internal order was to be maintained by a native gendarmerie and a local militia. An organic statute was also to be framed, and the powers and functions of the Governor-General defined by a European Commission. It is only necessary to add that the provisions of the treaty as they regarded Eastern Roumelia

---

[1] "The Struggle of the Bulgarians for Independence," p. 47, by Major A. Von Huhn. London: Murray.
[2] The treaty as published, and Holland, p. 287.

are now not of the slightest consequence, as both States are governed by the Constitution of Bulgaria.

After the close of the Russo-Turkish war, therefore, we find Bulgaria an independent Principality, under the nominal suzerainty of the Porte, but under the actual control and influence of Russia; and Eastern Roumelia still a Turkish province enjoying certain autonomous privileges. In the next chapter we shall see how the union of the two States was accomplished, and what degree of liberty the united monarchy has attained.

CHAPTER VIII.

ALEXANDER, THE FIRST PRINCE OF BULGARIA, THE UNION, AND THE SERVIAN WAR.

The career of Prince Alexander—Prince Dondukoff-Korsakoff and the Bulgarian Constitution—Accession of Alexander—Bulgarian sentiments of gratitude towards Russia changed through her despotism and misgovernment—Personal experience of the demeanour of Russia towards Bulgaria—Treatment of Prince Alexander by the Czar, Alexander III.—The Prince demands absolute power for seven years—It is conceded by the Sobranje—Withdrawn at Russian instigation—Generals Soboleff and Kaulbars, their unsuccessful attempt to kidnap the Prince—The revolt in Eastern Roumelia—The revolutionary committee at first favoured by Russia—The leaders of the rising—The Turkish governors, Aleko, Gavril, and Drigalsky Pashas—Account of the revolution in Philippopolis—Major Nikolaieff and Gavril Pasha—Deposition of the latter—Undignified conduct of the Roumelian leaders—The general of an army run in by two gens-d'armes—The revolt successful—Prince Alexander and the rising—Criticism upon Von Huhn's version of his connection with it—The rising premature—Russian professions and intentions—Alexander accepts the joint-rulership—Conference of the Powers at Constantinople—Intrigues of Russia—Inaction of the Porte—Attitude of Great Britain—Recall of Russian officers from Bulgaria—Its effect upon the Bulgarian people and army—The Servian invasion—Bulgarian perplexities—Presence of mind of the Prince—Reorganisation of the forces—Promotion of junior officers—Strength of the army—Macedonian and Turkish volunteers—Routes of the invading army—Partial successes—Halts at Vidin, Bresnik, and Slivnitza—Consternation in the capital—Confidence and exultation of the Servians and Russians—The enthusiasm at Philippopolis—To the front!—Difficulties of transport, how overcome—Patriotism of all classes—Devotion of the peasantry—Fatigue of the marching regiments—Devices for expedition—The Prince commander-in-chief—Slivnitza—The strength of the respective armies—The first day's fighting—The "Djumi-Maritza"—Bulgarian successes—The second day—Reinforcements—Continued successes—The third day—Rumour of Bulgarian defeat at Bresnik—The Prince hastens back to Sofia—Consternation there—Zankoff and the Russians arrange for a "Provisional Government"—A scare—Bresnik safe—The Servians beaten all along the line at Slivnitza—Rejoicings at Sofia—Disappearance of Zankoff—The Prince returns to the front—The Bulgarian victory—Reception of the news in Europe—Further reinforcements—The "Brigand Brigade"—Captain Panitza crosses the Servian frontier—March towards Servia—Tzaribrod—A Servian flag of truce—King Milan's deference for the Powers—Capture and entry into the Servian town of Pirot—Retreat of the Servians—Appearance of Austria on the scene—Threats of the Austrian Minister—Conclusion of peace between Bulgaria and Servia—The union of Bulgaria and Eastern Roumelia sanctioned by the Powers.

ALEXANDER, the first Prince of Bulgaria, has been the hero of a hundred biographers and journalists (see Plate I.). His story has been frequently published, in part or *in extenso*, and sometimes by men who were constantly near his person, and who followed him through his adventurous career. To emulate their descriptions would, therefore, be impossible, and all I can promise the reader is, that if he will follow me through the dry details of history in this place, I will endeavour farther on to introduce him to the Prince in person, to give him an opportunity of forming an estimate of his noble qualities, and, however imperfectly, to describe the present results in Bulgaria of the rapid progress made by the nation under his rulership. Like one or two of the Bulgarian Czars of old (to whom his successor, Prince Ferdinand, made a reference in his first manifesto on entering Bulgaria), he united and consolidated the Bulgarian nationalities under one rule, resisted the domination and tyranny of the most aggressive Power in Europe against great odds, and beat back the unjustifiable invasion of a jealous neighbour; whilst at the same time he beautified his capital, introduced mildness into the laws of his country, and managed, under the most perplexing political conditions, to secure the affections of his people. He was born on the 5th April 1857, and is, therefore, even now a young man, was a major-general in the Prussian, and lieutenant-general in the Russian army. He was related by marriage to the late Czar, being his nephew, and therefore cousin of the present Czar, and was a *persona grata* at the Russian court during the reign of the former, who recommended him for the throne of Bulgaria. Before he was elected, the Russian "Commissary" or Governor-General, Prince Dondukoff-Korsakoff, had assisted the Bulgarians to frame a Constitution, perhaps the most democratic in existence—a circumstance which has been the subject of much adverse criticism. It has been

ALEXANDER THE FIRST PRINCE OF BULGARIA

called a "Pandora's box," containing elements which would make an independent rule impossible, and what not;[1] but any one who has studied the history of Russia and her dealings with her subject races, knows well that she has a large stock of liberty, but that "she keeps it for exportation only." I am disposed to believe that the Constitution was given to Bulgaria in good faith, by the desire and through the instrumentality of the Czar Alexander the Liberator.

Be that as it may, after the Constitution was framed and passed, Prince Alexander of Battenberg, who was living at the time in modest quarters in Potsdam, was elected hereditary Prince of Bulgaria on the 29th April 1879, and ascended the throne on the 9th of July in the same year. At that time the hearts of the Bulgarians overflowed with gratitude towards Russia, whom they regarded as a disinterested liberator, and the progresses of Prince Dondukoff-Korsakoff throughout the country resembled those of a beloved sovereign. The enthusiasm of the Bulgarians for their rulers was, however, not perfect in its steadfastness (as I shall show hereafter), and the Russians soon gave them cause to change their sentiments of gratitude into others of a widely different character.

As far as the people were concerned, the Russians lost no opportunity to show them that the war had only brought them a change of masters. They treated them as an inferior race, or as they treat their own lower classes; sent wastrels to fill responsible offices, as they send them to Central Asia, and generally lorded it over the nation they professed to have liberated. In this all writers are agreed, and fortunately I had myself an opportunity of seeing one of the straws which indicated the course of the wind at that period. In 1881, whilst I was on a tour of observation in South-Eastern Europe, I happened to meet on the Danube steamer, between the Iron Gates and Giurgevo, a very communicative young Russian officer, who told me he was an Imperial messenger from St. Petersburg to Sofia, and whose conversation, to which I paid particular attention, was very instructive. I asked him where

---

[1] See Appendix II., "Most Important Decrees of the Constitution of Bulgaria."

he was going to land and how he would travel to Sofia, which was then more difficult of access than it is at present. He said, if I remember right, at Lom Palanka; that a carriage and horses would be in waiting for him, and that wherever he stopped on the road, everybody and everything would have to clear out of the way. He spoke with great arrogance, made no attempt to conceal his low estimate of the Bulgarians, and evidently considered himself the bearer of *orders* from St. Petersburg to the Powers at Sofia. That incident, and what I was subsequently told at Bucharest, quite confirmed the generally-received view, that the Russians committed a great mistake in not treating the Bulgarian people with consideration. But their blunders in higher places were even more serious. As long as Alexander II. was Czar of Russia, the representatives of that country were obliged to treat Prince Alexander with some degree of respect, for, as already stated, he was well-liked by the Czar; but after his death, on the accession of the present one (March 1881), who bears personal enmity against the Prince, such considerations ceased to have any weight, and, dismissing exaggerations, he was regarded as a Russian satrap, and treated accordingly. Unfortunately, too, he committed an act which gave the Russians a handle for agitating against his rule. Declaring that it was impossible to govern the country under the Tirnova Constitution, he demanded from the Sobranje absolute power to initiate laws for seven years, threatening to resign if it was not conceded to him. At that time his leading ministers were MM. Karaveloff and Zankoff, who were then, as they are at present, Russian tools and partisans. The National Assembly granted him the authority which he demanded (July 1881), but Russia, actuated no doubt by her well-known attachment to constitutional government (!), soon compelled the Prince to relinquish his powers. The ministers named resigned office, but were soon reinstated on the condition that the government of the country should proceed under the Constitution.[1]

Along with Messrs. Karaveloff and Zankoff, as the civilian

---

[1] For details of Russian intrigues at that time see "Causes Occultes de la Question Bulgare." Anonymous. Paris: Ollendorff, 1887.

representatives of Russia. Prince Alexander and his people had to put up with Russian military governors in the persons of Generals Soboleff and Kaulbars (brother of the Kaulbars who afterwards unsuccessfully stumped the country as a Russian election-agent); but those generals were obliged to leave the country in 1883 owing to a little misunderstanding in the shape of an unsuccessful attempt on their part (there were several altogether) to kidnap and carry off the Prince.[1] One night they attempted to enter the palace with an authorisation from the Minister for War, and asked for an audience with the Prince, but Lieutenant Marinoff, the officer of the Prince's guard, refused to admit them. When they tried to force a passage, he drew his sword and sent a messenger to the Prince to warn him of the danger. The two Russians then withdrew, and it is said that a carriage was found waiting at the palace gate to convey the Prince to the Danube, and that proclamations had been printed announcing his deposition.

Whilst these events were passing on the northern side of the Balkans, a silent movement was in progress in Eastern Roumelia, having for its object the liberation of that State from Turkish rule and its union with Bulgaria, as was originally intended by the Russians under the Treaty of San Stefano. With the connivance of the Russian Government, or at least with its knowledge and sanction, a revolutionary committee was formed, which had its ramifications throughout the country; but European complications caused Russia at a later period to suspend her plans for awhile. This was, however, not at all to the taste of the Roumelian patriots, who continued the agitation, and, under the direction of Dr. Stranski (the present Foreign Minister of Bulgaria), Major Nikolaieff, Karaveloff, and others, it burst into a revolt on September 1885. Eastern Roumelia had already enjoyed the privilege of one Turkish governor, Prince Vogorides, a Bulgarian Christian known as Aleko Pasha,

---

[1] "The Growth of Freedom in the Balkan Peninsula," p. 237-238, by J. A. C. Minchin Murray, 1886; and "The Kidnapping of Prince Alexander of Battenberg," p. 4, by A. Von Huhn. Stanford, 1887.

who ruled from 1879 to 1884. It is said that he was cognisant of the intended rising, and had hoped, by ingratiating himself with Russia, to help her to get rid of Alexander, and to secure the joint-sovereignty for himself. It is further stated that both he and his successor, Gavril Pasha Krestovich, followed the good old Phanariote practice of lining their purses during the five years at their disposal at the cost of the nation they were sent to govern. Along with Gavril Pasha, the Turkish military commander-in-chief was Drigalsky Pasha, with whom, of course, the insurgents would have to reckon. This was, however, an easy task, for the whole population, including the gendarmes and militia, were implicated in the revolt. It is recorded that on September 18, 1885, Major Nikolaieff quietly entered the Konak or palace[1] of the Governor-General, Gavril Pasha (see Plate V.), whilst the latter was breakfasting, and announced to him his deposition and temporary arrest, and that, seeing a battalion of militia in the courtyard of the palace, Gavril bowed to the inevitable. To the great discredit of the insurgents, they were not content with deposing him, but they subjected him to the mockery of a drive through Philippopolis in a carriage, accompanied by an armed schoolmistress, and of course well guarded. Photographs of this heroine, with a drawn sword in her hand, are still sold in that city! The story of Drigalsky Pasha's arrest and subsequent liberation is thus narrated by Major Von Huhn : " By this time the commander-in-chief of the Roumelian army, Drigalsky Pasha, had heard the noise in the streets; without much hesitation he buckled on his trusty blade and went to the market-square to see what was up. There he found drawn up a battalion of militia, with Major Nikolaieff at its head, and the following dialogue ensued :— *Drigalsky:* 'Sir, what are you doing there with that battalion?' *Nikolaieff:* 'I do not know you.' *Drigalsky:* 'What! you do not know me?' *Nikolaieff:* 'Gens-d'armes, take that gentleman home.' And two policemen took Drigalsky between them and removed him in the most approved style. This is probably the most remarkable thing that ever happened

---

[1] To be described in Part II.

to the commander-in-chief of an army. . . . It was not even found worth while to arrest Drigalsky Pasha." Only later on a sentry was placed at his door, and he was told to consider himself under arrest. . . . "And in the same way that the revolt succeeded in Philippopolis without bloodshed, so in the whole province; the military and the populace everywhere acknowledged the Provisional Government. In one forenoon the Turkish rule had been overthrown, and the whole undertaking accomplished." [1]

A few words in regard to Prince Alexander's connection with the revolt and acceptance of the post. He was charged with having been privy to the rising, and with having misled Russia as to his intentions. In his memoirs, Von Huhn defends him from these accusations, and says that he was forced by circumstances to accept the position. He seeks to substantiate his justification by a long statement, under inverted commas, in the first person singular, purporting to have been made to him by the Prince himself; but in so doing I am afraid he has proved too much for his own cause. What he does prove, however, is that the Prince is what I shall hereafter show him to be, namely, frank and honest, even where blame to himself is likely to be the result. If the reader will take the trouble to peruse this statement (assuming it to be correct [2]), I am sure he will agree with me that neither the Prince nor Russia, represented in this instance by M. de Giers, with whom he had a personal interview at Franzensbad, cared one fig about the Treaty of Berlin; that both were well acquainted with the intended Roumelian rising, and meant to benefit by it, but that the Prince would have preferred doing so under Russian auspices if he could have made his peace with the Czar; that the rising took place sooner than was anticipated, and that the Prince from motives of policy tried to arrest it for a time, but when he found it was a *fait accompli*, that he then, partly to save his crown, and also to prevent a civil war between Christians and Mohammedans, accepted the rulership of Eastern Roumelia without consulting Russia or seriously considering her interests in his line of action. These

---

[1] "Bulgarian Struggle for Independence," p. 31. [2] Ibid., p. 36.

appear to have been the facts; and inasmuch as Russia (one of the signatories, and a great stickler for the Treaty of Berlin, be it remembered) cared no more for the liberties of Eastern Roumelia than she did for those of Bulgaria, but merely sought her own aggrandisement; and seeing, moreover, that Alexander's successor has adopted precisely the same policy (for which he is not, in my opinion, to be blamed in the smallest degree), without the same powerful incentives, it is hardly worth while bestowing any further criticism upon the actors in this historical drama.

Three important events followed the union of North and South Bulgaria. Diplomatic action of the Powers, resulting in a Conference of the Ambassadors at Constantinople; the withdrawal by the Czar of all the Russian officers in the Bulgarian army; and an attack upon Bulgaria by the Servians. At first the Russians once more resorted to every possible device for getting rid of Alexander, and promised the Bulgarians that, if they sent him about his business, the union would be acknowledged. At the Conference, supported by Germany and Austria, they urged the Porte to occupy Eastern Roumelia with an armed force; but her statesmen, besides distrusting advice from such a hostile quarter, knew that if she attempted to use coercive measures, she would have to reckon, not with the Bulgarians alone, but with Macedonia, where a rising was also imminent. So she did what she usually does under similar circumstances—nothing! As subsequent events proved, her decision in this instance was a wise one, and employment was soon found for a Macedonian legion of volunteers in helping the Bulgarians to fight the Servians, which was better than effecting a rising against Turkish rule. But there was an influence more potent than the inaction of the Porte which greatly facilitated the union of the two Bulgarias, namely, the determination of Great Britain, expressed in unmistakable terms by her able representative at the Conference, Sir William White, not to support any hostile movement against Prince Alexander. So the Conference proved an abortion, and the union was consummated.

Having failed in the prosecution of her designs to extend

her own influence, the next move of Russia was to inflict as great an injury as possible upon Bulgaria, and that the Czar attempted to do by recalling every Russian officer out of the country, and leaving the army without leaders. The effect of this move, however—the most fatal to her interests of all the acts of Russia in the Balkan Peninsula—was the very opposite of what was anticipated. Whilst it opened the eyes of the people to the real feelings of Russia towards their country, it placed their army under their own control, made them self-reliant, called forth all their latent energies, and ended in giving them a humble but honourable place in the ranks of European monarchies.

Now came the severest trial of all for the young nation. Her army, only partially organised, was drawn up on the Turkish frontier, prepared to resist an advance from that quarter; her ruler was boycotted by the "Great Powers," just as they are boycotting Prince Ferdinand; dissensions were being sown by the largesses of a rich and powerful empire amongst her political parties; and all Europe was undecided how she should be disposed of; when, lo! a neighbouring state, Servia, which had passed through similar trials to her own, and had but recently acquired her independence, must needs take advantage of her perplexities and make a raid upon her, in order to obtain an extension of territory at her expense. I am not going to waste the reader's time by spinning a web of theories and surmises as to who instigated the unchivalrous acts of King Milan and his people, or what had been their original and what their ultimate intentions. They picked a quarrel with Bulgaria when she was hard beset; the King refused to enter into negotiations with Prince Alexander, refused even to receive a letter from him; declared war against him in November 1885, and led an army across the unprotected Bulgarian frontier, with what results we shall see presently.

And this is what happened in Bulgaria on the withdrawal of the Russian officers and during the hostile approaches of the Servians. The Prince, nothing daunted, began to reorganise the army as soon as the Russian officers had taken their departure. He appointed Captain Nikeforoff Minister of War,

Captain Petroff Adjutant-General, and promoted the junior officers and subalterns, Bulgarians who had been gradually working their way into the army, to the posts deserted by the Russians. " Captains of companies," says Major Von Huhn,[1] " assumed the command of regiments and brigades brought up to their war complement, and led them from Bulgaria into Roumelia " (for the defence of the southern frontier) " in the most exemplary manner, and without any signs of insubordination on the part of the troops towards their young leaders." So much for the officers, whose conduct under fire was soon to be put to the test. As to the strength of the army, it probably numbered at first 90,000 men of all arms: say 35,000 Roumeliotes and 55,000 Bulgarians, including reserves and volunteers, to which were shortly added 3000 Macedonian volunteers, the so-called " Brigand Brigade ; " and when the war broke out with Servia, 6000 Mohammedan volunteers spontaneously joined the Bulgarians in the defence of their common country.

The reader will have noticed that in this brief survey of Bulgarian history very slight references have been made to campaigns, battles, or sieges, for my intention has been mainly that it should be introductory to the observations which follow on the present position of the country and its future prospects; but it will be necessary to say a few words on the Servian war, not so much on account of its interest as a national military exploit, but because of the moral influence which it exercised, and still continues to hold over the destinies of Bulgaria. For I am convinced that one of the causes of Russian hesitancy to undertake a filibustering expedition against the new-born State is the knowledge that Prince Alexander's return in her defence would evoke such enthusiasm in the army, that if they had to fight Russia single-handed (which they would *not*), there would be few laurels to be won by the great military Power, and little permanent benefit would accrue to her from the enterprise.

Before the tactics of the Constantinople Conference were made clearly manifest, and ere the Bulgarians were assured of the safety of their southern frontier, they had to face their

---

[1] " The Bulgarian Struggle for Independence," p. 52.

aggressive western neighbour with an untried army, far removed from the post of danger, and with very limited pecuniary resources. But once more the energy and patriotism of Prince and people engendered a degree of enthusiasm which compensated for every disadvantage. The Servian army had made its entry into Bulgaria in three divisions, along the same number of almost undefended roads; and after receiving slight temporary checks here and there from small but well-armed bodies of Bulgarian regulars and volunteers, they had halted before Vidin, on the Danube, Bresnik, and Slivnitza, two villages about equidistant from one another (about thirty kilometres) and from the capital. There, at Sofia, all was consternation, and the inhabitants expected hourly to see the city occupied by King Milan and his army. That seemed to be the opinion, too, of the Russian partisans in the capital, who were jubilant and demonstrative, and, of course, the confidence of the Servians was unbounded. The latter had telegraphed their successes in inflated language to every point of the compass; and the feeling which success always inspires in nations as well as in individuals led the world to believe that poor, presumptuous Prince Alexander would soon be a fugitive at some friendly court (if he could find one), and that Russia and Servia would be dividing the Bulgarian spoils between them. (I wonder what Servia would have got out of the transaction if events had turned out as was anticipated.)

In Philippopolis the news of the Servian invasion created a sensation widely different from that nearer to the scene of action. The picked men of the army were stationed there, and they threw up their "busbies" and rent the air with never-ending shouts. In the course of a few minutes after receiving marching orders, they were *en route* (at first by railway as far as it could convey them) to the "front." The command of the railway was in the hands of the Bulgarians as far as a station called Sarambey, between Philippopolis and Sofia; but there the finished portion ends, and all the troops who had been ordered to the Servian frontier were obliged to find their way, hurry-skurry, as best they could by road. If the inhabitants had shown devotion to the Russians and Roumanians during the war of liberation, it may be readily imagined what succour they gave to their own soldiers in defence of their homes and liberties; and it has been a problem even to experienced military men how, without a regular transport service, the march from Sarambey to Slivnitza was so well and quickly accomplished. Every horse, bullock, and cart was enlisted in the service; they were in many instances offered gratuitously by the peasantry; and as the enemy was still far distant, no obstacles except the natural ones of bad roads interfered with the conveyance of food and the materials of war. As to the conduct of the men themselves, here (anticipating a little) is an example of how they came to the front:— . . . "Overnight our first reinforcements had arrived—four battalions of the Breslaff regiment and an Eastern Roumelian battalion. When the latter had reached Sofia under the command of Captain Kowatscheff, the men were so dead-beat that it was out of the question to continue the march. At Sofia, however, it was well known how small was the number of defenders at Slivnitza, and that every additional company was of the very highest importance; it was therefore quickly decided to send the battalion on to the front on horseback. Taking the horses of a cavalry regiment in course of formation at Sofia, two Roumeliotes were put on each animal, and the entire battalion just arrived in the nick of time to take part in the general action."[1] The Prince, who was at Philippopolis when the invasion began, travelled with all speed to Sofia, where he placed himself at the head of the army and directed the defensive operations. It soon became apparent that Slivnitza (on the main road to Servia) was to be the place of encounter between the contending forces; and whilst the Servians had concentrated from 25,000 to 30,000 men there, the Bulgarians could at first only muster half that number, of whom a considerable proportion were volunteers. The battle, of which a graphic and minute description has been given by Von Huhn,[2] lasted three days. The fortunes of the first day (November 17th) were various. The Servians fought with great

---

[1] "Bulgarian Struggle for Independence," p. 137.
[2] Ibid., cap. xi.

bravery, so also the Bulgarians, led by Captains Gutscheff and Bendereff,[1] with Captain Panoff in charge of the artillery. The Prince himself was everywhere in the thickest of the fight, leading and encouraging the men, and often exposing himself to great danger. The result of the first day's encounter was that, notwithstanding their inferiority in numbers, the Bulgarians occupied an improved position, from which they had eventually driven the enemy. Here is an account of part of the day's fighting, which must serve as an illustration of the capabilities of the young Bulgarian army:—

"As soon as the two battalions of the Danube regiment had joined Bendereff, he ordered the positions just seized by the Servians to be carried by assault. The moment when the Danube regiment formed for attack at the foot of the heights held by the Servians remains a memorable one in Bulgarian history, for it was the announcement of that wild and relentless onslaught under which the Servian army was eventually to break down. Without firing a single shot, with colours flying and drums beating, they rushed up the hill—a hill that it would have been no mean performance to have climbed in the quiet times of peace. It was here that the Servians first heard the strains of the national air, 'Djumi-Maritza,' which were alone sufficient later on to put them to flight.[2] Under the most violent Servian fire the hill was climbed,—a final rush, and the Servians were driven out of their positions at the point of the bayonet, and thrown down the other side. No sooner had the Bulgarian battalions reached the top of the hill than they disappeared behind it. There was a long pause, . . . then from a distance was heard once more the 'Djumi-Maritza,' desperate firing, the loud hurrahs of the storming Bulgarians, and the second position was taken. . . . Yet a third height had been stormed in the same way before Bendereff managed to come up and arrest the attacking columns."[3]

---

[1] The latter, sad to say, afterwards turned traitor, and headed the party who kidnapped the Prince.

[2] Major Von Huhn described this part of the battle at second-hand; so perhaps he is not responsible for this, it is to be hoped, figurative remark. He, however, repeats the assertion elsewhere.

[3] Ibid., p. 131-132.

On the second day (November 18th) reinforcements having meanwhile arrived for the Bulgarians, as described above, the Servians assumed the offensive; but they were not only repulsed, but towards evening the news arrived at head-quarters[1] that Captain Bendereff had in one place driven the Servians back a considerable distance. The third day was most eventful. At first information came that the Servians were marching from Bresnik on to Sofia (which was almost unprotected), and that they had defeated the Bulgarian troops stationed at the former place. Consternation prevailed everywhere, and the Prince hurried back to Sofia to check the supposed Servian advance on the Bresnik road. At Sofia there was a complete panic. The national treasures were removed to Plevna, and the Russian Consul, with his right-hand man, Zankoff, was making all the necessary dispositions for a " Provisional Government;" when lo! the news came that the whole thing was a scare. Bresnik was taken and held by Captain Panoff. The Bulgarians, having become the attacking force, had beaten the Servians all along the line at Slivnitza, and dislodged them from the Dragoman Pass, between that place and the Servian frontier. Then all was rejoicing at Sofia; the Russian party ceased to demonstrate; confidence was restored; the Bulgarian victories were telegraphed in every direction, and—Europe changed its views on the Bulgarian question!

The Prince had hurried to Slivnitza on the receipt of the welcome news, but on the following day he returned to Sofia in search of reinforcements and to give his army rest before commencing the march towards Servia. There he found two regiments and four battalions, who had " hurried up in gigantic marches through rain and through snow over the Balkans, without resting day or night, imbued with one desire—to come to the assistance of their fighting brethren."[2] Then came the

---

[1] A filthy little khan or wayside inn, where I had the pleasure of being detained three hours, between 8 and 11 P.M. My Servian driver, who had undertaken to bring me into Sofia at 9 P.M., arrived at Slivnitza at 8, and wanted to coerce me into stopping there all night. I, however, gained a victory also, and had the pleasure of entering Sofia at 2 A.M.

[2] Von Huhn, p. 173.

further joyful intelligence that the Bulgarian and Mohammedan volunteers had repulsed the Servian attack on Vidin, and that Captain Panitza (whom hardly any one had heard of before), who was acting as a free-lance at the head of the "Brigand Brigade" (Macedonian Legion, see frontispiece), had beaten the Servians in several encounters, taken many prisoners, with ammunition, and crossed over the frontier into the enemy's country; in proof of which he sent a bag containing the official Servian seals of the frontier custom-houses he had occupied. It was now time for Prince Alexander to be on the move, and after some more desultory fighting, the army entered Zaribrod, the last Bulgarian town, where messengers with a flag of truce appeared, who bore a letter from King Milan, asking for an armistice, and expressing his readiness, "out of deference to the wish of the Powers," to discontinue the war and conclude a peace. Prince Alexander and his victorious officers failed, however, to see eye to eye with the defeated monarch, and even with "the Powers" themselves, and the advance was continued. The frontier was crossed without any resistance on the 26th November, but on arriving at Pirot, the first Servian town, the Prince found the approaches defended by batteries. These were dislodged, the Servians were compelled to retire in the direction of Nisch, the Bulgarians entered Pirot in triumph, and the war was practically at an end.

For as soon as the Servians were defeated and driven back into their own territory, and Belgrade instead of Sofia seemed likely to change owners, it became apparent that the Austrians had been backing up the first-named in their unjustifiable invasion of Bulgaria. On the evening of the 28th November the Austrian minister arrived at headquarters and induced Prince Alexander to grant an armistice, assuring him (it is said, on his own responsibility, but that is doubtful) that Austria would not allow Servia to be crushed, and that if he advanced any farther, he would be opposed by her also. The Powers again intervened, certainly now with changed feelings towards Prince Alexander and his people, but the result could hardly be deemed satisfactory. A peace was concluded between Bulgaria and Servia, by which, greatly to the disgust and indignation of the young Bulgarian officers, the former gained absolutely nothing, not even a war indemnity. The union of Bulgaria and Eastern Roumelia could, however, no longer be resisted, and that was consummated by a treaty between Bulgaria and the Porte, with the assent of the Powers, Prince Alexander being nominated Governor-General for five years, and subsequently appointed by a firman of the Sultan.[1]

The Russians threw every possible obstacle in the way of a settlement, and when they failed to find any further justification for resistance, they showed their animus by refusing to allow the name of Prince Alexander to appear in the treaty, and insisted upon the insertion, instead, of the words " the Prince of Bulgaria." And now we arrive at a series of events, following one another very rapidly, with which the past history of Bulgaria must be concluded.

---

[1] For further correspondence respecting the affairs of Bulgaria and Eastern Roumelia, see Blue Book, " Turkey, No. 1, 1887." Harrison & Sons, 1887.

CHAPTER IX.

THE ABDUCTION AND RETIREMENT OF PRINCE ALEXANDER—THE REGENCY—PRINCE FERDINAND—CONCLUSION OF PART I.

The *Coup d'état* in Bulgaria—Events preceding it—Loss of Russian prestige—Resort to "diplomacy"—Open enmity of the Czar against Prince Alexander—His name struck off the Russian army list—Russian intrigues with Bulgarian leaders—Corruption of officers—Plan to carry off the Prince at Bourgas—Proofs of Russian complicity in plots against the Prince—Bulgarian disloyalty—Foreign views concerning it—Disaffection in the army—The traitors, Grueff, Bendereff, and Stoyanoff—Absence from Sofia of loyal officers—Warnings to the Prince unheeded—The mutinous Struma regiment—Occupation of Sofia—Attack upon the palace—Scene between Prince Alexander and the mutineers—Enforced signature of abdication—"God protect Bulgaria!"—Abduction of the Prince—Ignominious treatment of him by drunken conspirators—Comparison of the deposition of Prince Couza in Roumania and the abduction of Prince Alexander—The latter delivered to the Russians at Reni—Reaction in favour of the Prince—Mutkouroff and Stambouloff—Counter-revolution and fall of the "Provisional Government"—Arrival at Sofia of Mutkouroff and Popoff—Arrest of the conspirators and release of Karaveloff—Withdrawal of the mutineers from Sofia—Flight and capture of Grueff and Bendereff—Submission of the mutinous regiment—Release of Alexander—Stopped at Lemberg and recalled by the Bulgarian loyalists—Action of British representatives in connection with the Prince's abduction—England and Russia—Triumphant return of Prince Alexander to Bulgaria—An unfortunate telegram and the reply from the Czar—Why Prince Alexander abdicated—Russian assurances of non-intervention in Bulgaria—Appointment of the Regency—Abdication and departure of the Prince—His services to Bulgaria—The Regency—Mission of the Russian General Kaulbars—His demands and threats—Election riots promoted by Russia—Electioneering tour of Kaulbars in the Russian interest—A deplorable failure—Plot and insurrection against the Regency headed by Russian officers at Bourgas suppressed—Recall of Kaulbars and rupture of diplomatic relations with Russia—Unsupported charges of Kaulbars against the Bulgarians—Moderation and tact of the Ministers—Mission to European courts—Election and accession of Prince Ferdinand—Refusal of the Porte to confirm his election—His present position—Great Britain and Bulgaria—The proposed Danubian Confederation—Conclusion.

"HAVE you received any intelligence as to a *coup d'état* in Bulgaria? What is thought at Constantinople as to the course events will probably take?"

These were the words of a dispatch which was sent on the 22d August last year by the late lamented Earl of Iddesleigh (better known as Sir Stafford Northcote) to our representative in Constantinople, Sir Edward Thornton, and it announced to an astonished world one of the most audacious and dastardly outrages that has ever been recorded in the history of the civilised world—the abduction of a reigning Prince in the dead of night by a band of traitors and drunken ruffians, at the instigation (to speak with reserve) of the agents of what should have been a friendly neighbouring Power of great weight and influence. Messages flew in every direction, not only from our Foreign Office to our representatives at various Courts, but from capital to capital in every European State, and great anxiety was everywhere expressed as to the issues of the disgraceful transaction.

This is what occurred. The Russians had found that, through their blundering policy in quarrelling with Prince Alexander, in withdrawing their officers from the country at a critical moment, and in opposing the union of the two States, they had frittered away the advantages they had gained in Bulgaria through the war of liberation, and they therefore resolved once more to adopt what they call " diplomatic " measures in order to recover their lost prestige. Knowing the ill-feeling of the Czar towards the Prince, which he never hesitated to exhibit openly when the occasion offered, as in striking his name off the Russian army list, &c., and feeling that the Prince's courage and successes against the Servians had greatly increased his hold upon the people's affections, they redoubled their efforts, at any cost and in any manner, to effect his removal. Overtures were made to poor and willing popular leaders in Sofia to assist in a political revolution; the army was tampered with, and certain officers who were disappointed of promotion were bribed with money and promises of advancement to turn traitors to the Prince and commander to whom they had sworn allegiance; and their agents were charged with complicity in a plan, which was betrayed and counteracted, to seize and carry off the Prince at Bourgas. It may be said that these were only charges; but if the reader will take the trouble to look over the official dispatches of disinterested Powers relative to the subsequent successful plot against the Prince's person, he will find ample evidence to corroborate them and to prove their accuracy.[1]

These are some of the proofs: The Prince was taken in his yacht (commanded, according to some reports, by Russian officers[2]) *a prisoner*, and when he was landed at Reni, in Russian territory, he was handed over like a bale of goods to the Russian authorities, who refused to give him any information, and kept him as much a prisoner as he had been in the hands of his traitorous subjects. Even after the order came for his liberation, he was conducted to the frontier by gens-d'armes. The politicians who seized the reins of government after his departure were Zankoff and other notorious Russian advocates and instruments. The first place to which the conspirators in Sofia betook themselves when the daring deed was accomplished, and after they had made a pretence of holding a public meeting, was the Russian Agency, where they sought and were promised sympathy and protection. Immediately after the consummation of the conspiracy " a Russian colonel arrived at Rustchuk to act as Russian Commissioner in Bulgaria ;"[3] and although in its communications with the Bulgarians the Russian Government sought to allay their fears by blandly protesting that there was not the least intention to occupy their country, yet in treating with the Porte the Czar would only pledge himself " not to occupy Bulgaria unless civil war should arise, *or some other good reason present itself.*"[4]

I have not hesitated to anticipate some of the main facts of this infamous plot, owing to their recent occurrence, and because it is a matter of greater importance to us to know who were its responsible authors, and what were the motives that actuated them, than the recital of the deeds of their unworthy and misguided instruments. At the same time, if the Russians are to be censured for instigating and participating in the crime, what must be said of the Bulgarians themselves, in whose midst it

---

[1] These will be found *in extenso* in " Turkey, No. 1, 1887," already quoted.
[2] Dispatch No. 214, p. 105.   [3] Dispatch No. 142, p. 82.
[4] Ibid., Dispatch No. 240, p. 112.

was accomplished. Friendly writers (and I hope I may not be denied that title) have sought to hide the blot which stains the national escutcheon; but notwithstanding the noble efforts of such men as Mutkuroff, Stambouloff, Natchevitch, Stoiloff, Zivkoff, and others to remove that blot, notwithstanding even the friendly and self-sacrificing reserve of the Prince himself, strangers, however much they may sympathise with the Bulgarians, still regard the abduction of the Prince as a national disgrace. Almost the first question that is put to one by persons who are anxious about the future of the country is, "Will they treat their present Prince better than they did the last?" And indeed the disaffection and disloyalty must have been widespread which allowed such men as Grueff and Bendereff, who have escaped the punishment they merited, but have attained an unenviable notoriety for all time, to compass their treacherous designs. That they, with the help of Stoyanoff, the commander of the mutinous Struma regiment, and others, whose complicity it has been deemed politic to ignore, should have been able to secure, and even for a time hold possession of the capital, and with their lay accomplices to mislead the entire nation as to the actual state of affairs, seems inexplicable, otherwise than on the presumption that whole masses of men were indifferent to the national honour.[1] It is true that circumstances favoured the plot. The most trustworthy officers, Nikolaieff, Panoff, and others, were away on leave of absence, and the two leading conspirators had succeeded, at the risk of another national war, in obtaining the removal of a number of loyal troops to the Servian frontier to protect it against a pretended invasion; but, notwithstanding these advantages, they never could have compassed their ends if a considerable number of officers who were unwilling to participate actively in the crime had not lent it their silent support.

Twice the Prince was warned of his danger, but it is not surprising that he should hesitate to believe in the treachery of his most trusted officers. After disarming certain loyal troops in the neighbourhood of Sofia, the mutinous Struma regiment

---

[1] Dispatch No. 151, p. 85–86, Sir A. Paget to the Earl of Iddesleigh.

ABDUCTION OF PRINCE ALEXANDER.

entered that city on the night of the 20th–21st August, where, by order of their officers, they placed sentinels at the doors of the leading statesmen and others who were known to be loyal to their Prince and country. There they were joined or assisted by a regiment of artillery stationed at Sofia, and by the cadets of the Military College, who had been won over by Grueff, under whose charge they were placed. They then proceeded to the palace; and although the pen hesitates to record the disgraceful scene that was there enacted, it is necessary to do so, as it constitutes an important crisis in the history of the country. According to the account of Von Huhn, which seems in the main to be correct,[1] the Prince, who was asleep at the time (about 3 A.M.), was aroused by his servant, Dimitri, who placed a revolver in his hand, and cried, "Highness, flee; they are going to murder you." The Prince sprang from his bed, and, half-dressed, ran into a corridor whence a glass door led into a garden. This he found guarded by soldiers, who threatened him with their bayonets, and he retreated, and mounting to a higher storey, he saw that the palace was surrounded by armed men. Thereupon he descended, put on his uniform, and returned to face his mutinous subjects. These "pressed round him on all sides with wild cries, the officers threatening him with their revolvers, the cadets brandishing their bayonets in his face. Especially distinguished for bluster and noise was Captain Dimitrieff, who apparently had nerved himself to his crime by drink. In the middle of this wild tumult the Prince caught sight of his brother, Prince Francis Joseph, who, awaking with the first alarm, was on the point of hurrying to the Prince when he was stopped by the conspirators. These unanimously called on the Prince to abdicate, and demanded he should with his own hand write the deed. On the Prince refusing, Captain Dimitrieff seated himself at a small table on which generally lay the visitors' book, tore a sheet out, and attempted to draw up the document. What between excitement and drink, he was incapable of accomplishing anything beyond a few illegible

---

[1] "The Kidnapping of Prince Alexander," p. 30. Dispatch No. 157, p. 89; Dispatch No. 229, p. 109; Dispatch No. 261, p. 123, and elsewhere in "Turkey, No. 1, 1887."

hieroglyphics. He accordingly yielded his seat to a cadet, who at his dictation wrote out a formal deed of abdication. During this interval Grueff kept his revolver pointed in the Prince's face, but did not venture either to address him or look at him, not even when the Prince said, "So, you are also with them?" He had some feelings of shame left. The Prince paid but a scanty meed of attention to the document, which was read to him, and which he subscribed with the words, "Gott schütze Bulgarien.—Alexander." (God protect Bulgaria.—Alexander.[1]) It is needless to carry the description farther. Suffice it to say, that before his departure, which took place under a strong escort at 5 A.M., and subsequently, the Prince was subjected to the foulest abuse and the most ignominious treatment, which showed that his captors neither respected him nor themselves.

There is a curious circumstance in connection with this part of the plot which deserves a passing notice. The conspirators, or those who advised them, seem to have studied the account of the deposition of Prince Couza of Roumania, which happened twenty years previously, and to have taken it as their model.[2] (The result for the chief actors was, however, widely different.) At that time a number of leading statesmen conspired to depose Prince Couza on account of his long-continued misgovernment and gross immorality, and they adopted a course precisely similar (so far as it was requisite) to that pursued in the case of Prince Alexander. They pleaded as the justification for their violent proceedings that if they had moved more openly and deliberately, the Russians would have interfered nominally on behalf of the Prince, but really to accomplish their aims against the Principality. In the case of Couza, he was not even arrested, but after having signed his abdication was allowed to go his way, and no one gave him a second thought. A proclamation was issued with the sanction of the leading statesmen of all parties in Roumania, and a Provisional Government appointed, which was joyfully obeyed. In the case of Prince Alexander,

---

[1] "The Kidnapping of Prince Alexander," p. 31-32; also "Turkey, No. 1, 1887," Dispatch No. 229, p. 108.

[2] "Roumania," p. 230 et seq.

however, after the corrupt conspirators had assured themselves of Russian "protection," they too issued a proclamation, professing to emanate from men some of whom neither sanctioned nor approved the deed,[1] and shortly afterwards, when it was thought safe to do so, a second proclamation of a different tenor was circulated, bearing conspicuously the name (amongst others) of "The Commander-in-Chief of the Bulgarian Army, Major Grueff." As to the Prince himself, of course the conspirators had no fear of Russian intervention in *his* favour. What they apprehended was the interference of the loyal part of the population; so they spirited him away to Rahova on the Danube by a circuitous route, and thence to Reni, where they delivered him over to the Russians.

Events now moved quickly. After the nation had recovered from its surprise, and when the loyal portion of the army became aware of the true state of affairs, a great revulsion of feeling took place, and a counter-revolution followed almost immediately.[2] It had its origin with Lieutenant-Colonel Mutkuroff, who was in command of a brigade at Philippopolis, and M. Stambouloff, President of the National Assembly, who was at Tirnova. As soon as these two found that a sufficient number of troops remained faithful, they sent a telegram to Darmstadt to be forwarded to Prince Alexander (for his whereabouts was still unknown), praying him to return, and assuring him of the fidelity of the people and army; and at the same time they issued a proclamation denouncing as traitors and outlaws "the members of the Provisional Government, at the head of which is Clement." This was the Archimandrite at Sofia, whose name was appended to one of the proclamations circulated by the conspirators. Almost without an effort on the part of the loyal population, this "Provisional Government" fell to pieces like a house of cards. The members of it sent in their resignations to each other! Major Popoff marched into Sofia at the

---

[1] Forgery was largely resorted to by the conspirators. "Turkey, No. 1," Dispatch No. 229.
[2] Ibid., Dispatch No. 289, p. 139.

G

head of the loyal Alexander regiment; the mutinous regiments left the capital and encamped in the vicinity. On the 30th August Colonel Mutkuroff also arrived with four regiments of infantry, one of cavalry, and several batteries. The leading conspirators were put under arrest; amongst them Karaveloff, who played a doubtful part throughout the whole transaction, but he was soon liberated. Grueff and Bendereff tried to escape, but were arrested at Rahova (irony of fate!), where the Prince had embarked. The only serious obstacle to the complete re-establishment of order was now the presence of the mutinous regiments; but by a little judicious dallying on the part of Mutkuroff, that also was overcome without bloodshed. Many of the officers fled over the frontier; some of the men deserted; and in a few days the remainder laid down their arms and surrendered at discretion. The course was now clear for the return of the Prince, whom the Russians had been forced to release in consequence of the universal expressions of indignation throughout the civilised world. After his liberation he proceeded on his homeward journey as far as Lemberg, where he was met by his brother Louis from Darmstadt. Here, too, he received the intelligence of the reaction in his favour, and the message of Stamboulofl praying him to return, and the two brothers held a long consultation on the subject. It has been said by certain German writers that Great Britain failed to show proper sympathy with the Bulgarians in their hour of trial. Here is a telegram which was sent by Lord Iddesleigh to Sir Edward Thornton at Constantinople on the 25th August, immediately after he heard of the Prince's liberation:—" I requested your Excellency by telegraph to try to impress upon the Porte with great earnestness, that it would be politic on their part, now that Prince Alexander has recovered his freedom, to summon his Highness to return to the Principality and restore order there."[1] And if that be not sufficient to refute such a calumny, here is an extract from another,[2] from Mr. Condie Stephen, our representative at Sofia, to Earl Iddesleigh, recounting a conversation between himself and Grueff, the self-elected commander-in-chief, on the 26th August:—" I

---

[1] Dispatch No. 181, p. 96.   [2] Ibid. No. 289, p. 139.

began by informing him that I must decline to discuss any political questions with him, for I could in no way recognise the authority which he and his companions claimed, but I had come to warn him that, as military chief of the revolt, he would be held personally responsible for anything that might happen to Prince Alexander." But as it may be said that these were remonstrances addressed to weak Powers, I may be permitted, in order to show how firmly our Government supported the cause of freedom in the East, to make one more extract, namely, from a long telegram sent by Mr. Morier, St. Petersburg, to the Earl of Iddesleigh, narrating an interview with M. de Giers. After listening to the most bitter denunciations of Prince Alexander, to the impossibility of a reconciliation between the Russians and him, and charges of "untold ingratitude of the Bulgarians for their deliverer," "I said, if that were so, the prospect was a black one indeed. The point of view from which the British nation viewed the question was necessarily a very different one. They regarded his Highness as a Prince who had striven to the best of his abilities to create a free and orderly community in the territories committed to his charge, and they had throughout wished him success in his arduous undertaking. If, with the tremendous odds and the hostility of Russia against him, he now succeeded in once more grasping the reins of power with a steady hand, and again stood forth as the constitutional head of a law-abiding State, I believed the people of England would be deeply moved, and would scarcely look on with indifference should an attempt be made from without to disturb this state of things. His Excellency repeated, as he had on several occasions previously done, that there was not the slightest intention on the part of Russia to interfere" (sic!).[1] On the 18th September, however, an official announcement appeared in the *Journal de St. Petersburg* of the mission of "M. le Général-Major Baron Kaulbars" to study Bulgarian affairs in detail, and assist the Bulgarians with his counsels, in order to extricate them from the crisis through which they are passing." "Ja, er kam mit einer

---

[1] Dispatch No. 295, p. 146.

Knute" ("Yes, he came with a knout"), said one of the leading statesmen to me at Sofia.

As my readers well know, Prince Alexander returned in triumph to his people. At Rustchuk he was met, not only by a large number of his loyal subjects, but by the representatives of foreign courts, including that of St. Petersburg; and in an evil hour, in the belief that he would thereby conciliate his irreconcilable cousin, he was induced to send him a telegram which the world has pronounced humiliating. After thanking the Emperor for having allowed his representative to meet him at Rustchuk, he said it was his "firm intention to spare no sacrifice *in order to aid your Imperial Majesty's magnanimous intention to terminate the present grave crisis through which Bulgaria is passing.*" He expresses his anxiety that Prince Dolgorouki, who was coming as an emissary from St. Petersburg, should come to an understanding with himself, and, after professions of devotion, he wound up with the unfortunate sentence: "Russia gave me my crown; I am ready to return it into the hands of her sovereign."

The Emperor's reply, bearing his own signature, was as follows:—

"*His Highness the Prince of Bulgaria, Philippopoli.*

Have received your Highness's telegram. Cannot approve your return to Bulgaria, foreseeing the disastrous consequences to the country, already so severely tried. The mission of Prince Dolgorouki is no longer desirable. I shall refrain from all interference with the sad state to which Bulgaria has been brought as long as you remain there. Your Highness will judge what is your proper course. I reserve my decision as to my future action, which will be in conformity with the obligations imposed on me by the venerated memory of my father, the interests of Russia, and the peace of the East."

Prince Alexander appears to have committed a very weak act, though it is difficult to judge without knowing what assurances were given to him by the Russian representative, or what feelings actuated him; and he laid himself open to a retort which would have reflected little credit upon any gentleman, much less upon one enjoying the exalted position of the "Czar of all the Russias," who has never done one single act nor said a single sentence likely to recall the "venerated memory of his father," the Liberator. But if this action of the Prince was not justified and was unworthy of him, his subsequent conduct far more than made amends. Nothing is more common in England, and even abroad, than to hear the question put, "Why did Prince Alexander abdicate?" After his release, his reception in Austria and Roumania was most flattering and sympathetic; so too was the expression of feeling throughout Europe, excepting, of course, in Russia. His return to Sofia by way of Tirnova and Philippopolis was one continued triumphal march; even the King of Servia sent him a message of sympathy and congratulation. Then why did he abdicate? I fear the answer will not raise the Bulgarians in the estimation of my readers; but the truth must be told. First, he found that the military conspiracy had extended much more widely than was generally supposed. "Out of six commanders of brigades," he told our representative at Sofia, in a deep fit of depression,[1] "three were implicated in the plot, and twelve out of eighteen commanders of regiments. The army was in a complete state of disorganisation, and his Highness could place no reliance on any of the civilians. M. Karaveloff was certainly acquainted with the plot. . . . The people were with him, no doubt; but it was impossible to govern with the people, and the leaders were not to be trusted." Then, again, to a large extent the punishment of the military insurgents was thrown upon his hands, for he was commander-in-chief of the army; and there would have to be numerous executions, which would not only be distasteful to the Prince, but would render him liable to assassination. But even as regarded the most prominent traitors, Russia was clamouring and bullying for their release, and two of the leading European Powers were supporting her demand. Under such circumstances, discipline in the army was impossible. And finally, the Russian agents, taking advantage of the Prince's grave indiscretion in sending the telegram to the Czar, were constantly representing

---

[1] Dispatch No. 278, p. 134.

to him that his presence alone stood in the way of a reconciliation between Russia and Bulgaria, and militated against the freedom and prosperity of the latter.

These are the reasons why Alexander abdicated; but before doing so he formally applied to the Russian Government for a promise that, if he departed from the country, it would leave the Bulgarians at liberty to manage their own affairs; and having received that promise in the presence of his councillors, he next considered how he could best provide for the re-establishment and maintenance of order. At first he tried to induce the Powers to appoint a European Commission to take over the administration of the country after his departure;[1] but as that was not found to be practicable, he himself nominated Messrs. Karaveloff, Stambouloff, and Nikeforoff Regents, and they selected a number of leading men of all parties to form a Ministry. Then, and not until then, the Prince expressed his firm and final resolution to abdicate; and after issuing a suitable proclamation to that effect, signed once more "God preserve Bulgaria," he prepared to take his departure. This occurred on the 7th September, when, accompanied by his leading advisers and officers who had remained loyal, and followed by the regrets of the people of his adopted country, he drove in state from Sofia to Lom Palanka on the Danube, embarked once more on board the yacht *Alexander*, landed at Turn Severin in Roumania, and there taking the railway, returned into private life after a glorious but troublous reign of eight years. During that period he had consolidated the Bulgarian nation, successfully defended the country against external foes, and secured its prestige as a military power, and, as far as the unremitting plots and persecution of a great autocratic "liberator" would permit, he had established order and greatly developed the internal resources of the land.

Prince Bismarck was right when he said that the Prince's sovereignty of Bulgaria would be a pleasant reminiscence!

After the departure of Prince Alexander, the Regents set to

---

[1] Dispatch No. 284, p. 137.

THE RUSSIAN AGENCY, SOFIA, WITH BRITISH AGENCY ON THE RIGHT.

work in their arduous task of governing the country until a
new Prince should be elected. The Russians, too, manifested a
most laudable desire to see order re-established, and with that
view they sent General Kaulbars to advise the Bulgarians.
This he did first by demanding the immediate release of all
persons, including officers, who had been engaged in the revolt.
For a long time the Government resisted this demand, but eventually, after his threats had been backed up by the arrival of
two Russian vessels of war at Varna, with which he threatened
to bombard the town, they were obliged to yield. Another
demand of his was that the elections for the great National
Assembly should be postponed. This the Regents successfully
resisted, and the elections took place; but in order to throw as
much doubt as possible upon their validity, the Russian agents
and Consuls incited the opponents of the Government and
others to riot wherever it was practicable. This was notably
the case at Sofia, where a large number of peasants were bribed
to attack the polling-booth. Repulsed by the guardians of
the peace, they took refuge in the Russian Agency, which is
situated immediately opposite ours. A disturbance ensued,
and several shots were fired upon the crowd from the Russian
Agency (see Plate II.), where a number of armed Montenegrins
were kept as "lambs." Some of the bullets lodged in or "left
marks on the walls of the British and German Agencies;"[1]
and this had the effect of somewhat cooling the electioneering
ardour of the Russian agent, M. Nekludow. But what was
wanting in Sofia General Kaulbars himself endeavoured to
supplement elsewhere. He stumped the whole country on
behalf of his master the Czar, and brought ridicule and contempt upon his Government and himself by his arrogance and
undiplomatic conduct. His tour was a complete failure, and
the elections, resulting in a large Government majority, were
held notwithstanding his unjustifiable interference. After this,
Russian agents instigated a plot against the Government at
Bourgas, where a number of insurgents led by two Russian

---

[1] Dispatch No. 410, p. 200. All details connected with the acts of Russia
during the progress of the elections will be found in Dispatches in "Turkey, No.
1, 1887."

officers, Captain Nabokoff (who afterwards escaped) and another, had possession of the place for a brief period; but the rising was suppressed on the arrival of a body of regular Bulgarian troops. These and similar measures were taken by the Russian officials and agents " to restore law and order" in Bulgaria, but they ended in the recall of General Kaulbars, the withdrawal of the war-vessels from Varna, and finally of the Russian Agency and all Russian officials from the "ungrateful country."

It would have been surprising if the irritating and arbitrary proceedings of General Kaulbars and his associates, one of which was to distribute, or attempt to distribute, throughout the country a seditious handbill against the Government, had not led to some expressions of ill-will, or even retaliatory measures against the Russians, and their envoy complained to the Ministry that violence had been used towards Russian subjects in Bulgaria. When, however, he was asked to give some definite cases for inquiry and prosecution, his reply was that he declined to enter into a discussion with regard to the particular cases in which Russian subjects had been ill-treated, so many instances having came to his personal knowledge during the time he had been in Bulgaria, "acts of which the Bulgarian Regents were themselves well aware;"[2] and, if the statements of the Russian officials in London and St. Petersburg are to be credited, his reports made to them varied from his accusations at Sofia. But throughout the negotiations, and during all this trying period, the attitude of the Bulgarian statesmen presented a marked contrast to that of the Russian representatives. The threats and intimidation of the latter were met with firmness, moderation, and good sense, and where, for the sake of peace, they found it possible and politic to acquiesce in the demands of Russia, the Government did so, as the reader may convince himself by a perusal of the voluminous dispatches. Indeed, the tact and demeanour of the Bulgarian leaders at that time, and down to the election of Prince Ferdinand, have secured for

---

[1] Dispatches Nos. 554 557, pp. 280, 281.
[2] Dispatch No. 518, p. 254; and Enclosures, 11 and 12 in Dispatch No. 550, pp. 277, 278.

them the respect and sympathy of the whole of the civilised world.

After a futile attempt on the part of Russia to press upon the people the candidature of the "Prince of Mingrelia,"[1] and after the election of Prince Waldemar of Denmark, and his refusal to accept the post, and the mission of a deputation of Bulgarian leaders to the various courts of Europe to place before them the actual condition of affairs, a third, and this time a successful attempt was made to secure a successor to Prince Alexander. This was done in the person of Prince Ferdinand of Saxe-Coburg and Gotha, who was elected on the 9th of last July, accepted the sovereignty and ascended the throne[2] on Sunday, 14th August, at Tirnova, the ancient capital of Bulgaria. Up to the time of writing, however, the Porte has declined to confirm and the Powers to approve his election, which they (or some of them) say is not in conformity with the Treaty of Berlin. As a matter of fact, however, it is they who are completely violating *the spirit* of that treaty, which says that "the Prince of Bulgaria shall be freely elected by the population." He was so chosen, his election has been confirmed by a subsequent Parliament, and not one of the Powers (not even Russia) has ventured to find fault with the choice of the Bulgarian people.

Before closing this survey of the past history of Bulgaria and attempting to deal with her present condition, I feel bound, partly in consequence of the flippant criticisms to which I have referred, and at the risk of being charged with needless repetition, to say a few words concerning the part played by our country during the recent troubles; for although I would by no means affirm that it is incumbent upon us to go to war again for the integrity of the Ottoman Empire, which is rapidly falling to decay, yet it is clearly our duty, by every legitimate means, to assist the young and rising States of Eastern Europe to retain

---

[1] Dispatch No. 553, p. 280 (from Sir W. White, who succeeded Sir E. Thornton at Constantinople, to the Earl of Iddesleigh).

[2] The Prince of Bulgaria is not crowned. He takes the oath to uphold the Constitution, and is blessed by a bishop.

their independence, and to protect them from the wolf-and-lamb policy of Russia.

That Mr. Gladstone's action in connection with the Bulgarian atrocities was directed to the liberation of Bulgaria and not to the aggrandisement of Russia, no dispassionate thinker will deny; and any person who reads the dispatches to which such frequent reference has been made in these pages, and who has followed the course of events with care, is bound with equal readiness to admit that the Earl of Iddesleigh courageously and honourably sought to maintain our reputation as the champion of liberty in the East. But what must be gratifying to Englishmen is to feel that in their policy and efforts both political parties were admirably seconded and supported by our representatives at foreign courts. When, by the desire of the people, the union of the two Bulgarias was accomplished, Sir William White at Constantinople and Mr. Lascelles at Sofia threw their influence into the scale for the Bulgarians against Russian diplomacy. When the treacherous and corrupt, or rather corrupted section of his subjects plotted, for a time successfully, against the liberty of their Prince and country, Mr. Lascelles refused to acknowledge the military leadership of Grueff in Sofia, and although, from what I know of him personally, I am sure that our brave Consul-General at Philippopolis, Captain Jones, V.C., would in no way outstep his diplomatic functions, yet it is an open secret that when he was privately consulted by General Mutkuroff, one of the saviours of Bulgarian liberty, his advice was given on the side of loyalty and freedom; and he kept our Government completely informed as to the plots and the unwarrantable interference of Russia in the internal affairs of the country. And finally, whilst even the great German Chancellor stood in awe of the power of Russia, and professed at least to be playing into her hands, Sir Robert Morier at St. Petersburg did not hesitate to announce to the Russian Government that this nation would not look with indifference upon any attempt that might be made to rob the young nation of her liberties.

I trust that the British nation will tolerate no Government that will act otherwise than in this spirit, and if these remarks should meet the eye of my Bulgarian friends, I will ask them to ponder well over a question that was put on the 29th September 1886 by M. de Staal to the Earl of Iddesleigh, and the Earl's reply: "He also asked me whether her Majesty's Government were taking any steps to bring about an understanding between Roumania, Servia, and Bulgaria. I replied in the negative, though, I added, we desired to see those States in cordial amity with one another, and I had so expressed myself to the Governments of those States."[1]

I am not aware whether and to what extent our Government is acting on the lines of this conversation, and I am well acquainted with the obstacles to the establishment of a Danubian Confederation. The good feeling which now exists between Servia and Bulgaria has already led to a move in the right direction, and the nations themselves will have to undertake the task. One thing, however, is certain, namely, that the Earl of Iddesleigh was expressing the opinion of nine out of ten sensible Englishmen, that this would be the best and safest solution, so far as it can at present be solved, of what is known as the Eastern Question, to which I propose hereafter more fully to direct the reader's attention.

Here our review of the past history of Bulgaria must terminate, but some personal remarks upon her two Princes, her living statesmen and their antecedents, will be found in the Second Part of this treatise.

[1] Dispatch No. 373, p. 185.

PART II.

BULGARIA. TO-DAY.

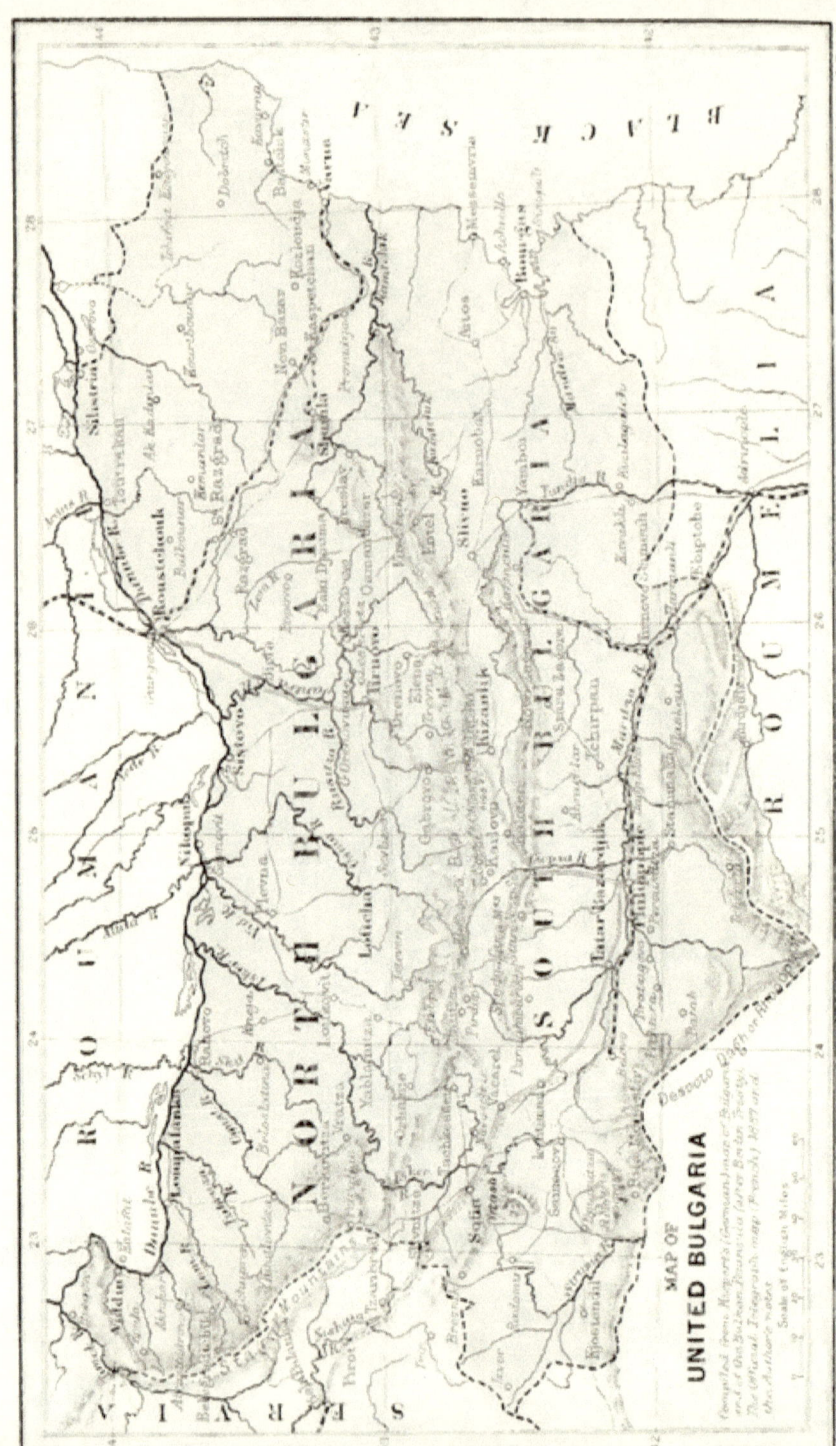

CHAPTER X.

GEOGRAPHICAL AND PHYSICAL.

Area of Bulgaria—Its mountain chains—Their shape and constitution—Configuration of the country generally—Ancient sea or lake beds—The plains—Tumuli and their contents—The surface soil—The rivers—Beauties of the Jantra—Towns—Roads—Railways.

IT is not my intention to treat my readers as schoolboys, nor to give them a lesson in the geography of Bulgaria, but before speaking of the institutions of the country, it may be interesting to refer to a few of its general characteristics. The boundaries of the united Principality, as they were defined by the Treaty of Berlin under the two heads of "Bulgaria" and "Eastern Roumelia," have already been given, and it may now be added that its area, about 38,500 square miles, is about equal to that of Ireland and Wales. The two provinces, North and South, are divided by the Balkan chain, which has been subdivided by some geographers into smaller groups or ranges. These take their popular names mostly from the towns and villages at their bases, as the Bercovića, Etropol, Zlatica, Trojan, Kalofer, and Karnabad Balkans. In addition to the Balkans there is the Rhodope chain in the south, which serves as part of the boundary between Bulgaria and Turkey; the Sredna Gora, or Middle Mountains, between the two; the Rilo and Vitosch Mountains, both (the last immediately) south of Sofia, the capital. The general height of these mountains is about the same as the Carpathians; none rising more than about 9000 feet above the sea-level. Their summits are, with few exceptions, rounded, and their composition chiefly limestone; but many different strata crop up at the surface in and near the mountains.

Some of these, as the vertical walls of sandstone at Belogradchik, are very bizarre; whilst at Philippopolis huge granite hills spring directly from the plain. A mineral which enters largely into the composition of the Balkans is argillaceous mica-schist, which gives them in places a very brilliant appearance as it glitters brightly in the southern sunshine, often reminding one of the Pass of the Tourmalets, between St. Sauveur and Bagneres de Bigorre in the Pyrenees. Another very striking characteristic of the Balkans, which the eye never tires of beholding, is the frequent recurrence of limestone escarpments, rising at different elevations and sometimes extending for miles. These resemble somewhat the Eagle Cliffs at Llangollen; and if the reader should ever approach Tirnova on the road from Biela, where these cliffs rise precipitously from the roadside, he will find them to be composed largely of fossiliferous limestone.

A striking feature of the country is the sudden transition from plain to mountain, the nearest approach to which is seen on the Worcestershire side of the Malvern Hills. You may drive for hours along a level road with a perfectly flat plain on either side of you, reaching miles and miles into the far distance,—a vast plain, absolutely no valley,—and then suddenly a high mountain range rises on one or both sides at the boundary of the plain. In some parts you have beautifully undulating country, as on the southern slopes of the Balkans, and then perhaps a long expanse of elevated plain; but the vast plateau, with its mountain ranges at the extremities, leaves the most durable impression upon the mind of the traveller.

Coupling together these level tracts of country with the escarpments of limestone or raised sea-beaches, the traveller, even one without pretensions to geological knowledge, is inevitably led to the conclusion that a great part of the country must at one time have been covered by the sea. Indeed, at one place, between Tirnova and Rustchuk, in the vicinity of Biela, the appearance of the landscape admits of no other inference. As you drive along the road, you see on your left a magnificent lake minus the water, for which is substituted a perfectly level grass-covered plain, and running round a great portion of its circumference for miles there is a range of hills, alternating with almost perpendicular limestone cliffs.

And these plains themselves possess another striking peculiarity, which is apt to puzzle the uninitiated traveller. Small hills, varying in height from twenty to fifty feet, generally overgrown with grass or a few stunted trees, rise from the plains almost throughout the whole country. These are tumuli or burial-mounds, and they may be counted by thousands. During a drive over the plain from Philippopolis to the Monastery of St. Kyriak (to be described hereafter), I counted in some places between thirty and forty such mounds visible at one time. They are of various periods, and will one day afford a considerable fund of information to the historians of the earlier ages of man. At present, most of the known facts connected with them serve as the foundation for guesswork, which is usually enveloped in a cloud of ambiguous verbiage. Some of them have been explored, and there have been discovered sarcophagi, skeletons, armour (such as helmets, &c.), arrowheads, &c.; but little or nothing definite is known with regard to the owners of these interesting objects. Two things are certain: first, that some of them have served as burial-places for chiefs, probably of most of the nations who formerly occupied the country; and secondly, that they have often been utilised as small fortified stations and look-outs.

The natural products of these plains and mountains we shall have an opportunity of considering as we drive through the country. The soil is, generally speaking, extremely fertile, and at present needs no manure. It varies, of course, in different localities, but is chiefly of the same argillaceous nature as elsewhere in the Danubian plains. There are, however, whole tracts where cultivation would seem to be almost impossible, owing to the presence of innumerable round stones, of which the superficial drift is almost entirely composed, and which choke the surface soil. The presence of these stones, of which I have never seen the like elsewhere, renders the introduction and use of our light Western ploughs very difficult; the old—I was about to say aboriginal—plough in use being better adapted for this almost impenetrable surface. The same beds of channelled clay which offend the eye on the hill-slopes of Roumania are seen here, and they often mar the beauty of the otherwise magnificent landscape.

The plains of Bulgaria are irrigated and drained by several important streams. Of the Danube, which forms one of its boundaries, I have spoken at length elsewhere.[1] Of its affluents in Bulgaria, the chief are the Isker, the Lom, the Vid, the Osma, and the Jantra, all of which, excepting the first, rise in the Balkans. The Isker has its sources in the south-west of South Bulgaria, and flowing northward, it breaks through the Balkans, which it divides into two ranges, not far from Sofia. Perhaps the most interesting of these rivers is the Jantra, whose course winds circuitously between high limestone rocks through and round Tirnova; and as one travels over the undulating country between the old capital and the Danube, every now and then he obtains beautiful glimpses of the river as it meanders along, often hemmed in by perpendicular walls of limestone. Another fine river is the Maritza, whose sources are near those of the Isker; it flows past Philippopolis (see Plate VI.), where it is already a broad river, crossing South Bulgaria from west to east, receiving many branches, and finally disappearing in the Ægean Sea. These rivers are crossed by fine stone bridges, as those over the Jantra at Gabrovo, Biela, &c., and over the Maritza at Philippopolis.

The most important towns in Bulgaria are Sofia, the capital, situated in an elevated plain at the foot of Mount Vitosch, in the south-west; Philippopolis, in the south, both cities being on the main road from Belgrade to Adrianople; Tirnova, north of the Balkans; Sliven or Slivno, a town celebrated for its manufacturing industries—" house-industries," as the Germans call them—namely, woollen rugs, clothing, &c.; Kezanlik, the seat of the otto-of-rose manufacture; Schumla, a strongly fortified place, and many other inland towns; also the ports of Varna, on the Black Sea, Lom, Vidin, Sistowa, Rustchuk, Silistria, and others, on the Danube. Many of these towns are united by good roads, as the trunk-road already named, from which there is an important branch at Philippopolis, crossing the Shipka

---

[1] "Roumania," chap. iii.

GEOGRAPHICAL AND PHYSICAL. 115

Pass in the Balkans to Tirnova, and thence to Rustchuk, with branch roads to Sistowa, Plevna, &c.; others there are from Lom Palanka to Sofia, from that capital to Köstendil, &c. There are two railways—the one, well known, from Rustchuk to Varna, which at present conveys passengers from most parts of Europe to Constantinople; and the unfinished line, which will eventually connect Vienna and Constantinople without the need of crossing the Black Sea. At present passengers cannot enter Bulgaria from Servia by that railway, although at the time of writing a locomotive engine has entered Sofia over the line. At Sarambey, in South Bulgaria, it recommences, and is thence available by Philippopolis to Adrianople and Constantinople.[1] Although the rails are not laid, and in some places the bridges wanting, the course of the line may be followed throughout, as given on the map appended hereto, and it will not be long before it is available for through traffic.

These few general remarks upon the country are necessary to enable the reader to comprehend the following detailed information.

---

[1] At Tirnova-Semanli there is a short branch on this line open to Jeni-Zagra and Jamboli.

CHAPTER XI.

BULGARIAN CITIES—SOFIA, THE CAPITAL—NATIONAL AND OFFICIAL LIFE.

Sofia—The new quarter—The old town—Its Oriental character—Absence of amusements in Sofia—Politics—A visit to the prison—The prisoners—Want of employment—A "Jack Shepherd"—The prison system—Administration of justice in Bulgaria—Courts of justice—Defects of administration—Biassed judges—Lenient treatment of criminals—Visit to the Technical School of Kniajevo—Its operations—Wood and iron work—Its beautiful manufactures—Teaching arrangements—Professor Athanasoff and his staff—Laboratories and collections—Cost of maintenance—Influence of the school on Bulgarian industries—Printing-offices—The citizens—Treatment of the Jews—Dr. Matincheff and the Jewish sick and poor—Bulgarian statesmen, their modest habits of life—M. Stambouloff, his career—Messrs. Stoiloff, Natchewitch, Zivkoff, Colonel Mutkouroff, Dr. Stransky, M. Radoslavoff, M. Karaveloff—Rapid rise of Bulgarian statesmen—Their consummate tact and ability.

IT would be difficult to conceive of three cities presenting greater contrasts than Sofia, the modern capital, Tirnova, the ancient capital of Bulgaria, and Philippopolis, the chief town in South Bulgaria, formerly Eastern Roumelia. Each has its marked peculiarities, and in describing them I propose also to refer to those national and social movements of which they are the centres.

Sofia is situated on an elevated plain in the south-west of Bulgaria, and more than one range of mountains is visible from its higher parts, conspicuously the Balkans to the north and Mount Vitosch immediately on the south. During my stay in the city there was unfortunately a change from very dry to wet weather. This had the effect of making the surrounding plain change from a parched brown to a bright green colour, but it prevented me from ascending Vitosch, from which there

NEW PART OF SOFIA

is a splendid view, as the summit was nearly always in the clouds. The atmospheric effects as these rolled over the mountain and around its slopes were, however, very grand and imposing. There is a gradually rising plain a few miles in extent from Sofia to the foot of the mountain, and it may then be easily ascended in any direction. The city itself, which covers a very considerable area, resembling in that respect Bucharest, contains about twenty thousand inhabitants. It may be said to have three distinct quarters. The new city, which was virtually planned and founded by Prince Alexander, is situated round about the palace, of which a fair idea may be obtained from the photograph; the old "Turkish" quarter, which resembles the narrow streets of certain Oriental cities; and a straggling series of streets and roads, with houses of moderate dimensions and some imposing buildings, as the barracks, the new printing-offices, and the boys' "Gymnasium" or upper middle-class school, &c.

The new part of the city comprises the palace, which is a very fine structure of modern French Renaissance (as may be seen from the photograph), resembling portions of the Louvre and Tuileries (see Plates III. and VIII.); the "Hotel Bulgaria" opposite, really the only fine hotel in the city; some good shops; the houses in which the Ministries are situated, very unpretending buildings, and near at hand the "Agencies" of foreign courts. These are situated at a higher elevation than the palace, and the finest is the Russian Agency, of which also a photograph is appended (Plate II.), showing the Russian and part of the British agency.

The old town is by far the most interesting to strangers. It consists of a series of streets containing shops with open fronts, enabling the visitor to see the artisans at work, and the trades are, as far as possible, grouped together—shoemakers, tinsmiths, cutlers making knives and dirks, brass-workers, butchers, bakers, clothiers, &c., and not the least conspicuous the furriers at work making the kalpack or cylindrical Bulgarian head-dress worn by the men. The better kinds are made of real fur, the commoner descriptions of sheep's-wool died black. In some places I saw very beautiful white kalpacks. In addition to these features the striking peculiarities of this and other towns are: first, the mosques, which have been converted to secular uses, as prisons, printing-offices, markets, &c. (in Sofia the baths, fed by natural hot springs); the execrable pavement, which makes progress in a carriage very difficult; the wooden skeletons of triumphal arches, which are permanently retained throughout the country, so that the people may not be put to any unnecessary trouble in preparing a joyous reception in turn for Russian general, German prince, or nationalist hero!

In Sofia there is no theatre, no concerts, and, as far as I could learn, no lectures nor systematic entertainments of any kind, except a military band, which plays very well, and one or two *cafés-chantants*. During my stay there the people were very much exercised, not only by the intrigues of Russia, but by the refusal of the Powers to recognise their Prince and the threat of the Germans to send men-of-war to blockade or bombard Varna on account of some petty insult in the shape of a newspaper article which had recently appeared reflecting on one of their Consuls, and that may have accounted for the serious aspect of the place. But to me it appeared that politics alone occupied all men's thoughts, and the whole place seemed to be in the throes of one vast mysterious conspiracy. That the political atmosphere was highly charged the reader will find when I come to describe a "meeting" which took place during my sojourn there. I was told that the Sofians are always either up in the skies or down in the mud, and I am afraid that it was my ill-luck to find them in the lower regions.

The places of interest to be visited there, besides those just named, are the Technical School of Kniajevo, which is situated a few miles out of the city, at the foot of Vitosch, and is unique; the printing-offices; the boys' Gymnase, which was unfortunately closed when I was there; and, for those who care to study the aspects of crime, the prison. Let us visit the last-named first. It is a (very slightly, I should say) converted mosque—the Black Mosque. You enter it from a kind of court or garden, and find yourself in a quadrangle, badly paved and slovenly, and containing a few stunted trees, with a series of buildings all round, consisting of large chambers or cells. In these there are raised shelves where the prisoners sleep, and where they stand in a row for inspection. The prison costume is white duck, and the prisoners are numbered. When I was there, there were about 170 men and (in another part of the building) seven women. One of the men was a priest, who was permitted to wear his long gown and silk hat. I understood that he had been implicated in the election riots.[1] The crimes of the others had been murder, manslaughter, highway robbery (or, as they call it, brigandage, of which I shall speak hereafter), and other heavy offences, and all but two or three were imprisoned for long terms, up to fourteen years or even longer. Two or three were sentenced to

THE BLACK MOSQUE (PRISON) IN SOFIA.

death, and I was shocked to see one man in chains standing amongst the rest, when I subsequently saw them in a body in the quadrangle, who was to be executed in a few days. He had previously sent me from his cell, where he was standing along with others, a belt made by himself of small beads, for which, of course, I gave him a trifle. Other prisoners voluntarily make similar objects of small, parti-coloured beads, as purses, necklaces, &c., which they sell to visitors, and that is the extent of the prison labour! The prisoners do abso-

---

[1] Or in a conspiracy in the interests of Russia, I forget which.

lutely nothing, as, with some trifling exceptions, they did in Bucharest, when I was there in 1881. The result of this enforced idleness and of the free association of the prisoners is that they are constantly conspiring to escape. About a fortnight before I was there two prisoners had escaped, and, I believe, up to that time they were at large. The very day previously another prisoner, it was believed in collusion with about ten more, was within an ace of making his escape. I was shown a key which he had cleverly constructed out of a piece of thin plate-iron, wherewith he was going to open his cell door, and another of wood for the outer gate. In case they had succeeded in reaching that, the prisoners would have overpowered, and probably murdered, the guard. The prisoner was afterwards shown to me in a strong cell, heavily loaded with chains round his breast, waist, and legs. The system of associating prisoners of various degrees is, however, not so bad as formerly. Some years since, if a soldier failed to salute his superior officer, or committed some slight military offence, and received a sentence of a short term of imprisonment, he was bundled into this and other gaols, and compelled to herd with murderers and highway robbers. The prisoners are well fed. As one of the Ministers said to me, " they live more comfortably than ordinary workmen." They have meat four times a week, bread in the morning, excellent nourishing soup (which I tasted) at noon, and another meal of some kind later on. They are nearly all well-educated, and three who could neither read nor write when they entered the gaol had been instructed by their colleagues. A few books were lent to them by a Missionary Society, but that was all that was done for their intellectual advancement. There is some kind of weekly inspection. I asked them whether they would not prefer to work, and was answered affirmatively; they even said they would petition for work; but I fear that is a reform of the future. Generally speaking, the treatment of prisoners is mild; the Government is averse to inflict capital punishment, and the prison officials are forbearing, intelligent, and attentive, and fully alive to the danger and inconvenience of the present system. And now a few words about the administration of justice generally in Bulgaria.

The police system in Sofia comprises four districts (including the central), called Ootchastoks, which take cognisance of crimes therein committed. In the central office, which was the one visited by me, a commissioner sits and disposes of petty cases involving not more than twenty-four hours' detention. Imprisonment for any longer period must be inflicted by higher courts. A second petty court is that of the Juge de Paix, who adjudicates upon cases not involving disputes or damages beyond 300 francs.

There are three superior courts. The Court of First Instance, the Court of Appeal, and the "Cour de Cassation." From the first, prisoners nearly always appeal to the second, and facilities are freely granted to enable them to do so. The Court of Cassation may revise the sentences of the Court of Appeal, order a new trial, or mitigate the sentence. So far the machinery of the law, which seems excellent; now as to how it is administered. I made searching inquiries, and received the following information from a great variety of sources. "Are the judges corrupt?" The answer is "No; not so far as bribery is concerned;" and this redounds greatly to their credit, for the salary of the President of the "Cour de Cassation," the highest court, is only £300 per annum! (Let me here add that a prefect receives at most £200 a year, a Minister of State £480. A Deputy gets fifteen francs per day during the session of Parliament, and his travelling expenses.)

On the other hand, it rests with the Procureur (public prosecutor) to give the prisoner a chance before the "Cour de Cassation," for his report is submitted to their consideration, and I was told on good authority that he is often biassed in his acts. Some even of the judges are influenced by political sympathies, especially in cases of riot or other matters connected with elections. If the prisoner belongs to their side, he is all right; if to the opposition, he may bid good-bye to his chances of justice. I shall be told that I need not go so far as Bulgaria for instances of that description; but as regards the judges of our superior courts, we need happily fear no such perversion of justice in England. Prisoners are often detained in prison for a long time before being brought to trial, and I heard of one case where a man was detained for a year before being *acquitted*. On the whole, however, the administration of justice is mild, capital sentences are often commuted, and no such severities are to be met with as killing prisoners by insanitary or exhausting employments.

From the prison and crime we will pass on to a more agreeable subject, namely, technical instruction in Bulgaria. After having visited many such institutions in Europe and the United States, I have no hesitation in saying that, plain and unpretending as it is, the "Ecole Technique" at Kniajevo is the most interesting and practical that I have met with anywhere. It is situated at the foot of Vitosch, about five or six miles from Sofia, and consists of three buildings—one on the roadside, another in the grounds in the rear, and the director's residence —and gives instruction to about seventy pupils, forty of whom work in iron and thirty in wood. The department of ironwork comprises a large fitting-shop, provided with excellent tools, and a forge and foundry; also a small blast-furnace, with crucibles for casting steel and other metals. The kind of iron and bronze work done is lamps, candelabra, bells for churches, gates, either of iron only, or beautiful wooden doors with iron grating and ornamentation, and with polished steel handles and locks. The lock-making is the strong feature, and some of the locks are very beautiful. In addition, there are balconies, kitchen ranges, and certain implements employed in agriculture, as ploughs, sieves for cleansing and separating wheat and flour, and many small articles of use and ornament. In the department of woodwork, cabinetmaking is the chief occupation, and the articles fabricated are second to none that I have seen elsewhere.

The woods employed are indigenous walnut, oak, beech, and pine, and from these are made chairs, tables, bedsteads, secretaires, bookcases, and almost every other article of household use. There was one beautiful secretaire of solid walnut, for which £2 was asked, but which in this country would have cost four or five times as much. There had been an exhibition a few days before I was there, of which I saw photographic representations, and the objects exhibited, I was told, were even more beautiful than those I had the pleasure of inspecting. But the sphere of usefulness extends beyond cabinetmaking, and embraces house-carpentry; for there were doors and many other parts of the interior of a dwelling. But whilst the students are taught to make all these varied and beautiful objects, it must not be supposed that theoretical instruction is neglected. The whole institution, which is supported by the State, is under the superintendence of Professor Athanasoff, educated at the University of Prag, who also teaches technology and chemistry. He is assisted by three practical instructors and three young assistants, who teach respectively casting and working in iron, locksmith's work, and cabinetmaking. There are two small but well-furnished laboratories, chemical and physical, for the use of the teachers, and as a preparation for lectures; small collections of minerals, metals, natural products of the vegetable and animal kingdoms; special cuttings of woods, most beautifully arranged; a general collection for instruction, and also collections for elementary schools. The library, although small, comprises the best technological works (about two hundred in number), in English, French, and German. In addition to these objects, there is an excellent set of models in plaster for instruction in drawing from still life, with models of implements of agriculture, &c., &c. The students live on the premises, and everything needful is provided for their comfort, excepting the sanitary arrangements, which are wretched throughout Bulgaria.

The cost of this institution is about £3280 per annum, or about £47 per head for each student; and the following is a very brief extract from the last annual account, showing in general terms how the money is expended:—

Teachers' and assistants' salaries	about £1200
Food and clothing of students and servants	,, 1000
Expenses of heating, lighting, and general maintenance	,, 205
Books, models, instruments, &c., for instruction	,, 350
Raw materials for work executed, fuel for engine (a new one is in course of construction)	,, 525
	£3280

I know of no other institution where such an amount of good is done with the same outlay; and from what I saw during my visit, I feel convinced that, if the country is only allowed to develop her resources and to multiply such institutions as this one, her progress will be rapid and her prosperity will be ensured. But I shall have much more to say that cannot fail to surprise my readers on the subject of education in Bulgaria.

The printing-offices in Sofia are at present located in an old mosque, but they will soon be transferred to a fine new building just completed. They are at present employed for printing State papers and postage-stamps, and contain the necessary apparatus for engraving, binding, &c.; but a good deal of work is done out of the country which could just as well be done in it; and a few weeks or months will probably see important changes, when the offices are removed to the more commodious building.

And now a few words regarding the people of Sofia. The population is mixed, consisting chiefly of Bulgarians, Turks, Greeks, and Jews. Of the latter, of whom there are about five thousand, nearly all Spanish. I heard a good deal whilst I was there; and my first question was naturally, "Are they persecuted?" They are not openly persecuted, but they are unfairly treated. The reader probably knows that in many Eastern countries certain organs of the press try to stir up bad blood against them;[1] and that is the case here. There are no direct attacks upon them or their dwellings, but offences are charged against them to create a prejudice. Last year a Christian child was missing; its absence was attributed to the Jews, and there was nearly an outbreak, which would have ended in bloodshed if it had not been suppressed by the Government. The trade of the city is largely in their hands, and they are extortionate; they are in consequence shunned by the Christian population, and any one who befriends them is regarded with dislike. This has, however, not prevented one good Christian, Dr. Matincheff, from devoting much time and labour to succour their sick and aged, and he is now earnestly endeavouring to found an hospital for indigent Jews. If a few of their coreligionists in England, who take such an interest

---

[1] "Roumania," p. 57-58.

MUTKOUROFF

STAMBOULOFF

NATCHEVITCH

STOILOFF

in the welfare of the Jews in the East, would help Dr. Matincheff in his laudable undertaking, they would do more practical good than by sending deputations to English statesmen to demand their intervention in behalf of the Jews in other countries.

I have already given the reader some idea of the modest remuneration which is received by Ministers of State, and he will therefore not be surprised to hear that their mode of living is most unassuming. Some reside in the smaller hotels, others in neat unostentatious houses. They are not above frequenting cafés. My first introduction to M. Stambouloff (a man of European reputation, and until recently one of the Regents) and M. Zivkoff, the Minister of Public Instruction, was in a restaurant which supplies the Hôtel de Bulgarie; and I was told that they sometimes go there just to see and hear what is going on.

A few words regarding the personality of the leading statesmen may not be out of place here. Two persons recently gave me their opinions on this subject. One, a foreign Consul in England, who must have been keeping Rip Van Winkle company, said, "I know Bulgaria well; there are no leading men there;" the other, an eminent traveller and litterateur in Budapest, told me, "Public opinion in Bulgaria is not yet formed; it is represented by about twenty clever fellows, and we ought to support them." The last statement is partially correct. Public opinion is represented by "twenty clever fellows" in whom the Bulgarian people have confidence. M. Stambouloff (see Plate IV.), who has rather a sad but determined expression, is about thirty-four years old, although he looks much older (indeed, as a rule, from the Prince and ex-Prince downwards, all the leading men are young). He was educated in, and expelled from Russia, and was a teacher, in which capacity he wrote several text-books. He has been a Deputy since 1878, and, if I have not been misinformed as to his age, he must have been elected, like a good many more, before he was of legal age, that being thirty years. Nevertheless he has preserved the liberties of Bulgaria more than once. Almost since his election to the Sobranje he has been its President. He is intensely patriotic, thoroughly *au fait* in Eastern and Western politics, and well fitted for his high office.

M. Stöiloff (Plate IV.) is a man of great culture. He, too, is about thirty-five years old; is the son of a merchant; was educated at Heidelberg (of which he is LL.D.), at Robert College, Constantinople, in Paris, Leipzig, &c. He arrived in Philippopolis, and entered public life in February 1878. Prince Alexander soon engaged him as his chief private secretary, and from that time until to-day he has taken an active patriotic part in the affairs of his country. He was the most prominent member of the deputation to European courts referred to in my historic record, and is now Minister of Justice. M. Stöiloff has a pleasant voice, an engaging manner, speaks English perfectly well, and his efforts for the improvement and better government of his country are only restricted by foreign interference.

M. Natchevitch, Minister of Finance (Plate IV.), is the son of a tradesman in Vienna. He is about forty-five years of age, and began political life about 1867. He was the Bulgarian Political Agent at Bucharest until about two or three years since, and has filled various posts. It is to him that I am indebted for a great deal of the statistical and other information which I received during my stay at Sofia. He has a dark complexion, rather an Italian cast of countenance, is very obliging and unassuming, knows a great deal more concerning the duties that devolve upon him, and regarding the social, political, and economical affairs of Bulgaria, than many leading English statesmen do concerning their country; and I found him generally one of the best-informed of the public men whom it was my pleasure to meet there.

M. Zivkoff, Minister of Education (Plate V.), was originally a schoolmaster, then a Government official, a Deputy, and one of the Regents. He, too, is very obliging, and has a most agreeable and "taking" manner.

Colonel Mutkuroff (Plate IV.), Minister of War, I had not the pleasure of meeting. He was educated at the Military Academy, St. Petersburg; commanded a division in the Servian war; gained his fame by the bold stand which he made against the traitors of 1885, in conjunction with M. Stambouloff, and

Plate V

KARAVELOFF

ZIVKOFF

RADOSLAVOFF

GAVRIL PACHA

promises to be a man of mark in the future history of his country.

Dr. Stransky is Minister for Foreign Affairs. He, too, is comparatively a young man. Took an active part in the Eastern Roumelian rising and the union of North and South Bulgaria. Whilst I was in Sofia, the relations of the Foreign Office with other countries were, and still are, somewhat perplexing to the Minister at its head, and our conversation, during a very short visit which I paid him, was naturally reserved. He was very courteous, and told me what steps to take to obtain an interview with the Prince, but his manner was not such as to favour friendly intercourse.

M. Radoslavoff (Plate V.) is in opposition. He, too, is an LL.D. of Heidelberg. I only spent a short time in his company, but found him very enlightened and polished. He is nearly always "agin the Government," in a legitimate sense, however; and, as far as I could judge, he is not treated with the respect to which he is entitled.

M. Karaveloff (Plate V.), who has boxed the political compass, and held several public offices, enjoys the proud distinction of representing Russian opinion, if not Russia herself, in Bulgaria. As my object was to obtain all the information about the country that was possible, and as such information could of course be best given by the leading officials, I did not indulge my curiosity to see and speak to a man who is generally looked upon as a dangerous enemy to his nation; for had I done so, the leading patriots would have been justified in regarding me with suspicion, and in withholding their assistance.[1] The reader must therefore be content to study his portrait, and as to his political views, he will hear those presently, as circulated by himself in his own organ.

M. Zankoff is an exile in Constantinople. He, too, has been everything by turns and nothing long; but, as the reader knows, he was one of the ringleaders in the abduction of Prince Alexander, I am sure I shall be pardoned for leaving him in his obscurity.

---

[1] Since my return, there was some talk of a Government prosecution of M. Karaveloff, which has, however, been wisely relinquished.

The most remarkable circumstance about all the gentlemen here referred to is the rapidity with which they have developed into statesmen and leaders of public opinion. Nearly all of them are of humble origin, all young men. We have scores, aye, thousands of intelligent politicians in England and Scotland, who have plodded all their lives, and have at best attained parochial eminence; but these men know how to hold their own against trained diplomats and scheming statesmen who have grown grey in political strife. My readers should just take up "Turkey, No. 1, 1887," and read the replies of the Bulgarian Ministers to the threats of Russian officials (mere mouthpieces of the Russian Ministers),[1] or the short but telling circulars which they issued to foreign Governments from time to time to acquaint them with the true state of affairs in Bulgaria. They have no doubt made mistakes occasionally; but what wonder that they should! His Majesty the present Czar was right when he telegraphed to Prince Alexander that Bulgaria is a country "*Déjà si éprouvé*" (already severely tried); but I am sure the verdict of history will be that in all her trials her young and rising statesmen were more than a match for her persecutors.

---

[1] The author of "Les Causes Occultes," &c., &c., endeavours to shift the responsibility of Russian misdeeds and mistakes in Bulgaria from the Czar and his counsellors to an interested Russian "coterie." This may suit the French views of the moment, but it will not be the verdict of posterity.

CHAPTER XII.

SOFIA—SOCIAL AND ECONOMICAL MATTERS—A POLITICAL MEETING—THE PRESS.

Medical affairs—The "*sage femme*"—The Medical Council and its system—Defective sanitary arrangements throughout the country—The working-classes of Sofia—Wages and cost of living—Number of working days and holidays—Amusements—"Bulgarian billiards"—Ardent politicians—A riotous political "demonstration"—Attack upon Karaveloff's house and printing-offices—Demeanour of Prince Ferdinand—The Bulgarian press—The leading organs of public opinion.

A FEW words concerning the medical and sanitary arrangements of Bulgaria. Until quite recently the only medical men (if I may be permitted a bull) who troubled themselves about the health of the community were old women. In many villages, and amongst the lower classes generally, this is still the case, and the witch of old is the "*sage femme*" of to-day. One of the Ministers told me that only a few days before my visit one of his servants who was ill refused to see a doctor, and preferred consulting the "*sage femme*." The foundation of a new system is, however, laid, which will in the course of time produce excellent results. Besides the hospitals in large towns (there are three in Sofia and one with 200 beds in Philippopolis), there is a regular medical staff throughout Bulgaria. Under this system, which was initiated in 1878, there are 140 State-paid qualified practitioners, spread over sixty-five districts, and about the same number of assistants (Feldschers or dressers). There is a Medical Council in Sofia, which has the superintendence of this staff, and they pay each medical officer 4000 francs (about £160), and each assistant 1200 francs (about £48) per annum. Unfortunately, the care of the army engrosses much of the attention of these doctors, but they are useful in promoting rational sanitary arrangements. Those are, as I have said, very bad. It is true there is a good fire-brigade and good water, collected and impounded from the slopes of Vitosch, at Sofia, but drainage is bad; and I was told by a leading medical man at Philippopolis that there the water from the Maritza is very poor, and that, coupled with bad drainage, it leads to frequent outbreaks of fever. There is no medical school attached to the hospitals, and the young men are educated and take their degrees in Germany, Constantinople, Moscow, and France. As for the traveller, he often turns sick with the filth, which is indescribable, in the sanitary arrangements at some of the smaller hotels; and the employment there of water, towels, ewers, basins, &c., is still in its elementary stage.

The working classes in Sofia are comparatively well off. What a Bulgarian must consider an evil, however, exists there, namely, that the work of skilled artisans in connection with the building and some other trades is performed almost entirely by foreigners. Such institutions as that of Kniajevo will doubtless soon supply the remedy. The Italian masons, &c., who perform this higher class of work, receive from 5 francs to 10 francs (3s. 9d. to 7s. 6d.) per day, of which they expend two-thirds on food and clothing. They eat meat, and generally live well. Bulgarian labourers receive 2 francs to 4 francs (1s. 6d. to 3s.) daily, and live on bread, fruit, and vegetables, which are cheap. The peasantry live chiefly on the products of their farms, and dress entirely in garments made by themselves.

House-rent in Sofia is comparatively high, ranging from £50 to £60 per annum for a moderately good house. Such houses as the Agencies average £400 per annum. Land is about £1 to £1, 10s. per square yard in the best neighbourhoods. Butcher's meat is about 4d. per lb.; veal, 8d. to 9d. Bread is very cheap, the commonest kind about 1d. per lb. Of the cheapness of fruit I will give an instance farther on. Vegetables, too, are exceedingly cheap. A favourite article of diet, which one sees everywhere, is "paprika," large red pepper, which is cooked in various ways at different stages of its growth. A workman pays about £2 for a suit of good clothes of home-made cloth, and 20 francs

16s.) for a pair of shoes. Taxes are moderate, as the reader will find when the Budget is under consideration, and schooling free. Fodder for horses and cattle ranges from 6 centimes to 8 centimes per oka (about 2 lbs.) for hay, 18 centimes for oats, and 5 centimes for straw.

As in Roumania and other Catholic countries, the labouring man works about 240 days in the year, the remainder being Sundays and festivals. Those English employers who are constantly railing at their workmen and talking of cheap labour abroad will kindly note this fact. The amusements of the working-classes in Bulgaria are not very diversified. As I have already said, there is little or no intellectual recreation for them. They like music, still more dancing, and I fear it must be added that they indulge very freely in the British habit of drinking. They have a curious game which is called "Bulgarian billiards," but is in reality a miniature game of nine-pins. It consists of a table, on which stands a kind of bagatelle-board divided into three parts. The first section is empty, in the second stand nine pins, and in the third five. At the flat end there is a hole, into which a top-shaped object is inserted, and round the stem which passes through the hole a string is wound, just as with us in a humming-top.

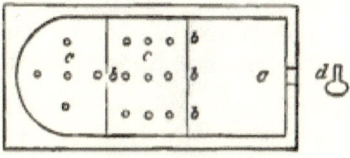

BULGARIAN BILLIARDS.

a, aperture in first division; b, b, b, apertures in second and third divisions; c, nine-pins; d, top-like object which is spun.

In the first division there are three arched apertures; in the second, one. The top is spun, and when free from the string it enters the first division and spins upright; presently it passes through one of the apertures into the second division, and knocks down one or more of the pins; passing into the third, it goes through the same performance. A clever player sometimes upsets the whole fourteen pins. I am told this game is generally played for drinks, excessive gambling being confined to the middle classes. The game may not be very common in Sofia; I saw it at Gabrovo.

The working-classes of Bulgaria, in the towns at least, and especially in Sofia, are ardent politicians. I had the privilege of witnessing one portion of a political demonstration during my visit. As I was sitting in my room writing, an acquaintance came and called me to see "a disturbance," as he termed it, before the palace, near which is situated the Hôtel de Bulgarie, where I was staying. My first impression, on looking at the scene from a suitable window, was that I had come in for a revolution; that the inhabitants did not like the new Prince, and had decided to make him abdicate in favour of the Prince of Mingrelia or of somebody else. But I was mistaken; it was a demonstration against Karaveloff, and a crowd of people, numbering probably 1000 or 1500, were assembled opposite the entrance-door of the palace within the grounds. Many of them had sticks, which they flourished vehemently, whilst every now and then loud cries were raised; and I was told they were calling for the Prince. They left a space clear before the door, and a court official was addressing them. Presently the crowd broke up and left the palace, apparently satisfied. I thought the "demonstration" was over from the quiet way in which the people moved off in different directions; but there again I was mistaken; and this is all I saw of the actual performance. In the afternoon I heard there had been a riot, and the following is what took place.[1] Let me preface the account by reminding my readers that in olden times political meetings were held in churches, as, for example, when Peter Asen was proclaimed Czar of Bulgaria, and that custom has descended to the present day.

It appears that after the state of siege was raised, and the suppressed newspapers reappeared, M. Karaveloff availed himself on the 11th September of the liberty to publish an article in his newspaper, *The Tirnora* (or *Tirnovska*) *Constitution*, in which he practically characterised the new Prince as a usurper. "Prince Ferdinand," he said, "is not the Prince of the nation, but of Messrs. Stambouloff, Stoyanoff, and Mutkuroff. Usurpation of rights and wishes of the people has taken place." The whole article was an invitation to Russia to intervene. Such an article appearing in the organ of any foreign country, in England, or in any well-established State, would be of

---

[1] For these facts I am indebted to M. Chadourne, the obliging young correspondent of the *Times* at Sofia, who was present throughout the whole affair.

little consequence, but it was feared by the patriotic party
that if it were passed over in silence it might be construed
into weakness by the Russians and their sympathisers. On
the following day, therefore (Monday, 12th September), at
about five in the afternoon, the bells of the cathedral church
rang out a tocsin, summoning the inhabitants to an indigna-
tion-meeting, which was to be held in the church under the
auspices of Zachary Stoyanoff, a supporter of the Government, Ilia Veltcheff, a "Radoslavist," and others, to protest
against the views of Karaveloff as expressed in his journal.[1]
Speeches were made by the organisers and others, and resolu-
tions carried denouncing Karaveloff and his Russian patrons
in language more forcible than polite, and the crowd then
left the church and adjourned to the palace. Here again
speeches were delivered, and the cries which I had heard were
"Down with the Roubladjis!" (rouble-bought men, referring
to the tools of Russia, paid with roubles), "Down with the black
souls!" Calls, too, were made for the Prince, when one of the
palace officials came out and told them he was out for a drive.
The crowd then left the palace garden, dividing into sections,
but these soon re-united, and hurried off to Karaveloff's house.
Meanwhile intimation had been sent to the police, who at once
took measures to protect the obnoxious politician. About
twenty gens-d'armes, led by the Prefect, arrived just in the
nick of time. The crowd had by this time swelled to three
thousand, including some of the most unruly spirits in Sofia,
and these gathered in front of the house. Not content with
uttering loud and menacing cries, they commenced an attack
upon it, and about a hundred of the most violent sent
such a volley of stones against the windows that in a few
seconds there was not a whole pane left. These men then
attempted to storm and enter the house, and there is no
doubt that, if they had succeeded, they would have lynched
the offender. The gens-d'armes, however, who were mounted,

---

[1] It was said that the Ministers had initiated the meeting, which they denied.
As far as I could gather from independent sources, they knew of and sanctioned
it, but did not expect it would result in disorder.

charged the crowd several times, and wounded many of the rioters. A large portion of the crowd then made its way to the dwellings of Messrs. Tzanow and Slaveikoff, two other Russian sympathisers, where the same scene was, or at least would have been enacted, had not the police taken the most energetic repressive measures. Notwithstanding these, however, the mob succeeded in making an attack upon the printing-office of Karaveloff's paper, and in completely smashing all the windows. After these exploits were performed, the crowd once more moved to the palace, arriving there just as the Prince was returning from his drive, and now they gave him a complete ovation. This was about seven o'clock. He soon appeared on the balcony, when one of the speakers harangued his Highness, telling him of the resolution which had been passed at the first meeting, and calling for the condemnation of the miscreants of the 9th August,[1] in conformity with the laws of the country, and for their banishment. The Prince replied in a firm voice in Bulgarian, "Be devoted to me; be patriots; thanks for your sentiments. Long live Bulgaria!" The crowd now burst into repeated hurrahs, and moved away singing the national march, the "Djumi-Maritza." From the palace they proceeded to the residence of M. Stambouloff, where the same orator delivered a similar harangue. Stambouloff stood upon the balcony with Mutkuroff, Zivkoff, and others, and appealed to the people to have confidence in the Prince and in the Ministers. The crowd then dispersed, and the demonstration was at an end. Besides those who were wounded (eight in all, I believe), several arrests were made, and the rioters punished. The next morning I went to view the field of battle, and found the window-frames in Karaveloff's house and offices, but glass there was none.

Before leaving the capital, it may be interesting to refer to the newspaper press. Considering that the country has only been free for a few years from the domination of two masters who carefully suppressed the utterances of public opinion in every form, and that there is little scope for advertisements, the

---

[1] Old style, still used in Bulgaria. The new style would be 21st August, the day on which Prince Alexander was kidnapped.

press is by no means insignificant. The most important journal, a very peculiar one, is the *Svoboda*, or *La Liberté*, the semi-official paper of the present Government, which we so often see quoted. It is a journal of eight pages, about 14 inches by 21 inches (as are most of the leading papers), and is published on Wednesdays and Saturdays. Although it is printed in the Bulgarian language, all information as to subscription, &c., is given in French. The price of the paper is 20 centimes (about 2d.), and the subscription 20 francs per annum, with proportionate rates for shorter periods. Its leading articles are signed, and it contains news, official announcements, &c. It is published at Sofia; but the Government have two other official papers, the *Plordiv* (Philippopolis), published in that town, and the *Derjavnii Vestnik*, a provincial organ. The "Liberal party" have a weekly paper called the *Narodae Sosnanje* (the "National Instructor"), published at Shumla; and the Russians have Karaveloff's journal, already referred to, and, I believe, another published at Philippopolis.[1] At Tirnova, the old capital, they do not boast of a paper of any kind. Besides the serious journals, there is a wretched little comic print called the *Eagle*, published at Sofia. It is a curiosity in its way, and I should think the men at Sofia who have seen *Kladderadatsch*, *Punch*, and the French comic papers must be heartily ashamed of it. On the last page of the number which appeared whilst I was there, there was what purported to be a picture of the attack on Karaveloff's house. If a British schoolboy of ten years did not draw better caricatures on his slate than this one, his companions would drum him out of the school! However, the press, as I have said, is by no means discreditable for a young nation just enjoying its liberty; and judging from the character and tastes of the people, I should say it will extend rapidly, and become an excellent public instructor.

[1] *La Science Bulgare*, of which the motto was "Liberty, Justice, Fraternity" (no Equality), is, I hear, discontinued.

CHAPTER XIII.

TRAVELLING IN BULGARIA—PHILIPPOPOLIS.

Absence of regular conveyances—A "phaeton"—Passports—Brigandage and highway robbery—The author's experiences—Cost and speed of travelling—Inns and travelling accommodation (want of)—Picturesque khans—Refreshment by the way—Two hotel bills—Scenery of the country—Turkish fountains and graves—Turkish *dayres* or military stations—Novichan—Shrub-covered hills—Philippopolis, its picturesque situation and aspect—Magnificent views from the granite hills of the city—Its quaint streets and houses—The hospitality of Philippopolis—Food industries—Picturesque Turkish costumes—Turkish women and their hidden charms—The Prefecture, formerly the Konak of the Pashas—Its garden and produce—The Alexander Gymnasium for boys—The curriculum, laboratories, drawing-models, library, &c.—Fine public library, with numismatic collection—Coins of the Bulgarian Czars—The girls' Lycée—Its curriculum—Clever girls.

IN order to see as much as possible of the country, and because there is little to be gained by taking the trains which run once or twice a day over the short distances on the unfinished railway, I travelled through Bulgaria in what is called there a "phaeton," a little open carriage with three or four horses. This mode of travelling is speedy, comfortable, but very dear. I heard of "diligences" or "posts," and once I had the advantage of a change of horses through an engagement made with a "post" contractor; but, as a matter of fact, the public conveyances are at present greatly in abeyance, and I was told that a few years ago the communication was better than it is to-day, on account of the recent interference with settled government. If I was rightly informed, another advantage accrued to me from travelling in my own carriage, for two days after I journeyed from Sofia to Philippopolis, the post was attacked on that road by highwaymen (brigands they call them), and the passengers as well as the mails were robbed.

For forty years I have travelled in various parts of the world, and, excepting in 1850 in Russia, my passport has been a form rather than a necessity. The one which I took with me this time (an old one of Lord Granville, by the bye) is a curiosity. It has eight visas, covering every inch of the back, necessitating twelve printed and stamped endorsements and six adhesive stamps. In Bulgaria the greatest watchfulness is no doubt necessary in consequence of the unsettled state of affairs coupled with Russian intrigues and intriguers, but I only experienced slight delays through the passport system; others told me they had not been so fortunate. As regards brigandage, the same cause which necessitates the inspection of passports, namely, the unsettled government of the country, militates against social order. The adventure of the M.P. for one of the Lancashire divisions in the Rilo Mountains cannot be seriously considered. According to his own account, he never saw the brigands, and it is as likely as not that the whole thing was a "plant" to secure a good reward for saving his life and property. Then, again, I heard of commercial travellers journeying in carriages being "*déralisé*," robbed of their portmanteaus, and allowed to proceed. It is as likely as not that in some such cases the travellers were drinking in a khan (a roadside inn), and had left their carriage and luggage exposed to the depredations of wandering gipsies, whom one meets on the roads, or other dishonest characters. My own experience is certainly opposed to the existence of systematic brigandage.

I arrived in Sofia two hours after midnight, and left it as many hours before daybreak. At Philippopolis I arrived late at night; so also at Kalofer, from which place I started at 4 A.M.; and I left Tirnova at 3 A.M. In no case had I the least annoyance from beggars, tramps, or "brigands." In addition to this, I frequently left my carriage and its contents in charge of the driver, and went alone, or with a travelling companion who was acquainted with the country,[1] for an hour together, walking sometimes over the plain, at others in the mountains,

---

[1] M. Isnian, a young Armenian lawyer of Philippopolis.

and this with a complete sense of security, and without carrying anything more formidable than a well-loaded stick. That highway robbery occurs from time to time there can be no doubt, and that it is more frequent when the Government is unsettled is quite natural. During the last Carlist war, when the guards were withdrawn from the northern frontier of Spain, bands of ruffians calling themselves Carlists roved about the country committing depredations; and a day or two before I visited Bosost such a band had entered and robbed the "Casino," and cleaned out the "bank" of the gaming-table. Not even honour amongst thieves there! In Turkey, where the Government is feeble, it is not safe to travel an hour's distance from Constantinople. In Ireland political disorder encourages moonlighting. Many similar instances occur to one.

To return to Bulgaria. In 1880 brigandage or highway robberies occurred in the vicinity of Osman Bazar, and repressive military measures had to be taken to arrest them; but that was the only case which occurred for many years, and it was attributed to Turkish intrigues, just as I heard at Sofia and Philippopolis the recent robberies attributed to Russian intrigue. In both cases the charge, so far as the principals were concerned, was probably groundless, the crimes being the indirect results of unsettled government and political disturbance.

To travel in such a carriage as I used costs on the average five napoleons, or, roughly speaking, £4 a day for short distances, for which, of course, two persons can travel very comfortably; and the distance travelled in twelve hours is about sixty or seventy miles. As a rule, it is advisable to start very early—at four or five in the morning—to let the horses rest two or three hours during the day. The same horses (three or four) make the entire journey. The traveller must take his own provisions, for at the roadside inns it is seldom possible to get anything excepting coffee, and perhaps eggs. The landlords are very obliging and attentive, but they are not accustomed to serving travellers. The khans are nearly all built on the same model—a quadrangular space, something like an English farmyard; round three sides, sometimes four, a two-storied wooden building, the lower floor devoted to the care of "horse," the upper of "man." Round the upper floor, which is approached by a more or less rickety wooden stair, runs a gallery and a series of doors leading to the sleeping apartments, which often contain—nothing. In some of the khans there are beds; in the larger towns, comfortable sitting- and bed-rooms with bedsteads. Meals are usually taken on the balcony, which occasionally projects into the court, forming a little square platform resting on wooden supports, and a roof to shelter the guest from the rays of the sun. The inns look slovenly and dirty, but during the whole of my stay in Bulgaria I never saw any kind of vermin. The bedsteads are of iron, the beds clean, the walls whitewashed, the ceiling of stained or varnished wood; and if there are carpets, they consist of one or two small ones of Bulgarian manufacture. Nor must it be supposed that there is no charm about these rude Turkish khans. Kanitz has drawn some wonderful pictures of the attractions of some of them, descriptions which have been justly called a *little* "idealistic" by German visitors. But the balconies of some of them are really picturesque. Vines cluster over the roof and round the wooden pillars, flowers in boxes and pots brighten up the plain surroundings, and it is interesting to watch the operations of drivers and stable-boys about the carriages and horses which stand in the court, and divide its occupancy with fowls, geese, dogs, pigs, and babies. To anticipate a little.

In glowing terms Kanitz describes the khan at Biela, between Tirnova and Rustchuk, where he seems to have slept. We dined there, and found it to resemble a rude country farm. Captain Jones, of Philippopolis, had given me some soup tablets, and one of these was put into a pan of water, and placed on the open stove to boil. My companion and I then looked round the kitchen and discovered eggs, onions, cabbages, and tomatoes, which, with salt and pepper, were sliced and precipitated into the soup, and helped to produce a *potage* such as we thoroughly appreciated, having left Tirnova at 3 A.M., and arrived at Biela at noon. I remember that dinner well. We had, besides the soup, baked potatoes with butter and salt, apple-tart, bought at Tirnova, grapes, of which my companion had bought four large bunches from a peasant woman on the road, who was carrying them to the wine-press—luscious little grapes, for which he paid what he called the excessive price of one penny!—bread and butter, Bulgarian light wine, and coffee and cigarettes for a finish. We did not always fare so well, and the traveller should take with him some German sausages or preserved meat, which does not necessitate cooking. They know how to charge in Bulgaria. The following bills give the two extremes of dearness and cheapness:—

Bill for Two Persons at Gabrovo at the "Grand Hôtel," a fair specimen of the better class of Khans.

	Francs.
One caviar (rubbish),	1 60
Our own soup,	...
Two portions of roast-fowl (skin and bone).	1 70
One do. of fish (rubbish, badly cooked).	1 0
Butter,	0 40
Bread,	0 30
Candles,	0 50
Coffee and milk,	1 50
Driver,	0 50
Two beds,	8 0
	15 50 = 12 3.

Cost of Dinner for Two Persons at the Restaurant of the "Hôtel de Sofia" at Tirnova (everything excellent).

	Francs.
Soup,	0 20
Beefsteaks, with eggs and dressing,	1 20
Two small bottles of light Bulgarian wine,	0 60
Bread,	0 20
Two cafés-noir,	0 30
	2 50 about 1 11.

With these superficial observations on the cost and nature of travelling in Bulgaria my readers must fain content themselves. Something more will be added concerning the prospects and surroundings of the traveller *en route*.

Between the Servian frontier and Sofia the scenery is in some places very fine, more especially about the Dragoman Pass, which rises to a considerable height and descends precipitously to Slivnitza. On the summit of the pass I experienced a sandstorm. Already on this part of the route the traveller is struck with two or three characteristic peculiarities. One is the presence of Turkish fountains of stone or marble, bearing inscriptions in that language, which are met with from time to time; another, the collections of Turkish graves. The latter are distinguished by numerous stones, more or less perpendicular, some of them surmounted by a turban. Between Sofia and Philippopolis a still more interesting feature comes prominently into notice, namely, the succession of ruined *étapes* or military

RUINS OF TURKISH ÉTAPE OR RESTING-PLACE FOR TROOPS AT NOVICHAN.[1]

stations, which were built by the Turks throughout the country, it is said, at intervals of thirty kilomètres, to afford rest and shelter to troops on the march. The most interesting of those structures that I saw, and the one in the best repair, was at Novichan (or Jenihan), the first halting-place between

---

[1] All the woodcuts, except the larger one of Tirnova, are from sketches made on the spot by the author.

Sofia and Philippopolis. The ruin consists of a building which may be compared to an enormous chapel, with large circular apertures, resembling stable windows, for lighting and ventilation, in the walls at either end. Attached to this main building is a very large quadrangular space with three walls enclosing it, the fourth side being the khan, or whatever may have been the name given to the main building. The length of the wall, and therefore of the building, is about 120 yards, which is the measurement of the four sides of the quadrangle. The building is constructed of rough stones and plaster, and is said to be 200 to 300 years old.

Another characteristic, this time of the country itself, which reminds one sadly of the destructive work of semi-civilised mankind, is the covering of oak scrub with which the hills are clothed. I have already referred to these in speaking of the ancient Slave customs, and it need only be added that in this part of the country, where the mountains are not high and the woods were easily cleared, the destruction has been complete. The hills are covered with what appear to be green plantations, but, on closer inspection, it is found to consist of low oak shrubs, and not a vestige of primeval forest nor of timber of any kind has survived.

Philippopolis, the chief town in South Bulgaria, possesses many features of interest which are not to be found elsewhere. It contains a very mixed population, numbering in all about 33,500 inhabitants. Many of them are Turks, who live very comfortably with their Bulgarian fellow-subjects; indeed, this remark applies throughout Bulgaria. The situation of the town is very remarkable. From an almost level plain there spring seven hills of granite, and upon and around three of those Philippopolis is built.[1] One of them very closely resembles the rock at Salzburg, as the reader will see from the photograph (Plate VI.). Narrow streets with picturesque houses run up another of the hills, and from the summit of this hill there is one of the finest prospects in Bulgaria, or, for that matter,

---

[1] Hence it was called by the Romans *Trimontium*.

VIEW OF JAMBASZ-TEPE PHILIPPOPOLIS.

BOYS LYCÉE CHURCH OF ST ALEXANDER, RIVER MARITZA AND BRIDGE.
PHILIPPOPOLIS.

anywhere else. To the south, on the borders of the plain, are the Rhodope Mountains; on the north is the broad river Maritza, which flows eastwards and westwards. The other six hills, the town below, and the wide surrounding plain complete the panorama. Not far from the Maritza two conspicuous buildings strike the eye, the Boys' Lycée and the Church of St. Alexander (Plate VI.). In the heart of the town is a large building, formerly an immense khan, now a market, in which are sold the cotton and woollen cloths of Lancashire, Yorkshire, Germany, and Austria. Thence, too (from the hill I mean), may be seen, at the summit of a lower hill, a quaint tower with a pointed roof or spire, which contains an alarm-bell to give notice of conflagrations. Another fine building to the left, as you face this tower, is the Girls' Lycée; and again outside the town large barracks lie to the right. Besides these secular structures, there are places of worship of every religious denomination, mosques with their attendant minarets, Byzantine churches of the orthodox faith, churches of the Greek, Armenian, and Catholic denominations, and synagogues. The streets upon this hill, which are narrow and precipitous, are remarkably picturesque, and some of the houses would delight the painter and the photographer. Every now and then you catch a glimpse of a house with overhanging cornice supported by curved wooden timbers, upon which the upper projecting front of the house rests; this is usually painted white, or constructed of white plaster covered with ornamental mouldings or painted with parti-coloured patterns. Many of the windows are barred, as in Venice and other Italian cities; and in one place an old gateway or arch forms a most picturesque break in the descent (Plate VII.). The rock known as the Jambaz Tépé, which I said resembles Salzburg, is smaller than the one we have just been visiting, but the combination of rock and houses gives it a very bold and striking appearance. The best hotel in the place, the Hôtel de Bulgarie, is very poor; so, too, are the cafés, but the hospitality of our Consul-General, Captain Jones (which is, I think, contagious in Philippopolis), leaves the traveller no opportunity for grumbling. The Consulates generally are situated at the outskirts of the town, from which

fine roads run into the country. The Ottoman Bank has a
branch here, where they are not over-liberal in the matter of
money-changing, and there is also a branch of the National
Bank of Bulgaria. Besides the usual open-fronted shops which
are found in every Bulgarian town, and where at Philippopolis
you may buy old arms (and new ones, for that matter), such as
damascened yataghans, knives, &c., at a very reasonable price,
a peep into one or two stores of a better description gives one a
very fair idea of the food industries of Bulgaria. There you
may see cheese of native manufacture packed in large sheep-
skins, salt from Bourgas, very fair soap made in Philippopolis,
and all more or less highly scented, for toilet or household use,
indigenous grains, "paprika," &c. In the streets you meet
men called "Bozadji," who sell a drink made from millet. They
carry a tray at their waists, on which stand mugs and tin
vessels containing the drink referred to, Bouza.[1] The streets,
too, are interesting on account of the costumes of the various
nationalities one encounters. The Bulgarians dress rather
quietly, and their distinguishing mark is the "kalpak," the
head-dress already referred to; but the Turkish men are a
marvel of bright colours. Here is one of them:—He wears a
red fez surrounded by a small bluish turban, a print jacket
without sleeves, coloured pale pink with a flowered pattern of
the same colour, but darker; through the arm-holes his arms
clothed in white shirt-sleeves protrude; round his waist is a
very broad scarlet waistband or thin shawl, in which his knife
is half concealed; dark blue trousers, white stockings, and
sandals. So far as the sexes are concerned, the order of Nature
is reversed. Look at that Turkish woman as she moves
stealthily along, apparently afraid of being seen; from the top
of the head to the shoulders, and a little way down the bosom,
she is wrapped in a thick white muslin veil or shawl, with

---

[1] Perhaps the reader will excuse me for referring to the account which I gave
of a drink of the same name in my work on the "History of Drink" (Trübner),
p. 4: "The Nubians make a liquor called Bonza from dhourra or barley, also a
kind of wine from the palm-tree, and from time immemorial intoxicating drinks
have been extracted from these two sources, and from other cereals in various
parts of Asia and Africa."

only her eyes and nose visible; the rest of her body is a black sack, partaking of the character of a barrister's gown. If you meet a Turkish woman on the highroad coming from her field-work, she draws her shawl or anything else she can lay hands on over her face until you are past, and so deprives you of the opportunity of admiring a face which, I am told (for of course I have never been permitted to see one), in nine cases out of ten is more attractive concealed than exposed! You see little Turkish boys, too, acting as shoeblacks in the streets of Philippopolis, but no beggars. Yes, I saw one, a broken-down fellow in broadcloth,—a "beat," as the Americans call them.

Besides these objects and places of interest, the traveller should visit the Prefecture, the Library, the Alexander Gymnasium for boys, the Girls' Lycée, and, if he has the chance offered to him, as I had, by my kind friend Captain Jones, the Monastery of St. Kyriak, the last-named being, however, situated at some distance from the city. This excursion deserves and will command a separate chapter.

The Prefecture was formerly the Konak or palace of the Pashas, where they dwelt with their harems, and next of the Governors-General, the last of whom was deposed there, as already described. It consists of a large hall, with smaller apartments at the side, where the ladies dwelt, but where now numerous clerks are at work, and at the farther end the Pasha's rooms, at present the official rooms of the Prefect. The most interesting adjunct is, however, the garden, which the Prefect was kind enough to show me with just pride. It is filled with flower-beds, and part of it is a fruit and vegetable garden. The fruits are remarkably fine, and represent fairly all the subtropical and temperate zones. The flower-garden is not, however, trimly kept, as with us; but it is possible that the time of the year (September) may have had something to do with its slovenly appearance.

The most interesting institution in Philippopolis is the Alexander Gymnasium for boys, a magnificent building, which cost nearly £26,000, and is maintained at an annual expense of more than £5000. It has been open two years, and affords instruction to about 500 pupils, varying in age from ten to twenty-two years. The instruction is given free of charge, excepting one of twenty francs per annum in the higher, and ten francs in the lower classes, which is devoted to the purchase of books and clothes for the poorest children. I may here mention that this rule seems to hold good in all the large schools in Bulgaria, and I was assured that it excited no prejudice in the minds of one class of students against any other. The school was only beginning to assemble, and I had not as good an opportunity of examining the boys in the different classes as afterwards in the public school at Gabrovo (to be referred to hereafter); but I saw and heard quite enough to satisfy me that, under the management of the Director, M. Demeter Agoura (formerly Bulgarian Minister of the Interior), a very high grade of instruction is reached. There are seven classes, and taking only the lowest and the highest, in the first-named the curriculum is as follows:—Orthodox religion, the Bulgarian language, elementary physics, chemistry, physiology, calligraphy, drawing, arithmetic, geometry, singing, gymnastics, and, strangely enough, geography, for which a charge is made! Objects of various kinds are employed for instruction. In the highest class the course is—Bulgarian, including the reading of translations from foreign authors; French; Latin and Greek in the classical section; history, logic, psychology, mathematics, algebra, geometry and geometrical drawing, physics, chemistry, laboratory practice, mineralogy, and drawing. All these branches of education seem to be well taught. The chemical teachers have a laboratory for preparing their lectures, a specially fitted-up lecture-room, and a second laboratory with twenty-four benches for the students. The teachers of physics have also a laboratory containing excellent apparatus and a separate lecture-hall. For natural history there are good cabinets of various objects; for drawing, a very fine class-room, with prints and beautiful plaster models of still life and statuettes. There is an excellent reference library of two thousand volumes; and the council and examination hall would be worthy of any university. As I only spoke to one or two of the boys here, it would not be fair to express an opinion of their efficiency; as already remarked, the reader will presently have a good opportunity to judge of the intelligence of the Bulgarian youth at the school at Gabrovo. In speaking of Sofia, I omitted to mention that there is a good public library, which was about to be arranged by M. Yovcheff, who was until recently librarian at Philippopolis, where that institution is well deserving of a visit. It contains about fifteen thousand volumes, of which about four thousand are English; all the best books in every department of literature, down to, or, as some may say, up to "Progress and Poverty." Besides these, there is a marvellous collection of foreign works in French, German, Bohemian, Sclavonic, Polish, Turkish, Armenian, Greek, and Latin. They are beautifully arranged around a fine reading-room, which is well furnished with journals, magazines, and the best European illustrated papers. Under the same roof is the museum, which is noteworthy only for its numismatic collection. The coins are in excellent preservation and beautifully arranged and classified. Some of them are remarkably interesting; there are Thracian, Asian, African, and Roman specimens (the latter of all periods), examples of Byzantine, and Barbarian imitations of them; coins of the Bulgarian Czars and of the Sveto-Slave kings. The coins of the Bulgarian Czars are of Simeon, the Asenidæ, and the Sismanidæ. The Czars' coins usually represent the Czarina as well as the Czar; they are very rude, and although attempts have been made to describe the dresses of the old rulers of Bulgaria from these objects, I hope it may not be presumptuous if I say that the imagination has had a large share in the process. The chief features of interest, which may be traced with tolerable accuracy, are the crowns and head-dresses of the princes, of which it would seem that pearls or other precious stones were a conspicuous ornament.

If I am unable to give the reader an account of the standard of excellence attained by Bulgarian boys at the public school at Philippopolis, I can at least tell him something about the girls, who had commenced work at their Lycée. It has been established six years, and is under the direction of Professor Joachim Grouew. There were about one hundred and fifty girls there, varying from eleven to seventeen or eighteen years of age, who are instructed by thirteen teachers having Austrian, Swiss,

English, and Russian diplomas. There are six classes, and in one or other of them the following subjects are taught:—Orthodox religion, the Bulgarian language, natural history, physics, chemistry, mathematics, arithmetic, general history, algebra, geometry, geography, drawing, singing, writing, sewing, gymnastics, French (grammar and translation), domestic economy, hygiene, and the art of teaching. I have taken the subjects at random, but as I cross-questioned the girls in every one of the classes, I know to what subjects the most attention is paid, or at least in which they attain the highest proficiency. Those are general history, in which some of the answers regarding foreign countries were surprisingly accurate; arithmetic (vulgar and decimal fractions); drawing. I brought back with me some illuminated initial letters and some designs which would be admired at South Kensington, executed by the girls of the third and fourth classes: unfortunately the cost of transference to these pages would be too great. To proceed: singing, in which the girls were very proficient: in geography also I received satisfactory replies to questions about some very out-of-the-way places; and natural history. In order to test their readiness in drawing and knowledge of plants, I got the teachers to direct them to draw certain flowers and cereals on the blackboard, which some of them did admirably; and, indeed, I have described them in my notebook as "remarkably bright and intelligent, fully equal to girls of any other country, drawn from every class of society." There is some little difference between the charge made to girls and that paid in the boys' gymnase. Here they pay in the four lower classes fourteen francs, and in the two higher twenty francs per annum, the money being devoted, as in the former case, to supplying indigent children (who are excused payment on presenting a certificate of inability to pay) with books and materials.

But I fear I am wearying my readers with dry educational details, so, by way of a change, will ask them to accompany our hospitable Consul Captain Jones, M. Shopoff, one of the professors at the Girls' Lycée, and myself on a picnic excursion to the Monastery of St. Kyriak.

CHAPTER XIV.

AN EXCURSION TO THE MONASTERY OF ST. KYRIAK.

Surroundings of the monastery—Voiina—Suspicious Greek women—The monastery—A sanatorium—Terms of residence—Occupations of visitors—Incident in a Bulgarian picnic—Arrival of a pilgrimage—The interior of the church—Miraculous cures and strange offerings—Religious ceremonies—The return home—Stanimaka—Arcadian simplicity, and reflections on the way.

IF the reader supposes that he is going to visit one of those sacred halls of which the great Staudigl sang so impressively, or to witness a long procession of cowled monks march round the dimly-lighted chapel, and if he has a taste for such things, he had better close these pages. He will see something of a pilgrimage and a little of divine service as it is conducted in Bulgaria; but the main object of our visit is to picnic in what is still a monastery, but is converted into a sanatorium for the people of Philippopolis and of a Greek town called Stanimaka, not far from the convent. The Monastery of St. Kyriak is visible from the windows of the British Consulate as a little white line far away in the woods that clothe the distant hills almost due south of Philippopolis. It was reached in a carriage, after driving about an hour and a half over a most uninteresting plain, and at the base of the hill we left our carriage, and proceeded up the steep slope on foot. The plain is about 550 feet over the sea-level, and the monastery stands at an elevation of about 800 feet over the plain. The plants which grow around as you wander through the woods and mount the hill are not without interest. The trees are chiefly elms, walnuts, and mulberries (cultivated for the silkworm). No more stunted scrub, but fine, well-grown trees clothe the mountain-sides. Vines, too, are met with from time to time, and the ordinary shrubs and herbs of the temperate zone. After leaving the plain and mounting a few hundred feet, we came to the Greek village of Vodina, a dirty place, built on the hill slope; and at the entrance to the village we saw a spring which is said to have the miraculous power of curing blindness and sore eyes. Here, also, we witnessed the primitive mode of extracting spirit from the skins and dregs of the grape after its passage through the wine-press. These are placed in a copper alembic, an old-fashioned still, and a coarse spirit is the product. A little farther on we saw a group of Greek women gossipping at the

THE MONASTERY OF ST. KYRIAK, FROM THE ASCENDING ROAD.

door of a cottage, and passing them, we looked into what appeared an empty store. Immediately one of the women moved towards us with an angry exclamation, and when I inquired what she said, one of my companions told me, "She wants to know what business we have there. The Greeks are very unfriendly and suspicious. Such a thing would never happen anywhere but amongst the Greeks in Bulgaria."

A little below Vodina a very picturesque view of the monastery, of which a sketch is here given, is obtained. It looks like a long building with a tower at the right extremity. This building is, however, only one side, and the tower is the termination of a higher side of the quadrangle which forms the monastery. The building stands out in a bright white colour against the dark woods in the background (it is white and grey), and above those are the grey bluffs, so often referred to, which here resemble the cliffs of Derbyshire. So close is the similarity, that during our descent I drew the attention of Captain Jones to some cliffs and hills resembling those in Dovedale. His answer was, "Yes; Thorpe Cloud without the Trout." Along the upper portion of the monastery you see a row of ordinary windows giving light to the chambers, of which further mention will be made; below the apertures are mere loopholes, evidently, in days gone by, for defensive purposes.

When you enter the monastery, you find it to be a large quadrangular building, enclosing a garden and a small Byzantine church. As already remarked, one side of the quadrangle along with a small portion of a second is higher than the remainder, and this part comprises a ground-floor with two fine wooden galleries, one above the other, supported by wooden pillars and connected by broad stairs of the same material; the rest of the quadrangle has only one gallery above the ground-floor, and that one of smaller dimensions. In the garden are a few trees (poplar, &c.), shrubs, and smaller plants. From the galleries you enter suites of chambers, which were formerly the residences of the monks; now only one resides there permanently; two brethren assist him when it is requisite, and there are besides men-servants and one old woman. The apartments are now let during the summer months to people from Philippopolis and elsewhere, in suites of two rooms (for males and females respectively) and a kitchen, and the amount paid for the hire of each set of rooms is from four to five liras or Turkish pounds per month (a Turkish pound = about 18s. sterling). In summer the monastery is often completely filled with visitors, as many as fifty families being sometimes accommodated; the average appears to be thirty. These take their meals in the galleries, where also they have music, and, as I was told, "dancing sometimes all day long."

In the gallery, too, we had our mid-day meal, but as I was the private guest of a hospitable host on that occasion, it would hardly be consistent with propriety to enter into details. Before the repast our hands were washed Oriental fashion, and during the meal we had to taste the excellent wine made in the convent. If I cannot speak of the dinner, at least I may be permitted to tell an anecdote which will give the reader an insight into Bulgarian life.

About a year previously my two companions were sitting on the same spot lunching, when suddenly a band of the so-called border guards entered the building, and rushed up and tied the convent-bell to prevent an alarm being given. These wild-looking fellows of the brigand type were armed with Martini-Henry rifles, and, according to all accounts, they seemed to be men bent upon plunder.

"What did you do?" I asked one of my companions.

"Do? Why, we went on lunching! They said they were in search of an Albanian who had outraged a girl, and not finding him in the convent, they went on to Philippopolis, where they found him and carried him off."

This is one of the *agréments* of a Bulgarian picnic. I wonder they did not bring him back and hang him, without benefit of clergy, in the garden of the monastery. Although not so exciting, we too had an interesting experience during our visit, for a pilgrimage of peasants arrived whilst we were there, and we followed them into the church. This is what we saw there. The interior of the church is completely covered with rude paintings of saints and legends in the gaudiest of colours; not a square inch is undecorated. It is hung with tawdry finery, such as would please the taste of the peasantry, and all around are the "ikons," or images of saints, loaded with offerings; amongst the latter the most conspicuous are little plates of gold, silver, or inferior metals, of an oval shape, about an inch in length, and punctured all over. They are intended as symbols that the worshippers have recovered their eyesight or been cured of ophthalmia by the miraculous water. First the peasants knelt in a group round the monk, who was robed, and placing a scarf which he wore over the heads of the kneeling worshippers, he asked them their names one by one in an undertone, and then said a short prayer over them. I was told that he was praying for immunity from disease for them, and that they have complete confidence in the efficacy of such prayers. The women went about the church kissing the "ikons," and then holding up their children and causing them to do the same. When the religious ceremony was over, the peasantry bought wax tapers, which were placed upon a table at the doorway, where they were sold by a monk. The worshippers took a taper, put their offering on the table, made a deep obeisance to the priest, crossed themselves, and one by one departed. I followed their example to the extent of taking and honestly paying for a taper; but not being a member of the Orthodox Bulgarian Church, I had to content myself with shaking hands with the amiable and kindly monk, from whom we had received much attention during our visit.

After this we returned to our carriage, making the descent by another route; and on the way down we got a fine view of the little Greek town of Stanimaka, which is most picturesquely situated. I am afraid it will not greatly enlighten my readers if I tell them that it resembles, though on a much smaller scale, the town of Kronstadt, at the foot of the Carpathians, on the Transylvanian side. Just as there, the streets and houses run up into the lateral valleys in the most capricious way; and the whole town somewhat resembles a star-fish which has been left by the tide and lost its symmetrical shape.

One more little incident before we return to Philippopolis and travel onwards from there. During our descent we heard the notes of a wind instrument, and turning round a bend in the path, we suddenly came upon a shepherd-boy discoursing melody upon a pipe to the sheep of his pasture. Such an idyllic scene, such Arcadian simplicity and pristine contentment, I have never witnessed elsewhere. It carried one back to the days when the city was founded, of which the distant spires were faintly visible on the horizon,[1] and made one for the moment forget monks and brigands, and "ikons" and convent wine, and tinned sardines, and all other modern innovations.

[1] Philippopolis was founded by Philip of Macedon about 350 B.C.

CHAPTER XV.

THE ROSE-FIELDS OF KEZANLIK—OVER THE SHIPKA PASS—GABROVO AND ITS GYMNASIUM.

Kalofer—Village politicians—The rose-fields of Kezanlik—The otto-of-rose industry—Ascent of the Shipka Pass—Signs of warfare—Memorials of the slain—Beautiful obelisks on the summit—A straggling cemetery—Reflections upon the Russian occupation—View from the Shipka—The king of the air—A novel drag—The descent—Gabrovo—Description of the town—Spinning women—Two visits to the Gymnasium—Ignorant candidates for admission—Elementary education in Bulgaria—The students of the Gymnasium—Their sharpness and great proficiency in every branch of knowledge—Foundation and history of the school—Report on its present condition by Professor Petroff—Remarks upon education in Bulgaria—Agricultural schools—Departure from Gabrovo.

THE journey from Philippopolis to Tirnova, the ancient capital of Bulgaria, occupies three days. The first day takes you to Kalofer, a small town near the foot of the Balkans; on the second you cross the Shipka Pass and reach Gabrovo, on the northern side; and the third brings you into Tirnova. Of Kalofer I saw but little, as we arrived after dusk and left before daybreak, and what I did see was not edifying. I had a letter to the Prefect, whom we found in a cabaret, or what we should call a country "pub," along with a few of the villagers, and he kindly returned with us to the poorest khan that I found in Bulgaria, to see that we were comfortable. The villagers had evidently been discussing politics, for the first question put to me by the schoolmaster of the village,[1] who joined our party, was whether I had heard anything of the mission of the Russian

---

[1] He told me afterwards that in the school at Kalofer there are 313 children of both sexes, and that he had seven male and three female teachers under him, who had been educated at the Gymnasium at Philippopolis.

General Ehrnroth. I told him that was ancient history, and that the proposal of the Russians to send a mission had fallen to the ground. In joyous tones he announced to the villagers that "Ehrnroth is not coming," a piece of intelligence which was received with undisguised satisfaction, for they seem to have stood in great fear of Ehrnroth and the Russians.

As I have said, we started before daybreak on the following morning, at 4.30, in fact, with the stars shining brightly overhead, and we had a magnificent sunrise over the Balkans. At nine we arrived at the village of Shipka, which is situated at the foot of the pass, having driven past many fields of rose-bushes on the way. These, as the reader doubtless knows, constitute the wealth of this part of the country, the district of Kezanlik, for it is here that in May and June the harvest of roses is gathered from which the essence or otto of roses is distilled. Of the weight of rose-leaves collected I can give the reader no idea, but it must be something enormous, and the following figures will enable him to judge as to the importance and profits of the industry. In 1883 there were exported from Eastern Roumelia 6500 lbs. of rose-water and essence, the value of which was estimated at £65,000, or £10 per lb.; in 1884 it was 7300 lbs., valued at £80,000, or nearly £11 per lb.;[1] and I am told that one wholesale perfumer alone in this country pays a firm in Kezanlik about £3000 a year for the essence. At the village of Shipka I bought a diminutive flagon of the essence for six francs; and judging from the infinitesimal quantity which is necessary to saturate a two-ounce bottle of pure alcohol, I should say that the profit on those little gilt glass flagons which are sold as otto of roses, but which really contain spirit perfumed with the essence, must be enormous.

The Shipka Pass, which is in reality not a pass at all, but a winding road over one of the Lower Balkans, rises immediately behind the village of the same name; and the ascent is so steep that the driver is obliged to unharness his horses, and

---

[1] Diplomatic and Consular Reports on Trade and Finance, No. 70. Report of Consul-General H. Jones on the Trade of Eastern Roumelia. 1886. Harrison & Sons, &c.

having made a noisy bargain with one of the peasants (who are always on the look-out for travellers), he substitutes a pair of oxen, hands over the carriage to the care of the peasants, and himself follows at leisure with his horses. The traveller may either keep his seat on the little vehicle or he may walk. My companion and I preferred the latter method of locomotion, and we reached the summit, which is about 2200 feet above the village of Shipka, with great ease in an hour and three-quarters, part of which time was employed in admiring the scenery and looking for evidences of the great battles that were fought there. Immediately on leaving the village you pass a fort, which is either in course of construction, or more probably being strengthened, and which is intended to command the pass on the south side; and shortly afterwards you see at a great height above a white obelisk, very conspicuously placed. This is one of several "memorials" of the great fight. It may be that I have no eye for what Lord Beaconsfield would perhaps have called "extinct batteries;" but with the exception of a few points of vantage in the ascent, which appear to have been levelled, I could see nothing to indicate that so recently as 1877 two great contending armies had converted the pass and the surrounding heights into one vast camp and fortress. As, however, you approach the summit, signs of "battle, murder, and sudden death" soon become apparent. First you see a crucifix or two placed up in conspicuous positions against the rocky eminences; then little enclosed spaces, containing the graves of fallen heroes; and at length you arrive at the obelisk, which is so conspicuously visible from the valley below. This turns out to be a plain monument, shaped very like another higher up, to be presently referred to, but smaller, and surmounted with a ball only. It was erected in memory of the slain of a certain Russian regiment (I forget which) by their surviving comrades. Mounting still, we soon arrive at the highest part of the road, and there we find an imposing obelisk, of which a representation is here given, which is surmounted by a ball and cross. It bears an inscription that it was erected during the reign of the Czar Alexander II., to commemorate the capture of the Shipka Pass by General Gourko, 7th July 1877. Now we seem to be in a straggling cemetery, for at short intervals, in every direction, there are crosses, crucifixes, and more or less imposing monuments and obelisks.

I can imagine some patriotic Russian, if he reads this description of the Shipka, exclaiming, "Are we then not justified, after shedding the blood of our brave soldiers, in demanding a foothold and our just influence in Bulgaria?" No more than we

RUSSIAN MEMORIAL OBELISK ON THE SHIPKA SUMMIT.

should be justified in demanding possession of Sebastopol or the heights of the Alma! If the campaign was one of many that were undertaken with a view to secure Constantinople, it was a hypocritical proceeding, which only verifies the adage that "Man proposes and God disposes." If, on the other hand, it was a disinterested sacrifice to liberate a people of the same race and religion, they should have been left to govern themselves and to carve out their own destiny, and their country should not have been made a hotbed of conspiracy and intrigue by their "liberators" for their own selfish and ambitious ends.

The view on the south side of the pass, all the way up from the village of Shipka, is very fine. Below, you see a vast fertile plain, with the Rhodope Mountains in the distance, but it is not to be compared with the scene that greets you at the summit. This is simply indescribable, and must be seen to be appreciated. In every direction, as far as the eye can reach, there are wood-clad hills, with here and there a few grey peaks, covered with a thin veil of snow. The summit itself is very peculiar. From where you stand at the large obelisk (on which, by the bye, the Russian eagle is conspicuously carved), the road descends for half a mile to a guard-house and khan, and thence rises again for the same distance to an elevation similar to the one on which you are standing. There the real descent commences. As we walked down to the khan where we were to lunch, we saw a frontier guard run out with a gun pointing upwards, and looking in his direction, we perceived a splendid eagle sailing over the pass. Whether the man was afraid of creating an alarm, or for whatever reason, he refrained from firing at the bird (which he would probably have missed), and the king of the air, after circling majestically for a few moments over the summit, swooped down into the valley below. In the khan we stayed half an hour to rest and refresh ourselves, and then followed our carriage. When we reached it, we found that a novel kind of drag had been improvised in the shape of an enormous bundle of branches with their leaves, which effectually prevented the carriage from slipping down the hill. We afterwards overtook our driver with the horses, which he was coolly taking on to Gabrovo, pretending that he thought we had walked on to that place. He knew well what he was about, and wanted to save his horses, for the road is so steep and rough that we soon left the carriage and walked to the foot, as we had climbed to the summit.

We arrived at Gabrovo at four in the afternoon, and taking up our quarters at what they are pleased to call the "Grand Hôtel," a somewhat better khan than the generality of such places, we at once sallied forth, first to have a look round, and then to pay a visit to the most noteworthy institution in Bulgaria, the Boys' Gymnasium, most noteworthy because it represents the renaissance of Bulgarian intellectual life and literature.

Gabrovo is a superior Bulgarian country town, with about 10,000 inhabitants. The River Jantra, spanned by three fine bridges, flows through it, and on one of these you see a tablet bearing the following inscription:—"This bridge was constructed by the private benevolence of the Sultan Abdul Medjid, for whose long life we pray. Date 1855." They were not such bad fellows after all, those old Sultans! The town itself has nothing particular to distinguish it. Streets narrow, pavement execrable, we had to creep through them on entering and leaving it in our carriage. There is a Byzantine church of rather imposing appearance, with its zinc dome glistening in the bright sunshine. The shops are open, resembling the smaller kind in the capital. Many of the houses are gaily painted, and the way in which the vines are trained over and about them is something marvellous. A beautiful example of this is to be seen in the "Grand Hôtel," where the little projecting balcony for meals was one mass of festoons and drooping vine branches. The bazaar or market was very gay and animated, women bargaining for fowls and vegetables, and all the while spinning away most vigorously. Indeed, I never saw such an amount of spinning done anywhere. I should think, if the women had been ranged in rows, they would have constituted a very respectable Oldham cotton factory!

But the Gymnasium was the *pièce de résistance* here, although at first it disappointed me greatly. Of the building it can only be said that it is large, very plain, and indeed rude in appearance, both externally and within. When we entered it, accompanied by the landlord of the "Grand Hôtel," who had sent to announce our intended visit, we were very courteously received by the Director (whose name I am sorry I forgot to note), the handsome priest who gives instruction in religion, and some of the masters, including Professor Petroff, the teacher of English and some other subjects. I was told that my visit was a little inopportune, as only a few boys were there, who had not yet entered the school, but were being examined prior to admission; that they had been educated so far in elementary schools in different parts of Bulgaria, and the object in examining them was to ascertain the degree of proficiency they had attained and to select their class. But that was precisely what I wished to know, as it would give me an insight into the character of the education in elementary schools, and I therefore begged permission to hear one or two of the boys examined. Accompanied by the Director, M. Petroff, and one or two other masters, we adjourned to a class-room, where we found a few grown-up lads, one of whom was working out a wonderful problem in algebra with sines and cosines and what not, something far above my comprehension, which completely filled a large black-board. The master who was examining him told me the result so far was not satisfactory, and he was ordered to stop for awhile. I said, "Tell him to add one-eighth of a franc to nine-tenths of a franc in decimals and show the result." He was absolutely unable to do it, and all the other boys were equally unsuccessful. Indeed, when I gave them a simple sum in decimals only, taking care to add the word *francs* (as I wanted to ascertain how their education would serve them in after life), they could not work it. I then asked the first boy where Canada is, and he said "America." "North or South?" "South." Another said Spain, thinking I meant Granada. The lads were, no doubt, nervous; my questions had to be translated (though I have no doubt they were correctly translated), and these boys may have been "pushed on" to enable them to enter the higher school. However, the masters appeared ashamed of the results, and M. Petroff asked me to return on the following morning, when the regular classes would be assembled, and I should hear a different story. This I should have done in any case, for it would be obviously unfair to judge of the education given in a high school from the examination of boys who had never been taught there. On the following morning we visited the Gymnasium again, and all I can say is that I wish we had a few such educational establishments in England.

In the lowest class of students (there are seven in all) I found the same evidences of defective elementary education amongst boys who had been there a year as I had met with the evening before in those who were candidates for admission, and I am therefore convinced that the lower schools of the country are too ambitious in their course of instruction, and devote too little attention to its practical details. The higher classes showed signs of rapidly-advancing knowledge, and when I got into the highest of all, it was *I* who felt ashamed of my ignorance! This prevented me from examining the boys in the higher branches of mathematics; but when I asked them how they would, under various conditions, ascertain the height of a building or a mountain, their answers were prompt and clear. As to the addition of fractions of a franc (they had no doubt heard of the *fiasco* of the night previously), it caused considerable amusement, and I was told by the master, " That is elementary." In universal history their information was very fair, and they answered questions relating to every age. So, too, in geography and in physical science. Chemistry, and that of the most practical kind, was a strong point, and when they were asked to draw plants on the black-board, they did so neatly and correctly. In all the various branches of a higher education they excelled the pupils in nine out of ten schools of a similar grade in England.

As I have already said, the Gymnasium at Gabrovo represents the revival of Bulgarian intellectual life and learning. It was the first school in which that language was systematically taught, and its foundation was due to a generous merchant, M. Apriloff, and to the self-denying labours of a young priest, Neofyt Rylski (educated at the Ryl Monastery), who in 1835, when the first school was founded, published the first Bulgarian grammar. It would appear that the present building was erected at a later period, but in this and other matters connected with the management of the school, the reader shall have more authentic information than any I can give, for the Professor of English favoured me with the following report, which I publish verbatim, without even correcting one or two minor inaccuracies, in order that the reader may have an opportunity to judge of the proficiency of master as well as of student (it must not be forgotten that it is a Bulgarian who is writing English) :—

"SOME INFORMATION ABOUT THE GYMNASE OF GABROVO.

"The bases of the Gymnase were put in 1850; the construction of it was finished in 1867. The founder of the Gymnase is M. Apriloff, born in Gabrovo.[1] In the time of Turkish rule there were seven classes with ten professors. The Gymnase gave graduates" (degrees) "for the first time in 1875. Most of the present higher military and civil officers are graduates of the Gymnase of Gabrovo.

"At the beginning of the present college year are inscribed as regular students 420. There are seven classes with fourteen parallel divisions. The number of the teachers is twenty, with one director. Most of the teachers are graduates of different European universities. The following are the studies in the Gymnase:—Mathematics, natural sciences, chemistry, descriptive geometry, history, geography, logic, Bulgarian literature, general literature, the ancient and modern Bulgarian language, French, German, and Russian languages" (he has forgotten English), "drawing, and religious instruction.

"The library of the Gymnase counts about 4000 volumes. There is a museum containing a large quantity of old coins, most of them found in the neighbourhood of Gabrovo. There are physical, chemical, and zoological cabinets connected with the Gymnase.   (Signed)   PETROFF.

"GABROVO, 23 September, 1887."

A few words more concerning education in Bulgaria. I have spoken to the reader about the higher-grade boys and girls' schools and colleges, and about the technical school of Kniajevo. Let me add that there are two agricultural colleges, one at

---

[1] M. Petroff is quite correct in saying the founder was M. Apriloff, who was born at Gabrovo, but he was not, as this report would imply, the founder of the present building if it was commenced in 1850. M. Apriloff was at school in Moscow in 1800, in business in Odessa in 1810, founded the first school in 1835, and died in 1848, consequently, according to M. Petroff's report, two years before the foundations of the present school were laid. I believe it has been enlarged once at least.

Sadowa near Philippopolis, where they have forty-eight pupils and eight teachers, and another at Rustchuk with fifty scholars and five teachers. The pupils are mostly educated at the cost of the State, but there are some who pay 300 francs per annum. The curriculum is very imposing, but I was told by those who know that a good deal of it remains on paper. Besides the usual scientific (and even to some extent elementary) education, they profess to teach such subjects as agriculture, the anatomy, physiology, and habits of domestic animals, gardening, stock-raising, veterinary surgery, vine-culture, and wine manufacture, bee-culture, silk-culture, forestry, drawing, and mechanics. There is, besides, a theological seminary and an "Ecole Militaire."[1] Education is compulsory, but in the large majority of cases "compulsion" is quite unnecessary; the children are eager to learn, and their parents that they should be taught. There are inspectors, who, as with us, do their best, but cannot bring all the children into school. This information rather surprised me, for, with the exception of the gipsies, there is no class such as our Arab element to contend with.

However, these minor defects will soon be outgrown, and whilst I leave the reader to ponder later on over these details, and judge for himself whether or not the Bulgarians are fit for self-government, I must now ask him to take a final drive with me through this interesting town. In quitting it, he will once more anathematise its execrable pavement, which, however, gives ample opportunity to admire the painted houses with their vine-clad trellised balconies, its busy artisans working away visibly at kalpak, metal-work, and all other household wares, and its women picturesquely dressed, and spin, spinning away as though it were for dear life itself.

---

[1] The one in which the cadets rebelled and helped to carry off Prince Alexander was, I believe, dissolved.

CHAPTER XVI.

FROM GABROVO TO TIRNOVA—LAND-CUSTOMS AND AGRICULTURE.

Drenovo—Its wretched khan—Oleomargarine—The northern slopes of the Balkans—Beautiful scenery—Fine roads—Wealth of the land—Trees and fruits, wild pears, cereals, tobacco, &c. Paprika—Domestic animals—Herds of cattle, sheep, &c.—Caravans—The Bulgarian araba—The peasantry, men and women—The draught-oxen—Charms against witchcraft—Perennial triumphal arches—Well-to-do peasantry—Land-tenure in Bulgaria—Méra or common land—Establishment of a peasant proprietary—Customs of the Méra—Migrations of peasantry—Bulgarian gardeners—Hidden property of the peasantry—Rotation of crops—Agriculture—Wealth of the country.

THE drive from Gabrovo through Drenovo to Tirnova is remarkably interesting, and in order that the description may, at least, not be interrupted by anything very disagreeable, I would like first to say a few words about Drenovo, where you stop to lunch. It is a long, straggling village, through which you could easily drive in a few minutes, were it not for the pavement, if you can dignify with such a name the heaps of stones over which you have to jolt and rumble for nearly half an hour. The khan is wretched; no beds; mats on the floor as substitutes, and no comfort whatever for travellers. Strangest of all is the fact that when, after a good deal of solicitation, I succeeded in getting some butter, it turned out to be veritable "butterine"—"oleomargarine" with a strong flavour of tallow. When I hinted this, the landlord honestly confessed that it was an imported mixture, and he regretted exceedingly that he could not supply me with genuine butter.

The road from Gabrovo to Tirnova is in the Balkans, that is to say, it runs over a series of hills, a magnificent, undulating country, nearly the whole way. The road itself is excellent, and it passes over very good stone bridges, which span the streams that have to be crossed *en route*. The surrounding landscape is highly picturesque, consisting of fine hills clothed with woods, and backed up by the higher Balkans. The soil is a rich dark-coloured loam, sometimes almost black, but here and there you find fields which are one mass of stones, caused by the nature of the drift turned up by the plough. And what a wealth of vegetation of every kind! Amongst trees I noticed oaks, poplars, cypresses, acacias, willows, and mulberries, all fine well-grown trees; the oak being the most conspicuous. Besides mulberries, grown for silk-culture, the fruit-bearing trees are walnuts, in great numbers, filberts, plums, pears, cherries, apples, and enormous quinces; but one fruit I saw here which I do not remember having noticed elsewhere, namely, wild pears. In some places they quite ornament the roadside with their fruit, which is either gold colour or bright pink. They resemble small apples, are larger and more astringent than our Siberian crab, and not so pulpy. Our ordinary English shrubs are there in abundance, and, judging from the wealth of bright red berries, I should say that in summer the thorns and roses must, in some places, constitute an unbroken mass of blossom. Besides the tree-fruits, there is a succession of vineyards, which, at the time of my visit, were just being harvested, and the little, luscious grapes grow in good-sized compact bunches. The gourds, interspersed in the fields amongst the maize and other cereals, are sometimes gigantic in their proportions, whilst melons and egg-plants are just as fine and plentiful. Besides maize and the other cereals, which had already been reaped, there are fields of tobacco with beautiful pink flowers resembling the convolvulus, and occasional broad expanses of pasture. The only fern that I noticed was the common bracken. All ordinary vegetables, such as potatoes, carrots, cauliflowers, and cabbages, are plentifully cultivated, and most conspicuous is the characteristic "paprika," or red pepper, whose large pods, strung like onions, hang in rows before every cottage. They are served up at table boiled, red and green, and pickled and *farcie*, and probably in many other ways.

On the pasture-land every species of domestic animal is nourished. Oxen and buffaloes, which are used for draught;

horses, large black and white flocks of sheep, herds of black and white cattle, goats, pigs, and geese. As you drive along, you meet "caravans" of merchandise, timber, and farm produce. These usually consist of clumsy "arabas," or native carts, but sometimes they are composed of horses carrying ballots of manufactured goods and light materials. An araba is a primitive cart, and this is how it is framed :—Each side is formed of two long trunks of trees slightly dressed, and connected together some distance apart by sixteen or eighteen thin wooden poles; the bottom is constructed according to the purpose for which it is required; it has no springs, and the wheels are what a fast young gentleman would call a "caution." They have no tyres, and the rudest kind of felloes are attached to a rough nave by equally rough spokes. I had frequent arguments about those felloes. When you see them offered for sale, they are a little apart, and I maintained that they are intentionally left so, in order that as they revolve they may close up and form a complete circle, if the hexagonal wheel can be so called. As they rumble along the roads, these wheels roll to and fro like drunken men, and if you shut your eyes as they approach, you would think that you are listening to the groans of a lot of patients moaning with pain from cramp in the stomach. The arabas are nearly always drawn by a couple of patient and docile buffaloes, and are often full of firewood, hay, or other produce, which is heaped up so high as to make the cart on its rickety wheels top-heavy. Thus loaded they struggle along, I should think often not over a mile an hour, deepening the deep ruts on the road, and groaning away loud enough to awaken the seven sleepers. On the plain between Tirnova and Rustchuk one of these arabas loaded with fresh hay had got a lurch, and the joint efforts of the driver, his boy, three of us, and sundry peasants could not raise it to the perpendicular; so we had to leave the perplexed owner to remedy his grievance alone. The carts of produce are accompanied by Bulgarian or Turkish drivers, who walk alongside their charge, always carrying a long pole. If a Bulgarian, he wears the kalpak (no Bulgarian would wear a turban), is dressed in homespun cloth, or in summer in the long white blouse and girdle, common, with slight modifications, to the peasantry in all the Danubian States. The men are, as a rule, very fine fellows, well built, of average height, with bronzed faces, shaven except the moustache. You meet the women in great numbers going to market with their produce, and often very picturesquely dressed. A circumstance which cannot fail to strike you is, that when the carts are drawn by oxen, their front hair between the horns is nearly always dyed a bright yellow. This is done to keep off the evil-eye, or prevent them from being bewitched. I never could ascertain exactly what virtue it is supposed to possess, and in strict confidence, reader, I think the oxen are just as well informed on the subject as their owners. As you enter villages, you often see the perennial wooden triumphal arch, which, as I said before, bears fresh foliage of love and loyalty whenever a new ruler appears upon the scene. I do think a few of these should be removed, just to let Prince Ferdinand see that the assurances of eternal fidelity which he is receiving from his subjects are genuine.

Speaking in general terms, the peasants of Bulgaria are all well-to-do. Each of them has at least one pair of oxen and forty or fifty sheep; very many have two pairs of oxen and 200 to 300 sheep, besides goats, pigs, geese, and fowls, all of which are allowed to pasture on the " Méra " or common land. This leads us to the customs and tenure of land in Bulgaria, concerning which a few words may be of interest. According to my information, which was obtained from the most trustworthy official sources, there are now really only two kinds of property in land—private property, and Méra or common land, which is held in the proportions of one-tenth private and nine-tenths Méra or rural property. Nearly every peasant has his farm, rarely of less than five to six hectares (12½ to 15 acres), and a number of these farms, with their cottages and huts grouped together, form a village, to which is attached a large extent of country as "Méra." In the plains this "Méra" is pasture, in the mountains woodland; but wherever it is situated, the community to which it belongs has the usufruct, including the right to cut wood. The Government is endeavouring to limit the latter right, for the reason frequently given, namely, that forests have already been denuded or are fast disappearing. There is no limit to a man's right of pasture; he may send ten or 10,000 sheep (his own property, of course) on the "Méra." In towns the owners of houses have their gardens, sometimes of considerable extent. If a man wishes to sell his land, he is bound to give his immediate neighbour the first offer of it. No peasant belonging to one community is allowed to send his cattle on to a neighbouring "Méra," but he may buy a hut in the community to which it belongs, and with it he acquires the right of pasture. Titles must be registered, and ten years' occupancy gives an indefeasible title. About thirty or forty years since a change in the tenure of land occurred in Bulgaria, in effect the same as that in Roumania in 1864;[1] but in the former country it was brought about by a firman of the Sultan. From what I can gather, the Begs, who were the chief owners of the land, not only oppressed the peasantry, but failed to pay their taxes to the Porte. By the firman the peasants were to pay an annual tax, and to receive the titles to the land. What the nature of the arrangement was between the Begs and the Turkish Government, I am unable to say—that is of no consequence; it suffices to know that the result has been the establishment of a prosperous peasant proprietary. There are some minor matters still unsettled between the Bulgarians and the Turks,[2] such as the terms on which the Vakoufs, or lands belonging to religious foundations, are to be paid for, but these are questions of little moment so far as our inquiry is concerned. Similar attempts were made by usurers (Armenians and Greeks) in Bulgaria to get hold of the Turkish land to those in Roumania, and here too the difficulty has been met by a temporary law which prevents them from acquiring such lands. A somewhat remarkable and important change has taken place of late years in the occupations of the male peasantry. Before the introduction of machinery into the northern plains of the Danube, about 100,000 peasants migrated there every year for the purpose of harvesting, just as the Irish come over to this country; after the harvest they returned to their homes. During their absence

---

[1] "Roumania," p. 82-86, and Appendix iv.
[2] See Treaty of Berlin. "Holland," p. 286.

their harvesting and other work was done by young Bulgarian boys and girls, who descended from the mountains for that purpose. Since the necessity for employment of so many harvest-hands has ceased, the men have still gone in large numbers to Constantinople, Hungary, Servia, and Roumania as gardeners; and at Bucharest they will tell you that they are far superior to the natives in that vocation. Another incident in peasant life is that, whilst under the oppressive Turkish rule thousands of able-bodied peasants took refuge in and congested the mountains, they are now descending and settling in the plains, where the inhabitants of villages allow them to use the "Méra," but not to cultivate the soil. The statesmen of the country are, however, endeavouring to secure the right of tillage for them; indeed, their aims seem to be to prevent forest waste and encourage the planting of trees, to increase the acreage of arable land, and to reduce the extent of " Méra."

That the peasantry are well-to-do is proved not only by their visible wealth in kind, but, as I have already said, by the money which they are known to secrete. That this is an acknowledged fact is proved by a very naive reply which was given by a Bulgarian peasant to an English traveller when he was asked whether it is true that the Bulgarian peasants hide their money in the ground. "Where," he replied, "do the English peasants hide theirs?"

A large proportion of the revenue of Bulgaria is naturally derived from taxes on products of the soil and on sheep, goats, and pigs; but there is no tax on horses and cattle, the breeding of which the Government is desirous of encouraging; and in this, as in other branches of industry, there is no doubt that the Bulgarians, with whom agriculture is still very primitive, will soon make rapid progress, for they possess all the elements of prosperity. They have no need to use manure, owing to the richness of the soil; but they practise rotation of crops—wheat (or maize), barley, rye, and two years fallow. Their rose-culture is the most lucrative in the world. Tobacco grows well.[1] The

---

[1] The tobacco of Eastern Roumelia is of the ordinary Turkish quality, and is largely exported to Egypt and Austria.

silk industry is capable of great development. Cotton is now being successfully cultivated. Their vines are of the best kind, but they spoil the wine through careless manufacture; and their climate is such that they are able in many instances to secure two harvests against one in higher latitudes.

CHAPTER XVII.

TIRNOVA AND ITS ANTIQUITIES.

The first glimpse of Tirnova—Its wonderful aspect and situation—Natural fortifications—Illusions dispelled—The Prefect, M. Bondareff, and Professor Grinchoff—Their attentions—The "Bella Bona" and the Khans of Tirnova—The hall of the Great Sobranje—Its desecration—Irregular plan of Tirnova—The "Hissar" and the "Trapezitz"—The causeway of the "*Rocher-coupé*"—Fortified approaches to the "Hissar"—Baldwin's Tower—The hill slopes—Vestiges of the palaces of the Bulgarian Czars—The mosque on the "Hissar"—Regard for Mussulman piety—The "Church of the Forty Martyrs"—Roman remains—Columnar inscription of John Asen II.—The metropolitan church—Its memorials and antiquities—Fanatical Moslems—Roman relics—Dismal prisons—Phanariote vandalism—Copper doors and Byzantine ornamentation—The Church of St. Demeter and its reminiscences.

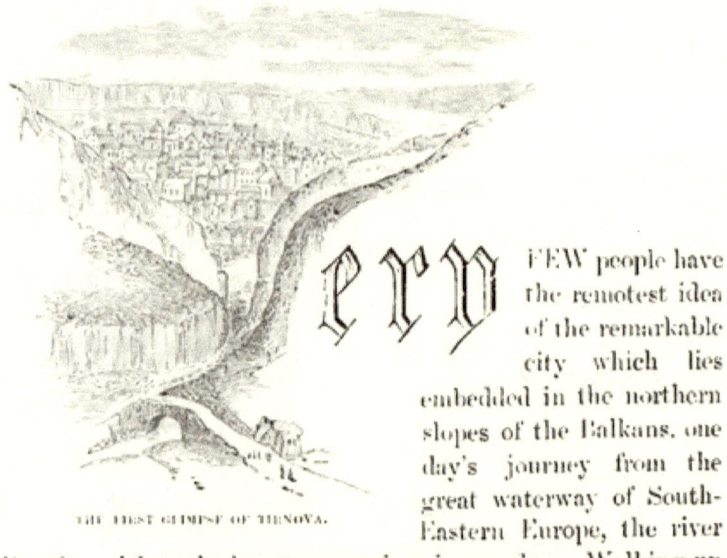

THE FIRST GLIMPSE OF TIRNOVA.

FEW people have the remotest idea of the remarkable city which lies embedded in the northern slopes of the Balkans, one day's journey from the great waterway of South-Eastern Europe, the river Danube. I have had many surprises in my day. Walking up the valley of the Visp for the first time, I have been struck with amazement by the great rock of the Matterhorn, towering, like the equally magnificent Langkofel at St. Ulrich in the Dolomites, high up into the blue sky. Stepping out upon the balcony of the Clifton House Hotel at early morning, my sense of wonder has been delighted with the great cascade of Niagara; driving along the road from Piræus to Athens, the appearance of the Acropolis, with its marble temples, has filled me with awe and reverence; and often has my memory dwelt upon the quaint and imposing aspect of Berchtesgaden, perched upon its rocky eminence. And yet, accustomed to look upon such marvels of

PART OF TIRNOVA, FROM THE PROMENADE (FROM PHOTOGRAPH BY O. MALCOLLM(?)).

nature and art as these, my surprise and delight were not one whit diminished when I obtained the first glimpse of Tirnova, framed in limestone cliffs, as it appears on the road from Gabrovo. The road runs through a gorge of fossiliferous limestone rocks about a mile from the city, and when you enter this, as you should always do on foot, the city, rising high up the hill slopes, is gradually exposed to view. To depict or describe the scene that breaks upon you as you emerge from the narrow pass is simply impossible. High hills rise on every side, covered almost up to their summits, at an altitude of at least 700 or 800 feet, with streets of houses gaily painted in various colours, domes, minarets, clock-towers, steeples, large buildings, and a long causeway of rock, intermixed with trees and gardens. Below flows the Jantra in its winding course, spanned by bridges, and rising from its banks are precipitous rocks covered with green shrubs, upon which houses are romantically built. In the distance you see hills, which appear (as they really were in former days) to be fortified with strong lines of ramparts. Perched upon one of these hills, the Hissar, or fort, a mosque stands conspicuous, and far away in the distance behind that rises another range of hills, walled round like those already named. Let me mention at once that these lines of fortification are really limestone escarpments, which were applied to defensive uses by the old Bulgarian Czars, and into the crevices of which strong stonework was ingeniously inserted here and there, to give solidity and symmetry to the natural ramparts. Entering the city as usual over an execrable pavement, you soon arrive at narrow, precipitous streets. You find the houses, so picturesque from afar, to be in many cases poor and dilapidated, the public buildings few and far between, the churches striking in appearance, but not equal in proportions to some that you have seen in smaller towns, the same open booths, the same handicrafts, the same spinning women.

I had a letter of introduction from the Prefect of Philippopolis to the Prefect of Tirnova, and the latter received me most courteously, sent for his secretary, M. Jean Boudareff, and requested him to introduce me to Professor Gnincholf, a well-known archæologist in Tirnova, and to show me all the antiquities deserving of inspection. I cannot express in too warm terms my obligations to these two gentlemen, both of whom are good French scholars, for the attention they paid me, and the interest they showed in the object of my visit. The Prefect recommended us to put up at the "Bella Bona," which he said was the best hotel in Tirnova; and remembering that Kanitz described its accommodation in glowing terms, I expected to find at least a comfortable hostelry.[1] But again the talented and

---

[1] "Donau Bulgarien und der Balkan," vol. i. p. 173.

circumstantial German writer has been a *little* " *idealistisch*," and I could hardly believe that the miserable shop through which we entered, and the wretched chambers upstairs, were the place to which he referred. It was so, however, and we were obliged to take our meals in the restaurant of another khan, the " Hôtel de Sofia." This one had greater pretensions than the " Bella Bona" (although you may easily lose yourself in the stables in trying to find your way up to the dwelling-rooms), and we were well cared for in the matter of commissariat. Let us not be ungrateful to the " Bella Bona," however, for we shall there have, before leaving, an interesting experience in Bulgarian politics. Having arranged to spend the following day in visiting the antiquities of the city, and as it was now becoming dusk, we contented ourselves with a ramble through the streets, and amongst other places I was shown the Public Hall, in which the great Sobranje meets, and the house where Prince Ferdinand was lodged when he visited Tirnova to mount the throne. The second is a kind of place in which an English country-doctor would decline to dwell (although, no doubt, they offered their new Prince the best accommodation at their disposal); the first resembles the public hall of some small English provincial town. Within I was shown the stage on which the ceremony was performed, but its appearance was somewhat marred by the apparatus of a *prestidigitateur*, who was going to perform there in the evening, and the boxes in which on that particular occasion the representatives of foreign courts were *not*, but ought to have been seated, but from whence the noblest and most patriotic of the nation viewed the scene below. My Bulgarian friends must not imagine that I am sneering at their State accommodation and ceremonies. I am bound to describe things as I saw them; but as for the significance of such empty parades, they matter but little, especially for a young nation just escaped from the toils of two oppressive masters, and struggling to secure its complete emancipation.

It is very difficult to give the reader a correct idea of the plan upon which Tirnova is built. Its streets run up the slopes of hills, and in places its houses are perched upon rocks forming the banks of the River Jantra, which winds in the shape of an S through and round the town. Looking from the balcony attached to and behind the "Hôtel de Sofia," which is situated close to what may be called the main street, two hills are visible, separated by a curve in the Jantra. The lower of these is called the Trapezitz (spelt Trapezić, or sometimes Trepevic), and it lies immediately opposite on the other bank of the Jantra; the other, farther off to the right, is the "Hissar." Both are surrounded by the semi-natural, semi-artificial walls already referred to, and upon both stood, in the days of Bulgarian greatness, the palaces

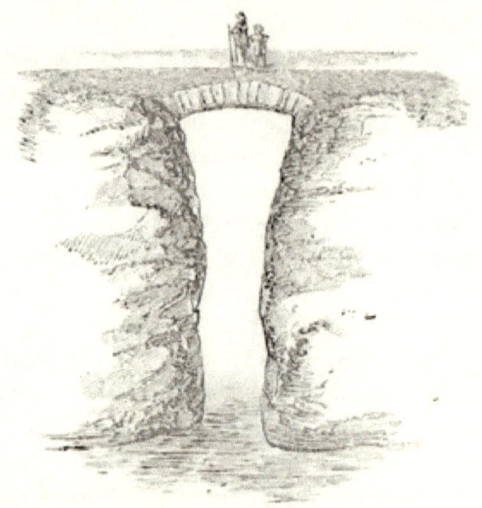

THE ROCHER-COUPÉ, OR CLEFT ROCK AND BRIDGE AT TIRNOVA.

and churches of the reigning Princes or Czars. In order to visit the "Hissar," you go along the main street from the westward towards the east, leaving the Prefecture, a fine plain building, to your right, and immediately beyond you enter upon a long, high, natural limestone wall or causeway, known as the Rocher-coupé, from the fact of its being cut about half-way along its length down to the ground beneath by a deep chasm. Some believe this chasm or incision to have been artificially cut, and that a drawbridge was thrown across, which, being raised, closed the access to the fortified hill and its buildings. It seems to be natural, and to-day a solid bridge affords a free passage. Having crossed this bridge, and walked along for some distance, you pass a ruined gateway, and find yourself within the fortified burgh. The causeway upon which you stand is from 180 to 200 feet above the Jantra, which flows below to the right and left as you approach the hill. The walls which you are passing are from six to eight feet thick, and in some places nearly fifty feet high, and are composed of stones and strong cement, with here and there remains of a strong tower of defence. Presently you come upon a ruined castle, Baldwin's Tower, as it is called,[1] where, as the reader no doubt remembers, Kalojan is said to have confined Baldwin, one of the Frank Emperors of Constantinople. At present this castle is interesting only from its situation, which is at an immense height from the plain below, and accessible in that direction only by a narrow winding pathway through what is to-day an old ruined arch. The tower stands at one of the corners of a small walled space, overgrown with grass and weeds, and containing a couple of stunted trees. Passing the tower, you ascend and wind round the hill, and there you may find numerous vestiges of the grandeur of its former edifices and their occupants. Attached to the palaces of the Czars there are said to have been gardens and fruit-trees, of which few traces remain; but if you search amongst the fine limestone *débris* on the ground, you will be sure to discover unmistakable signs of the former existence of palaces. I have before me whilst penning these lines a number of little objects of a somewhat cubical form, made of glass and quartz enamelled with gold, and with the various colours of the spectrum; these are mosaics; also a fragment of stone moulding, which has been cut by hand and decorated with silver; and a piece of plaster, forming part of what has evidently been a fresco either in a dwelling or in a place of worship. These were found either by myself or by my companions, M. Bondareff, Professor Guincheff, and my travelling companion, M. Ismian, during our ramble over the hill; and the second-named gentleman has quite a noteworthy collection of such objects.

---

[1] See vignette letter to chapter iv.

Near the summit of the hill stands a mosque, which is still used, and, as we were about to descend, I walked along a path in the direction of the mosque; but M. Bondareff signalled, and asked me to go by another path, "for," he said, "service is being performed there." I mention this to show that all phases of religious belief, even that of their former oppressors, are not only tolerated, but respected by the Bulgarians. From the Hissar we looked down upon the Trapezitz, the hill on the opposite side of the Jantra, which flows round a great part of both eminences. The reader will understand this better if he imagines an S with a hill within each curve, as I have endeavoured very roughly to show in this little woodcut. There is nothing of particular interest on the Trapezitz beyond the fact that palaces and churches were certainly built upon it also; and on a hill in the far distance, much higher than either of these, and also fortified, the Czars are said to have kept their harems.

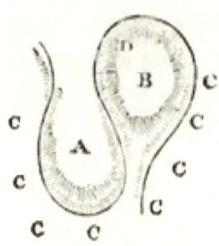

DIAGRAM SHOWING RESPECTIVE POSITIONS OF HISSAR AND TRAPEZITZ.

A. Trapezitz. B. Hissar. D. Mosque on Hissar. C. City. The line shows the course of the Jantra.

We will now descend the side of the hill opposite to the one we mounted, to visit some of the edifices still existing, but erected contemporaneously with those which were destroyed by the Turks, and have disappeared from the two hills just described. The first of these is the "Church of the Forty Martyrs," now a military church, on the external wall of which you may see a tablet bearing the following inscription by my learned guide and companion, Professor Guincheff:—"Built in the name of the Forty Martyrs, 1230, by the Bulgarian King, John Asen II., to commemorate his victory over the Greeks; converted into a mosque during the Turkish occupation, and retransformed into a Christian church in 1877." This is, in brief, the history of the edifice. The interior of the church, although it is very plain, is remarkable for its interesting antiquities. The pillars are of polished marble, with old Roman pedestals, of which the dado is ornamented with bulls' heads and wreaths, and it is almost certain that they were brought from the old Roman town of Nicopolis. On one of these pillars we find the inscription to which reference has already been made as having been placed there by John Asen II.[1] It is engraved round the column in Cyrillic characters, in the manner shown in the woodcut, and the following is the translation, as it was deciphered for me by Professor Guinchoff:—

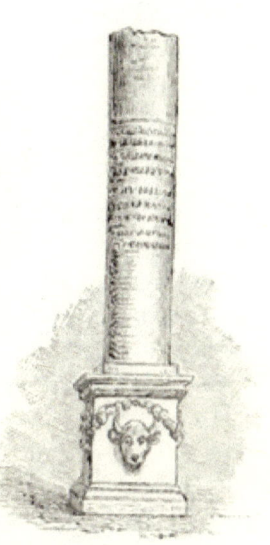

ROMAN COLUMN WITH INSCRIPTION OF JOHN ASEN II., CHURCH OF THE FORTY MARTYRS AT TIRNOVA.

"A.M. 6738" (= A.D. 1230). "I, John Asen, son of the Great Asen, under God Czar and Autocrat of the Bulgarians, did begin and finish this holy church, and I have adorned this church in memory of the Forty Holy Martyrs in the twelfth year of my reign; in the same year having painted the church, I went out on the 2nd of May against the Greek army, and their king himself, Kyr Theodor Komnena, I took prisoner with all his notables, and I conquered all the Greek country from Adrianople to Durazzo, the Greek peoples of Albania and Servia, all those countries with their towns, the environs of Czarigrad,[2] which town alone continued to be held by the Franks, who also submitted to my rule, and ended their days under me, as they had no other king except me. For it was thus ordained by God. For without Him neither word nor deed can be accomplished. To whom be honour and glory in the ages."

From the Church of the Forty Martyrs, with its interesting record, we proceeded to the metropolitan (also Byzantine) church, situated in a monastery, which is inhabited, as the name of the church indicates, by the Metropolitan Bishop. Historically this is perhaps one of the most noteworthy edifices in Bulgaria, for it stands much the same as when it was originally founded, and, both externally and within, it bears evidences of the barbarism as well as of the devotion of nearly every epoch in Bulgarian history. The church itself is a small one, and from the court in which it stands, surrounded by the monastic

---

[1] Part I. p. 17.   [2] Constantinople.

buildings, you can see on the white metal dome the bullet-holes made by the enemies of the faith. When you enter the edifice by its copper portal, to be referred to presently, you are made further acquainted with the religious fanaticism of the Moslem conquerors through the numerous gashes and punctures of their spears and yataghans or scimitars, still distinctly visible upon the frescoes representing Christian saints and legends. Examine the structure of the interior, and you are carried back still farther into the historic past, for there too

COPPER DOORS OF THE METROPOLITAN CHURCH AT TIRNOVA.

you may see polished pillars from Nicopolis or some other Roman colony; and when you are conducted beneath the church, you find yourself in the vaults and dismal prisons where the wicked or unfortunate of every age have languished. The prisons are damp cells of narrow dimensions, lighted by a slit in the wall capable only of admitting an infinitesimal supply of light and air. But there is another period of which mementoes are to be found here. At the back of the church is a small crypt or chamber, in which stands a large empty chest, and you are told that it formerly contained many valuable records on parchment of the time of the Bulgarian Czars; but that the Phanariote priests, eager to propagate their faith and to establish their authority, and determined to expunge from the page of history every memorial of ancient Bulgarian power and conquest, had emptied the chest of its literary treasures and made a holocaust of them in the courtyard of the monastery. Yes, and still one more trace of past Oriental grandeur! The heavy portal of the church is made of panelled oak coated with thick sheet-copper and embossed with crosses; and upon the arch, which is constructed of thin red bricks alternating with layers of cement, you may see a row of little discs; these too are of baked clay enamelled with green glaze, and they were probably borrowed from the Byzantine ornamentation of some edifice in Constantinople, just as the Czars clumsily copied the Byzantine coins of the Greek Empire. I shall have to refer to these little discs again. Meanwhile was it not correct to say that the church has a noteworthy history? The columns tell of the highest flourish of ancient Rome, when her legions held the banks of the Danube, and her emperors planted their indestructible monuments of her power and greatness; they tell, too, of her "decline and fall," which left her temples in ruins, to afford shelter for barbarous Asiatic hordes. The church itself, with its curious ornaments, its dismal prison vaults, its shining metal dome, and its monastic surroundings, speaks plainly of the rise and domination of the second Greek Empire, and of the influence which it exercised over all the nations of Eastern Europe, including the semi-civilised Bulgarians; and then the spear-thrusts and the bullet-marks proclaim the conquest and servitude of the Sclavonic people under the fanatic Moslem rule; whilst the old empty chest is typical of the Turkish treasury, which sold the most sacred offices in its vassal realms to the profane, venal, and debauched denizens of the Phanar!

One other church, this time a ruin, and we must close the archaeological page. The Church of St. Demeter (all these churches, by the way, are within easy walking distance of one another), of which only the walls are standing, is the one, the reader will recollect, that Asen founded where the meeting was held which chose him for Prince and inaugurated the second Bulgarian Empire, after the return of the brothers from Constantinople. The only noteworthy feature about the ruin is that, in addition to the little row of discs upon the arches, there is also a row of crosses. The discs are of green-glazed pottery, as in the Metropolitan Church, the crosses of red tiles, which

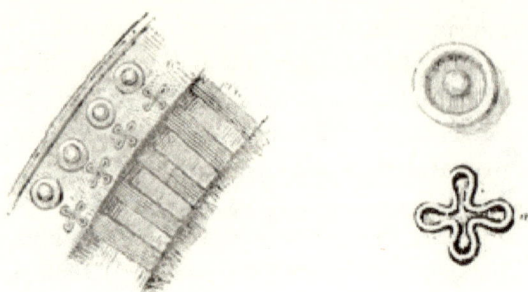

DISCS AND CROSSES IN THE ARCHES OF THE CHURCH OF ST. DEMETER, TIRNOVA.
a Enlargement of the same.

appear to have been moulded as short tubes, and then pressed into the form of crosses by indentation at four opposite points in the circumference.

Many sacred stories and legends are associated with this church, such as that the holy St. Demeter appeared in the midst of the multitude during the Asenite meeting and extended his protection over the revolt. But these interesting traditions must be left to some other abler pen than mine, for I wish the reader to return with me to the " Bella Bona " khan, and there to read another short chapter in modern Bulgarian history.

CHAPTER XVIII.

TIRNOVA—INNKEEPER'S POLITICS—TO RUSTCHUK— FAREWELL, BULGARIA!

The "Bella Bona"—A political lesson on the bed-chamber walls—An innkeeper's all-embracing loyalty — Sunday at Tirnova — A Bulgarian wedding-day — Journey to Rustchuk—Brave guardians of the peace—An expensive luxury—A gipsy horde closely watched—An unexpected escort—"Slivovitza," a great stimulant for gens-d'armes' courage—Splendid equitation of our escort—We lose the benefit of their guardianship—The beautiful Danube—Rustchuk—Bucharest.

ON the morning after our arrival at Tirnova, my curiosity was piqued by the sight upon the walls of my bedroom of a number of framed prints, and I thereupon made a tour of inspection. The first was a full-length portrait of the Czar Alexander II., the Liberator, printed in Moscow in 1877. "Ah!" I thought, "the Russians know how to improve the occasion." The second was Alexander, Prince of Bulgaria, printed at Vienna. The third was a small picture, resplendent in gold and colours, of the Czar Alexander III. and the Czarina, in their coronation robes. The fourth was an allegorical picture intended to commemorate the liberation of Bulgaria, which was represented as a bellicose female figure standing upon a rock, with a drawn sword in one hand and a standard in the other, on which the lion of Bulgaria was depicted. Hovering above her head, in the attitude of a protector, soared the double-headed Russian eagle, with the words, "San Stefano, Feb. 10," upon a band or ribbon which it held in its claws. Standing by was another Bulgarian lion, whilst pieces of yataghans, broken fetters, and other objects symbolical of the ruptured ties of Ottoman rule lay in profusion at her feet. Conspicuous amongst these was the date of the Treaty of Paris subsequent to the Crimean war; wherefore, I was at a loss to imagine, unless the Russians wished the Bulgarians to believe that that war also was undertaken for their liberation! Close to Bulgaria liberata was a portrait of the Bulgarian Exarch, and next to him that of the patriot Rakoffsky, who had headed an unsuccessful rising against Turkey. So it would appear that all the Powers that had been from time to time were represented. No! where was the memento of Ottoman rule? I went out to call my travelling-companion, who slept in an adjoining room, when, lo! the tale was complete. On the wall of the passage hung one more engraving commemorative of the great White Czar who had freed the country; it was the funeral procession of Alexander II., and by its side was a portrait of the Sultan Abdul Aziz, surrounded by miniature likenesses of all his leading generals! Of a truth, the landlord of the "Bella Bona" was prepared for every political contingency, and I was once more reminded of the perennial Bulgarian *arcs de triomphe!* There was one hiatus, however: Prince Ferdinand was not yet favoured with a niche in the political pantheon; probably that omission has since been repaired.

In Tirnova on Sunday nearly all the shops are closed during the whole day, and the amusement of the people is to walk in the neighbourhood of the city, admire the magnificent scenery, and smoke and drink coffee at a large café in the outskirts. On the Sunday we were there, a wedding took place between a Bulgarian officer and the daughter of a wealthy trader of Tirnova, I believe. The girls of Bulgaria, I was told, "dote on the military," and no one except an officer has a chance of getting married. This wedding, although it was commonplace, was largely attended, the church in which the ceremony took place being crowded to the roof by persons of every class. But, so far as picturesque costumes or interesting ceremony was concerned, the function might just as well have taken place in a Greek church in London. Every one was dressed after Western fashion, bride and bridegroom (who wore his uniform) included. The bridesmaids were young girls wearing artificial flowers in their hair; and it was very amusing after the ceremony was over to see them come running out of the house to which the happy pair had adjourned for a reception to fetch chairs from the neighbours, which they carried back without any feeling of impaired dignity.

From Tirnova to Rustchuk is a long day's journey, but by dint of early rising (for we departed at about 3 A.M., with the stars as usual shining overhead), we managed to arrive at Rustchuk at about 5.30, before the departure of the boat which crosses to Giurgevo. Our feast at Biela, half-way between the two places, I have already described whilst speaking about travelling in Bulgaria, but one more incident of the journey remains to be mentioned. I had been told at Sofia that the road from Tirnova to Rustchuk was not safe from brigandage, that is, highway robbery; but from what I had gathered generally, it was of little use to take a gens-d'arme, as they generally bolt and leave those whom they are sent to protect. The secretary of the Prefecture at Tirnova did not deny that the mail had been robbed near Vacarel, between Sofia and Philippopolis; and when we came to discuss the matter, my travelling-companion admitted that at Drenovo he had seen two travellers who said they had been *dévalisé*, that is, robbed of their luggage, and permitted to proceed, and that they were making a reclamation from the authorities. Of that I thought nothing, for reasons already assigned; and when I inquired about a mounted gens-d'arme, I was told that one could readily be supplied to me *at a charge of twenty francs*, " but they are not much good if you are attacked!" I declined the escort, and although we gave the "brigands" between two and three hours of night-travelling before sunrise, they failed to put in an appearance. Still we were to be honoured with a bodyguard, and it fell out this wise. At some distance beyond Biela, it may have been at about three o'clock in the afternoon, as we were driving quietly along, we suddenly heard a great tumult in front of us, and our carriage was surrounded by a wild horde of gipsies begging alms. We threw them some coppers and they passed on, but they were immediately followed by a couple of mounted gens-d'armes, who carried, besides their rifles unslung, naked revolvers very handy in their belts, and ready for use. We had not travelled far when two other mounted gens-d'armes appeared, this time riding in our direction; and when we overtook them they let us pass, but in the course of a few minutes we saw them galloping full speed over the plain at a little distance from the road, shouting and whirling their rifles about like Arabs of the desert. It was a very interesting but by no means an imposing sight.

Presently we came to a Turkish fountain, near which was a cabaret. One of the gens-d'armes, whom we found to be a serjeant, entered, no doubt to have a drink of water—it may have been slivovitza; but in whatever liquor he indulged, when he made his appearance again, it was clear that both he and his companion were considerably the worse for drink. We sat still for a time in our carriage whilst our driver watered the horses and our heroes commenced grooming their steeds. The serjeant tortured his by twisting its tongue and feeling in its throat for something that was evidently not there. The driver said he must stop for half an hour, so we descended and walked on. In about three-quarters of an hour he overtook us, and the first thing he told us was that the gens-d'armes were the worse for drink: *that* was no news. Next he said they had asked him all about ourselves, and I imagine he had in no way understated my rank in the information he gave them. Then they inquired what we had been talking about on the road; and he said he was sorry he could not enlighten them, as we spoke in a language he did not understand (we spoke French). Whether they took us for brigands or Russian spies I do not know, but, from whatever cause, they hastened after us, and very soon they were again galloping along a bye-path on the plain, howling and yelling like Buffalo Bill's Indians, and keeping us in a constant state of apprehension lest their rifles should go off unawares, and they should injure each other or their horses. They continued to follow or precede us, making short cuts across the plain whenever we passed them; and every now and then they favoured us with an exhibition of horsemanship. At length, as we neared Rustchuk, they dropped behind and disappeared, depriving us of the advantage of their escort and protection. I was sorry for this, as I had an introduction to the Prefect of Rustchuk, and would gladly have stopped there to recommend them for promotion on account of their remarkable equitation and sobriety! Two such knights-errant at twenty francs a piece would have been rather a dear bargain, reader!

It is a beautiful sight, as you descend from the high plateau which lies between the Balkans and the Danubian plain, to see winding far away in the distance the silvery course of the great stream. I have been on or near the Danube several times, have travelled along it on shore, crossed it at Donauwörth, steamed through the Kazan Pass of the Carpathians, and through the Iron Gates, and traversed it twice at Giurgevo, and it has never been my good fortune to see the "Schöne blaue Donau," the beautiful *blue* Danube; but I never wish to see a more welcome sight than that which greeted me after the long weary day's journey from Tirnova to Rustchuk, in the glittering watercourse, as it wound through the plain east and west as far as the eye could reach. And, strange though it may appear, when I stepped on board the steamer that was to convey me from the Bulgarian to the Roumanian shore, although I was perhaps at a greater distance from Old England than at any previous part of my journey, I felt myself "at home." I was just in time to catch the boat which runs in connection with the last train from Giurgevo to Bucharest, and am therefore unable to give my readers any further account of Rustchuk (the terminus of the Varna railway) than that its streets are tolerably wide, its pavement is not intolerably bad, and that it contains some fine buildings and a busy quay. Possibly, if I had remained there for any length of time, I could have told him no more; but I did not, and it was with feelings of considerable satisfaction that four hours later, after a journey of nineteen hours by road, river, and rail, I drove through the well-lighted boulevard of Bucharest (which has vastly improved in appearance since my visit in 1881), entered the comfortable "Hôtel Brofft," and told the waiter to be good enough to let me sleep the next morning until I awakened of my own accord.

CHAPTER XIX.

BULGARIAN TRADE—AGRICULTURAL RESOURCES—GAME AND THE CHASE.

Imports and exports—Order of importance of various European States—Brief statistics—Trade with Austro-Hungary and Great Britain—Articles of import and export—Order of importance of seaports—Consular reports on trade—Considerations connected therewith—The author's recommendations to English traders and manufacturers—Resources of Bulgaria—Consul-General Jones's report—Cotton recently introduced—The chase in Bulgaria—Wealth of game—Bears, deer, chamois, smaller game, wolves—Game birds: pheasants, partridges, wild-fowl, water-fowl—Localities where they are found, and centres for shooting excursions—Fishing: sturgeon, trout—Absence of regulations for the preservation of game—Its probable extinction.

IN the preceding chapters I have endeavoured to give my readers an outline, imperfect though it be, of a country which at the present time possesses considerable European interest, and in this one I propose to say a few words concerning its commercial and economical importance to other States. To speak in general terms, Bulgaria has as yet no manufacturing industries of note, although these are capable of indefinite development; and whatever mineral wealth she may possess is almost entirely below the surface. She is strictly agricultural, and such objects of household and personal use as are not made by her industrious peasantry are to a large extent imported from other countries. The order of importance in which these stand in their commercial relations with her are:—(1.) Austria-Hungary; (2.) Great Britain; (3.) Turkey and Greece; (4.) Roumania; (5.) France. The trade with Russia, Italy, and Switzerland is small, but on the increase. Owing to the recent union of the two States (Bulgaria and Eastern Roumelia), and to the frequent changes of Government, no official statement of the imports and exports of United Bulgaria has as yet been printed; whilst the data which have been given to our Consuls, and by them returned to the Foreign Office, contain some serious discrepancies, and are, as they themselves admit, untrustworthy as regards values. I have therefore been cautious in the use of figures, and the amount of information which I am able to present to my readers is necessarily limited.

The only trustworthy official statistics concerning Bulgaria (now North Bulgaria) date back as far as 1882–83, although they have been issued during the present year,[1] and from these I have compiled the following short table:—

IMPORTS. Average value for the two years 1882-83.		EXPORTS. Average value for the two years 1882-83.	
From Austria-Hungary and Germany (chiefly Austria-Hungary)	£622,500	To Austria and Germany	£94,970
„ Great Britain	439,660	„ Great Britain	298,600
„ Turkey and Greece (nearly all Turkey)	227,537	„ Turkey and Greece	365,720
„ Roumania	124,975	„ Roumania	346,814
„ All other countries	387,600	„ All other countries	497,720
Aver. tot. imports, 1882–83, £1,802,272[2]		Aver. tot. exports, 1882–83, £1,603,824	

A glance at this table will give the reader a very fair idea of the volume of trade done with foreign countries by the province of North Bulgaria. South Bulgaria was until recently a province of Turkey, and the figures for the above years have not been at my disposal. From the Consular reports referred to,[3] however, I have taken the following data, which are no doubt quite correct so far as the tonnage of vessels is concerned, but

---

[1] "Statistique du Commerce de la Principauté de Bulgarie avec les Pays étrangers pendant l'Année 1883." Sophia, 1887. (This publication really contains statistics of both 1882 and 1883.)

[2] In converting francs to pounds sterling I have taken the exchange at 25·10.

[3] No. 1, Bulgaria, Report on the Trade of Varna for the year 1885, by Vice-Consul Brophy (Varna); No. 70, Turkey, Report on the Trade of Eastern Roumelia for the year 1885, by Consul-General Jones (Philippopolis); No. 185, Turkey, Report on the Trade of Eastern Roumelia for the year 1886, by Consul-General Jones (Philippopolis) and by Vice-Consul Richards (Bourgas). Another Report (No. 237), of which an abstract is given in Appendix IV., reaches me whilst these pages are going to press.

the value of imports and exports must be taken with considerable reservation:—

TONNAGE OF VESSELS WHICH ENTERED THE BULGARIAN BLACK SEA PORTS, 1885.

	Tons.
Into *Varna* (nearly all steam; about one-half Austrian, one-fourth Russian, and one-seventh British)	359,645
Into *Bourgas* (about seven-tenths Russian steamers)	104,066
Total	463,711

In addition to this, there was a small tonnage, not returned, into Kavarna and Baltschik, on the Black Sea.

The clearances are about the same as the entries.

IMPORTS AND EXPORTS INTO AND FROM THE BLACK SEA PORTS, 1885.

	IMPORTS.		EXPORTS.	
Varna	£579,050	(nearly one-half from Great Britain).	£652,345	(about one-half to Great Britain).
Bourgas	166,446	(a fair share from Great Britain).	213,850	(chiefly to France).
Kavarna and Baltschik			173,000	(almost entirely grain).
Total imports, £745,496			Total exports, £1,069,195	

These figures, I must repeat, can only be taken as approximate, for the reports do not agree with one another; and as it would be illusory to add the statistics of 1882–83 for North Bulgaria with those of 1885 for South Bulgaria, especially as I find great variations in the amount of trade in different years, the reader must content himself with a rough general estimate that the imports of United Bulgaria circulate about £2,500,000, and the exports about £2,650,000; beyond this I shall spare him any further trouble with statistics of trade.[1]

---

[1] These estimates are, if anything, in excess of the actual trade, for both sets of figures on which they are based include the interchange of commodities between North and South Bulgaria (Bulgaria and Eastern Roumelia), which amounts to about 10 per cent. of the whole in both imports and exports. According to statistics which have kindly been furnished to me by Dr. Giffen of the Board of Trade, the value of the imports from Bulgaria (not Eastern Roumelia) into Great Britain in 1885 was £302,411; of the exports for that year, £103,743.

Although we have been obliged to proceed with great caution in dealing with exact values, our information in regard to commodities is more precise; and a glance at the pages of the voluminous report already referred to [1] gives one a very fair idea of the relative importance of the articles imported and exported, and of the seaports through which they are passed. In connection with the first, I propose only to deal with Austria-Hungary and Great Britain, the two countries with which Bulgaria does by far the largest trade.

From *Austria-Hungary* she imports (in the order of approximate values) salt, spices, sugar (chiefly beetroot from Trieste), potables, stone, clay, and glass wares, machinery, metal wares, textile fabrics, paper, and ready-made clothing; and she exports cereals, skins, leather and fleeces, otto of roses, &c.

From *Great Britain* she imports textile fabrics (cotton cloth, &c.), twist, stuffs and clothing, metals and metal-wares (chiefly iron, in rods and sheets), coals, coke, articles of food, colonial produce (coffee, cocoa, sugar, &c.), glass, earthenware, chemical manufactures, &c.; and she exports cereals, malt, vegetables, otto of roses, and a little wood-ware. Our trade in cereals with Bulgaria is very important; we received from there in 1883 cereals and vegetables to the value of about £458,000.

The duties on commodities imported into Bulgaria is 8 per cent.; on those exported, 1 per cent. *ad valorem*. As far as the ports of transit are concerned, Varna on the Black Sea is by far the most important. It does about a third of the whole import and a quarter of the export trade of South Bulgaria. Bourgas, on the same coast, is also an important seaport; whilst on the Danube, Rustchuk, Sistova, Lom, &c., rank in the order here given, and a considerable trade passes through the custom-houses on the Servian and Turkish frontiers.[2]

The carrying trade by sea with Bulgaria is to a large extent in the hands of the Austrian Lloyds and the Russian Steam Navigation Company, but that by British vessels is on the increase, especially in the conveyance of grain, the greater

---

[1] "Statistique du Commerce," &c.
[2] "Statistique," &c., A. Tableau vi. to xi., pp. 15 to 23.

part of which comes to this country ; and in 1885 the Vice-Consul at Varna reported that about fifteen steamers discharged annually part cargoes from London direct.

Austria-Hungary is our chief competitor in the supply of manufactured goods, the reasons being. (1.) closer proximity ; (2.) the supply of a cheaper description of goods ; (3.) the willingness to run more risk and give longer credit. Taking the last item first, our Vice-Consul at Varna recommended in 1885 that our manufacturers should be " willing to take a leaf out of the book of their Austrian and German competitors, that is to say, risk more." On the other hand, Consul-General Jones tells us in his report of the following year (1886) that "there has been a general restriction of credit by the wholesale houses of Austria and Constantinople, causing a widespread bankruptcy among the petty traders here, whose always precarious business collapsed on the first strain on their slender resources." Captain Jones adds that the foreign trade of the country has been languishing, and the consumption of foreign goods has very considerably declined since the departure in large numbers of the Turkish population. This means, incidentally, that the Turks, who wear cottons, are now nearer to the Mediterranean and Ægean Seas, farther from Austria, and nearer to Great Britain, in the long-run, therefore, it should be an advantage to us ; whilst the Bulgarians, who take their place, are wearers of home-made clothes and materials, by which their country will eventually be the gainer. So far, however, as increased credit is concerned, it is clearly not advisable that our wholesale houses should extend their operations.

As to the quality of manufactures, the Consuls also express somewhat divergent opinions. Vice-Consul Brophy (Varna) says that there are many slop-shops where ready-made clothing, boots, shoes, hats, &c., &c., "are sold; but this trade is exclusively in the hands of Austrian Jews, who can sell cheaper than French or English houses of the same description, because their goods are also of inferior quality."

Consul-General Jones, writing of the same year, says:— " Austrian (always including German) trade is rapidly extending in the province. The goods supplied do not, however, seem

such as will compete with British imports, and are chiefly
broadcloth and ready-made clothing, glass and pottery, cutlery,
matches, fancy articles in brass and iron, stationery, and beer.
The quality of all except the last is the very lowest; but here, as
throughout the East, cheapness is the great desideratum." The
last sentence seems to contradict the first part of the paragraph;
but what I take the writer to mean is, that persons who want
good commodities will not be induced by low prices to buy inferior articles. This is what I have found to be the case wherever
our manufacturers come into competition with those of other
countries, both on the continent of Europe and in the United
States.[1] It is a pity that when the Royal Commission on the
depression of trade held its sittings, it did not decide to take the
step of sending *experts* to various parts of the world, and especially to countries like Roumania, Bulgaria, &c., where trade is
just beginning to develope, to ascertain the prices, qualities, and
demand for English goods as compared with those of foreign
fabrication, and thus afford some practical aid to our hard-
pressed manufacturers.

And lastly, the proximity of markets is sure to be a permanent advantage to Austria; but one of the Consuls also tells us
"that the Austrian houses have the advantage of position and
transport, besides being represented by a ubiquitous and poly-
glot tribe of Jewish commercial travellers."

The general conclusions which may be deduced from these
reports, coupled with what I myself observed whilst in the
country, are these:—As regards the export trade from here,
large English houses desirous of extending their trade should
engage trustworthy persons, *conversant with French and German*,
to travel through Bulgaria (and the other Danubian States), to
inquire into the tastes and necessities of the people, and seek
to form respectable local connections. Manufacturers of agri-

---

[1] Vice-Consul Richards at Bourgas confirms Captain Jones's views. He says:
"English imported goods are mostly articles of the first necessity, which are not
likely to be undersold by foreign importers." I have not burdened these pages
with notes referring to the reports, for they are very short, and can be purchased
at 1d. each from the printers, Harrison & Sons, or Eyre & Spottiswoode, and
of Black, Edinburgh, and Hodges, Dublin.

cultural implements should watch the progress of agriculture there, for the new machinery is adapted to a very large extent of country already under cultivation, or about to become so. Cattle-dealers should keep a sharp eye upon the Bulgarian " Méra." With meat selling at a very low price at Sofia, a railway opening through the country, over which cattle can be conveyed to London in a few days, with only one change *en route*, and with a demand at home which brings live cattle or dead meat from every part of the world, it will not be long before large meat-supplies are drawn from Bulgaria. The tax upon the resources of the country during the Russo-Turkish war acted very prejudicially against cattle-breeding, as the best beasts were slaughtered wholesale; but notwithstanding that, meat is very low in price.

To the corn-factor I can teach nothing. As one of them told me lately, when I mentioned that the whereabouts of Bulgaria is to many still a mystery, "We are obliged to know geography;" but the extension of railways, which is sure to revolutionise the whole trade of the country, will also have a material effect upon the charges and facilities for the transport of grain.

And now a few words on this question from the Bulgarian point of view. There cannot be the least doubt that for some time to come it will answer the purpose of the inhabitants to cultivate agricultural rather than manufacturing industries. I know well the patriotic feeling which prompts nations to make efforts to become manufacturers, and the desire on the part of statesmen and politicians to train artisans rather than peasants. But, besides being a free-trader on principle, I cannot help seeing that in the case of Bulgaria, for the present at least, her prosperity is intimately associated with her agricultural and pastoral development. It will pay her far better to produce and export good cattle, sheep, hides, wool, and silk, good wheat, maize, tobacco, fruits, and even vegetables; to extend her otto-of-rose industry, and to increase her land under cultivation, leaving it to Austria, Great Britain, France, and other countries to compete for her custom in such articles of daily use as she cannot herself at present manufacture, than to invest large sums of money in costly machinery to enable her, even with the aid of high protective duties, to compete with nations of unlimited resources, which have long been the centres of manufacturing activity. Even in England we are going back to cottage or village industries; and it would indeed have been a blessing to this country, where the peasantry crowd into towns for employment, if they had been accustomed, as they are in Bulgaria, to spin and weave their own wool and make their own garments.

Consul-General Jones says in one of his reports:—" The Bulgarian peasant shows no tendency to make use of foreign wares, or to depart from the habits of extreme thrift so characteristic of the race. Even in the matter of cotton-twist—almost the only article of foreign origin which he regarded as a necessity hitherto—he sees an opportunity for further economy by spinning the same with his domestic help from country produce, and with this view patches of cotton are now being planted beside every Bulgarian cabin." Does not this sentence completely confirm the opinion above expressed, that it is better for the people to allow foreign manufacturers to compete for the supply of their modest needs, and to develope the resources (limited only by the extent of their vast plains and mountain slopes) of their soil and climate, the latter of which enables them to gather their rose-harvest in May, and to enjoy the blessings of summer until the middle of November?[1]

This leads me to say a few words on another of the natural productions of Bulgaria, which will be interesting to a large section of my countrymen—I mean the game of the country, which is at present found in great abundance. There is sport for lovers of the chase of every calibre, and the Bulgarians themselves are ardent sportsmen. Not only did I frequently see small parties of three or four with one or two dogs walking across the plains during my drive through the country, but on more than one occasion I was asked to allow a gentleman carrying his gun to ride alongside of my driver for a short distance

---

[1] The reader is specially referred to Appendix IV. The caution, as well as thrift, of the Bulgarian peasant is shown by his attention to fire-insurance. The agents of insurance-offices are frequently to be met with, and I noticed on a great many cottages and houses in villages the plates of Continental, American, and even English insurance-offices.

from town, until he should arrive at a spot where he was to commence the day's sport.

Bears are found in the more secluded districts of the Balkans and of the Rhodope Mountains, especially where these two chains unite, to the north-east of Macedonia. Red and roe deer are also fairly numerous in the same quarter, and Peruschtitza and Jchtiman are good centres for sporting excursions. The chamois is found amongst the snows remaining on the Rilo and the neighbouring peaks throughout the summer; wild swine abound in the marshes of the Danube and on the shores of the Euxine, and more or less in all the larger oak forests of the plains. Wolves are numerous and common; they commit considerable ravages among the flocks during severe seasons, and even enter the towns to prey upon the street-dogs. The inhabitants of the villages take various precautions to keep them at a distance. Of the presence of eagles I have already spoken in describing the Shipka Pass. Bustards of both varieties are found in considerable numbers on the plains in the months of November, December, and January; pheasants are found in many places, but their chief habitat seems to be the dense scrubs in the district of Jamboli, to which place there is a branch from the Philippopolis-Adrianople (trunk) line. This almost impenetrable jungle secures them, in a great degree, from the approach of man; but the native hunters lie in wait for them near the springs where they resort to drink, and often succeed in killing several brace in a single day. Wild-fowl of all descriptions and snipe are found abundantly in all the marshes throughout the country. Partridges and hares are also very numerous and general. Woodcock and quail, especially the latter, appear in great numbers in their proper season; for the former, the month of November, and for the latter, August and September. The capercailzie is said to exist in the mountain forests, and also the hazel-grouse, but they must be rare.

Of the sturgeon I have spoken elsewhere, in connection with the River Danube,[1] where it is found in considerable numbers,

---

[1] "Roumania," p. 25.

and trout are found towards the sources of nearly all the streams issuing from the mountain chains. Unfortunately, there are no regulations either as to game or fishing. Trout are caught in nets at all seasons, and there is no closed time for game. When the Bulgarians are visited in greater numbers than at present by strangers for the purposes of the chase, they will learn to estimate the wealth of game which they possess, and the attraction which it will afford to tourists; and then, no doubt, they will take measures for its preservation. Should they not do so, every bird and fish worth taking will be extirpated.[1]

---

[1] I have to thank my friend, Consul-General Jones (Philippopolis), for the particulars concerning sport in Bulgaria, and the reader will find more detailed information in the two works by Barkley and Baker, named in the Bibliography appended to this treatise.

CHAPTER XX.

THE BUDGET AND THE NATIONAL SERVICES.

A few figures from the last Budget of Bulgaria—Direct and indirect taxation—Mode of levying taxes—Expenditure on war, education, and the Civil List, compared with that of Great Britain—The national debt.

IT is hardly fair to dissect and criticise the national balance-sheet of a young State just on the threshold of its existence; but there are some points of interest in connection with the Budget of the Bulgarian Minister of Finance which throw light upon the condition of the country, and speak well for those who have the care of the public purse. In order that the reader may possess a thoroughly authentic statement of the finances of the country, I will attach to the end of this volume (see Appendix II.) an abstract of the financial statement for the year 1887, which M. Natchevitch, the Finance Minister, was so courteous as to make for me; and if the reader wishes to have the precise amount of any one item, he can easily convert the francs into pounds sterling at any exchange he thinks fit. At the rate of 25·10 francs, the two sides of the balance-sheet run up to close upon £1,890,000.[1] I take no notice of the small balance which stands to the debit, about £8500, because M. Natchevitch assured me that there will be in reality a surplus of nearly 800,000 francs. From this balance-sheet the reader will see that about 63 per cent. of the revenue is derived from direct, and 37 per cent. from indirect taxes, the latter consisting largely of excise and import duties on luxuries. The tendency of late years has been

---

[1] In Whitaker's Almanack the revenue for Eastern Roumelia alone in 1886 is stated to be £1,873,016 (at least, so it will be understood by any ordinary reader). This should, no doubt, be the amount for United Bulgaria. At any rate, it is incorrect as it stands.

to commute every kind of impost which has militated against industry into cash payments. Such of my readers as know anything, for example, of the system of levying what we should call "tithes in kind," as it was formerly practised in Bulgaria, and is still elsewhere in the East, will understand what I mean by saying that it often led to the destruction of whole crops of farm produce. This impost now takes its place upon the balance-sheet as "dimes" or tenths; and if (as the reader will see on calculating the amount) that tax yields about £645,000, a rough estimate may be made of the annual *rateable* value of the products of the soil in the whole country, which should be about £6,450,000. I say *rateable* value, because, no doubt, a considerable proportion of the actual products of the soil, such as the fruit, vegetables, &c., which are consumed by the peasantry, escape taxation altogether.[1]

It will be observed, too, as already stated, that there is a tax upon goats, sheep, and pigs, but not on horses and cattle, the object being to encourage breeding. Again, the item of road-tax, about £74,000, represents a very large amount of labour liberated for more useful purposes. Formerly the peasantry were compelled to give up a certain portion of their time for this work, but by an Act of the Sobranje in 1883 the labour was commuted for a cash payment. The roads in Bulgaria are in some places well maintained, but on the plains the driver often makes a detour to avoid them! They are there only excelled by the pavement in the towns.

There are some interesting items also on the other side of the account. Taking first the war expenditure, a comparison with our own outlay is not without interest. For the purpose of calculation, we will estimate the population of Great Britain roughly at 37,000,000, and that of Bulgaria at 3,000,000, and the expenditure for what ought to be defensive purposes in Great Britain at £39,000,000, and in Bulgaria at £720,000. This gives for Great Britain more than £1 per head of the population; for Bulgaria, 2s. 10d. per head. Of course there are many things to be considered. We have troops in various

---

[1] The crops are valued as they stand by special assessors.

parts of the world, and a powerful navy to maintain; on the other hand, the little State has to watch a very extended frontier, and to counteract the hostile action of the agents of a great military Power, which is constantly at work in her midst. With the above expenditure she supports a standing army and a reserve amounting together to 70,000 to 80,000 men of all arms; besides which, there would be a Landsturm of 20,000 to 30,000 in case of an invasion, making in all about 100,000 men.

Concerning education I have already said something. Looking at her recent emancipation and the influence still exercised by a conservative priesthood, I consider that the foundation of an excellent system of public instruction has already been laid. As the reader knows, attention is given, not only to the usual branches of education in which every citizen should be proficient, but special institutions are rising up for the industrial training of the artisans of her towns and the peasantry of her fields. She has as yet no university, but the instruction given in her "Gymnasia" is of the highest order. As our universities are to a large extent maintained without State aid, these need not be considered in comparing the cost of education in the two countries. Taking the same estimate of population, then, we expend on all agencies for instruction in education, science, and art, £5,200,000, or 2s. 10d. per head of the population; in Bulgaria the cost is £92,000, or 7d. per head. I am not giving these figures for any other purpose than to enable the reader to judge of the financial operations of the young State. In this country our war expenditure, roughly speaking, is between seven and eight times as much as that for educational purposes; in Bulgaria the proportions are as one to five.

In Bulgaria the members of the Sobranje are paid. There are 364 or 365 members of that body, who receive 15 francs per day during the session, and their expenses. The "Civil List," i.e., cost of maintaining the head of the State, is covered by 600,000 francs, or about £24,000; the total expense of the Crown and national representatives is about £60,000. In this country the annuities paid to the Royal Family amount to £543,000, and the national representatives work for nothing and pay their own expenses!

A word more and we have done with this dry subject. On the balance-sheet the reader will find the item of 2,239,898 francs (or about £89,200) interest on public debt ; but according to treaty stipulations, Eastern Roumelia (now South Bulgaria) ought to pay to the Porte an annual tribute, or, to speak more correctly, a proportion of the interest on the debt of the Empire, which amounts in English sterling to about £168,000. If this were paid, the interest on her public debt would be about £267,000. The interest and charges on our national debt at the time of the Revolution of 1688 were £39,835, and last year they amounted to £23,449,678.

Coupled with the stipulated payment to the Porte of the annual sum named above was the condition of the autonomy of Eastern Roumelia. Since then the inhabitants of that province have joined Bulgaria, with the consent of the Porte, and the Government of United Bulgaria has, I believe, recently offered to pay this tribute or annual subscription, contingent upon the recognition of her Prince, who has been " freely elected by the population," according to the same treaty as the one which stipulated for the payment of an annual tribute by Eastern Roumelia (the Treaty of Berlin). On this question more will be said when we come to consider the political problem ; but so far as the finances of Bulgaria are concerned, I believe all matters have been touched upon which will interest the general reader.

CHAPTER XXI.

THE TWO PRINCES, FERDINAND AND ALEXANDER.

The author's reasons for seeking interviews with the Princes—The interview with Prince Ferdinand—Interior of the Palace at Sofia—Objects of interest in the reception-saloons—A faithful follower—Prince Ferdinand—The author's reception—Conversation with the Prince—Fallacies concerning him—His policy in Bulgaria—Meeting with Prince Alexander in London—His presence and manner—Conversation with him—Cause of his abdication—His present views and intentions—Will not sanction "Battenberg party" in Bulgaria—His loyalty—Great abnegation and unselfish expression of feeling—Still devoted to Bulgaria.

SOME of my readers may wonder why I have associated under the same heading the Prince and ex-Prince of Bulgaria. As a matter of fact, their stations are not so far apart as at first sight appears. According to those who claim the right to decide—I mean the European Powers, parties to the Treaty of Berlin—Prince Ferdinand is not yet the rightful ruler of Bulgaria; and one of them, namely, Russia, declares that he never shall occupy that position. On that matter I hope to be permitted to say a few words hereafter. As regards Prince Alexander, as I have already said, I believe he is exercising a more powerful influence over the destinies of the young State than he is himself aware of, for I think the knowledge that he is still available is a very important factor in the calculations of cool-headed Russians as to what would be the result of a descent upon Bulgaria. Nay, I will go farther, and say that I believe it is largely owing to this contingency—the possibility of the "hero of Slivnitza" being in the saddle again—that Prince Ferdinand and his people have been so far left unmolested. Holding these views, and remembering the conspicuous part which both Princes have played in Bulgaria, it was natural

THE PALACE, SOFIA

that I should wish, if possible, to see and speak with them, so that I might be able to give my readers some personal impressions concerning them. As regards Prince Ferdinand, in asking for a meeting, I told two or three of the Ministers frankly what object I had in view, and there is therefore not the slightest breach of decorum in describing our interview. There was, I think, at first some little hesitation in the matter, for one of the Ministers told me he had expressed the opinion to his colleagues that "there could not possibly be any harm in his seeing me," and remembering that his Highness then occupied, as he still enjoys, the distinguished honour of being boycotted by every European Power, and that even our own diplomatic representative in Sofia could not approach him in his official capacity, it is not to be wondered at that he should have felt some little delicacy in receiving even a private individual whose object was to describe his person and attributes. The influential introductions to the Bulgarian Ministers of which I was the bearer, however, secured me the desired interview, and I received a letter through the customary channel (the Maréchal de la Cour), informing me that I should be received at 10 A.M. on the following day (the day previous to my departure from Sofia).

Of the external aspect of the palace, which was built by Prince Alexander, I have already spoken. It is a very handsome edifice, standing in a large garden, with flower-beds and fountains; is approached through a beautiful light portico (Plate VIII.), and presents a very imposing appearance as you enter the fine large hall, from which there rises a magnificent staircase. On my arrival, I was received with the utmost courtesy, and was conducted into an antechamber, which was beautifully furnished, and contained many objects of interest. Conspicuous amongst these was the handsome ceiling, carved in wood by a Bulgarian sculptor, in imitation of one in an old convent; hence the chamber is known as "the Bulgarian chamber." Upon the walls, besides other objects, there was a trophy of standards which had been carried by the militia (Landwehr) during the Russo-Turkish and Servian wars. Here I was requested to be seated for a while upon a lounge placed against the wall, Bulgarian fashion, nearly immediately underneath a portrait in oils of the Czar Alexander II., and I had a pleasant preliminary chat with an elderly good-natured aide-de-camp of the Prince, who had accompanied him from Vienna. He told me his Highness was having a lesson in Bulgarian, which I took to signify "he intends to stop;" but from what I could gather, he (the aide-de-camp) very much preferred life at Vienna to that at Sofia. No wonder! Presently I was ushered into the "audience-chamber," and finding no one there, I had an opportunity to take a rapid survey. The visitor is here at once attracted by two fine oil-paintings, representing scenes from the Russo-Turkish war—the fights at Genova and at Shipka, in which the Bulgarians took a prominent part. Whilst I was examining these, the door of an adjoining apartment opened, and the Prince entered, but at the first moment, although I had several times seen his photograph (Plate IX.), I did not recognise him. His face is not so broad as in his photograph; he has a Roman nose, and what I should call shrewd eyes. He is tall in stature, and, as far as I can remember, has a slight stoop. His dress, a military uniform, was decorated with two or three ̤ ̤ters. The impression he gave to me was that he is much older in mind than body. He *stood* on his dignity, and made me *stand* on mine—I mean, he did not offer me a seat.[1] His manner was intensely German; he might have been a German student; and the natural bent of his mind, I should say, is quite in the direction of study.

After saying inquiringly, "So you are come to study our country?" and receiving my thanks for giving me an opportunity of seeing him, he asked me how I found things in Sofia. He seemed pleased to hear me praise the Technical School at Kniajevo; and when I told him of the state of things in the prison, that the prisoners would gladly work, he said, "Aber sie haben uns ja anatomisirt!" ("Why, you have dissected us!"), adding, "For the moment, as you may imagine, I have more earnest things to think about, but later on I will look into it, and see what can be done."

---

[1] I was told by an Italian gentleman of good family, who had an interview with him on the same day, that he was similarly received.

He then spoke of his travelling experiences, and made inquiries about the road from Nisch to Sofia, and that led us to the question of Bulgarian railways. I told him that I believed when the railway was open from Belgrade to Constantinople it would be a grand thing for the country, as I thought no one would travel by Varna and the Black Sea if they could get into the Orient Express at Paris and leave it at Constantinople. He quite agreed with me; spoke of the bad landing at Varna, and said the temporary difficulty was money.[1] The subject of loans followed, as a matter of course, and I ventured to say that it would be a mistake for the Bulgarians, with their great internal resources, to depend upon foreign countries for loans of money, instancing the Porte, its position in Egypt, and its financial difficulties at home, as the results of such a policy.

Let me here say that during the whole of our interview not a word was mentioned of a political character; for, so far as I was concerned, it would have been most indelicate, looking at his position, to refer to politics; and he must have known, from the conversations I had with his Ministers, that he could learn nothing new from me. When, however, we spoke of the condition of Turkey, he smiled, and made a most peculiar gesture, which certainly appeared to me to have a political significance; but as his Highness is an obedient vassal of the Sultan, I may have misunderstood his meaning.

Returning to personal matters, he told me of his experience in the Balkan districts, with its disingenuous and warm-hearted peasantry; and added, that people said his ignorance of the language would prejudice him with the Bulgarians, but that he always found that a few sincere words went farther with them than long speeches. Sometimes he became very earnest and animated, and then he would suddenly burst into French (we had been speaking German; his mother is a Bourbon), which language he seemed to prefer. After we had chatted for a short time about his travels, and about scientific matters, he suddenly turned round, shook hands with me, saying, "Auf's

---

[1] I see he received the first engine in state which arrived at Sofia from Belgrade.

Wiedersehen" (Au revoir), and retiring through the door by which he had entered, he left me to find my way back to the place from whence I came.

Let me correct what I believe to be one or two misconceptions concerning the Prince, and express my views in regard to him with frankness. I know nothing of his military attainments; and, as far as I can learn, he possesses none. That he has great moral courage is clear from his presence in Sofia; and that he has physical courage also, *and tact*, is proved by the circumstance that he takes his walks abroad without any guard, and attended only by an aide-de-camp. Silly stories have been told about his childish fancies and his stilted manner. His childish tastes I believe to be love of study. He is not haughty nor stilted in his demeanour, but he is a great stickler for court ceremony, just as all the German princes are, especially those of the smaller States; and I am not sure that it won't stand him in better need with the Bulgarians than undue familiarity. He is believed by some to be very rich, by others this is said to be a mistake; but one thing is certain, he knows how to take advantage of the love of ostentation and State ceremonies which is entertained by the *democratic* Bulgarians; and his displays of wealth on great occasions are to them exceedingly impressive. I for one should not blame him in the least if he covered and hid every rouble he finds in Bulgaria under two thalers! His ability as a statesman can only be measured by his success in overcoming his external political difficulties; and, so far at least, that has not been conspicuous, but for the sake of his country, if for no other reason, every one must wish him a prosperous future. One thing is certain, if the Bulgarians are not united in their loyalty to him, they will not long retain—nor do they deserve to retain—their freedom.

Whilst I was at Sofia a great friend and admirer of Prince Alexander told me that I should have no difficulty in obtaining a friendly interview with him, and that I should find the contrast between him and Prince Ferdinand very interesting; and certainly it would be impossible to find two more distinct personalities than the two young princes, for the oldest, Alexander, is only just over thirty years of age.

PRINCE FERDINAND.

I wrote to him from Budapest, but only received his reply on my return home, as he had been absent from Darmstadt when my letter arrived, and in answer to my expressed wish to see him, he invited me to meet him at the Buckingham Palace Hotel on the 14th of September last, where, divested of all the insignia of rank, and dressed in a plain tweed suit, he received me on the appointed day. As the reader has doubtless often seen his portrait, and has again the opportunity of doing so here (Plate I.), there is no necessity to speak of his personal attractions: suffice it to say that he is handsome, frank, and genial. I spent over an hour and a half in his company, and there was hardly a subject connected with "Bulgaria, past and present," that was not, in its turn, the subject of conversation and discussion. He confirmed a great deal of the information which I had obtained during my visit to the country, and explained many things that were not clear to me. Our conversation was to a large extent private;[1] but since we had our interview I find that many observations which he made to me are identical with what he had already said to others in Sofia, and are contained in the dispatches to which reference has already been made. So candid and unreserved was he, that I did not hesitate to put questions to him, concerning matters of historical interest, which I should hardly have ventured to ask an intimate, personal friend.

He assured me that before he abdicated he had received a formal promise from the Russian Government that they would not attempt to interfere in the internal affairs of Bulgaria. Nekludoff, the Russian agent at Sofia, furthermore told him that if he left the country the cause of Russian enmity towards Bulgaria would be removed. These promises were not made by an agent only, whom his principals might repudiate, but by telegraph from St. Petersburg, and the message was read to him in the presence of his Ministers and advisers. He mentioned also that he was embarrassed by the interference of other European Powers. When he arrived at Sofia, the two chief traitors, Grueff and Bendereff, had been condemned to death, but he received messages from Vienna and Berlin saying that they must not be shot. As commander-in-chief of the army, he saw

---

[1] I have committed no breach of confidence in publishing it.

that if the officers were allowed to rebel with impunity, there would be an end of all discipline.

We had some conversation about the new Prince, with whom, however, he was better acquainted than I was, and the little that passed between us in regard to his position and prospects was of a private nature. I then ventured to ask him whether he thought he should ever go back to Bulgaria; and he said that, although it would be an indiscreet thing for him or any other public man to say what he might or might not do under unknown conditions, he had not at present the slightest intention to do so, nor to do anything that would unsettle affairs in Bulgaria, and that he had told his friends so. I then had no hesitation in telling him that whilst I was over there a warm friend of his, and an acquaintance of my own, had said that he ought to take that course; and I added, "I should like to be able to say that you are quite opposed to any movement on your behalf which would interfere with the tranquillity of Bulgaria." "Yes, certainly," he replied; "and I hope you will say that I have written to —— and ——, who were anxious to lead a Battenberg party, that I wish them to give their whole allegiance to their Prince; that I have been Prince of all Bulgaria, and don't wish to be the candidate of a party; that their country, not I, must be their first consideration; and I have received letters from them promising to follow my wishes."

I asked him whether it was true that he was at first a Russian partisan,[1] and he admitted that he was, giving me at the same time cogent reasons, with which the reader is well acquainted, why his sentiments towards the Russian Government had changed. "What *could* I do?" he asked me. "I had to choose between Bulgaria and Russia." When I inquired why he had wished to alter the Constitution, he said that the Ministers and he were constantly at cross-purposes at that time, and he had asked for exceptional powers for seven years to enable him to make headway in the government of the country. (As a matter of fact, Karaveloff and Zankoff, although professedly constitutional, were mere tools of Russia.)

---

[1] As I had stated in the preface to my "Roumania."

We conversed on many subjects that were of interest to me in connection with this work ; but what I should like to convey to the reader is the feeling of admiration that I experienced for his modesty and utter abnegation of self. He had nothing but the kindest expressions for the country, its people, and the friends he had left behind, although he made no attempt to gloss over abuses. Not a syllable of reproach for those who had maltreated him escaped from his lips throughout the whole conversation; indeed, in one or two instances, he mentioned things he had done to prevent the world from knowing his true feelings concerning them. He never spoke of the good he had done in the country, excepting in answer to my questions, and the subject that seemed always uppermost in his mind was the welfare of Bulgaria. Where he preferred silence it would not become me to speak. I told him that whatever the world might say to-day concerning the events of his reign, posterity would recognise the good he had done to his adopted country, and his answer was, "Well, that is the chief thing to be considered."

He spoke excellent English, although from time to time he used an occasional expression in German to give point to some observation ; and my only regret is that, instead of reading this tame and imperfect account of our interview, my readers cannot enjoy, as I did, the advantage of a friendly chat with the Prince himself on the affairs of his adopted country.

CHAPTER XXII.

THE EASTERN QUESTION AND BULGARIA.

The decline of the Ottoman Empire—Hallam's reflections—Its condition to-day—The "European concert" a discord—Its effect on the liberties of the Balkan States—Russia likened to an octopus—The Czar: his peace policy; his critical position—The war party and its aims—Why Russia does not occupy Bulgaria—What Russian "diplomacy" means—Turkey: her dependent condition and perplexities—Russian threats and temptations—Danger from Macedonia and Greece—Should ally herself with, and strengthen the Balkan States—Greece: her aspirations; enmity towards Bulgaria; illusions—Servia: Russian intrigues in; her disposition towards Bulgaria after the war; friendly relations to-day—A Danubian confederacy—Roumania: her position towards the Eastern question; too confident; a Danubian confederation needful for her safety—Austria-Hungary favourable to Bulgarian independence—Hungarian sympathy for Bulgaria; esteem for her statesmen—Germany: "is not primarily interested;" desires peace—Prince Bismarck's policy—The recent threat to attack Bulgaria—Germany, France, and Russia—France engrossed in her own affairs—Great Britain: before the cession of Cyprus, &c., and now; her sympathies for Eastern liberty platonic—What the Continental nations think and say concerning us—Why not express readiness to acknowledge Prince Ferdinand?—European diplomatists waiters upon Providence—A few words to Bulgarian statesmen: how to meet Russian enmity and intrigue—A "king" for Bulgaria in place of a Prince—Conclusion—"May God protect Bulgaria."

DIVINE prescience, and not human forecast, is needed to predict the ultimate issue of the conflict between the Crescent and the Cross, or perhaps it would be more correct to say, the precise conditions under which, in Europe, the Cross will displace the Crescent. To judge from past and passing events, it would seem natural enough to anticipate, as many statesmen and historians have done, the disappearance of Mohammedanism from this side of the Bosphorus, and indeed the dubious prophecies of some high authorities are the best guides of all to the probable future. Hallam, for example, was by no means sure of the complete downfall of the Ottoman power in Europe. Writing as recently as 1848,[1] he said: "The two monarchies which have successively held their seat in the city of Constantine may be contrasted in the circumstances of their decline. In the present day we anticipate, with an assurance that none can deem extravagant, the approaching subversion of the Ottoman power, but the signs of internal weakness have not yet been confirmed by the dismemberment of provinces; and the arch of dominion, that long since has seemed nodding to its fall, and totters at every blast of the North, still rests upon the landmarks of ancient conquest, and spans the ample regions from Bagdad to Belgrade. Far different were the events which preceded the dissolution of the Greek Empire. Every province was in turn subdued; every city opened her gates to the conqueror; the limbs were lopped off one by one; but the pulse still beat at the heart, and the majesty of the Roman name was ultimately confined to the walls of Constantinople."

What a strange and instructive picture the great historian has presented to us! What wonderful changes a few years have wrought, and what a lopping of limbs![2] It is true that in the modern phase of the struggle between the Cross and the Crescent the "conqueror" has gained little by his victories, but it has certainly not been for want of the will to profit by them, and all the same the arch that "spanned the ample regions from Bagdad to Belgrade" is fractured and "tottering" to its fall, and soon nothing will be left, as of old, excepting the keystone on the Bosphorus. Of the Turkish possessions in Europe, Servia and Roumania are independent kingdoms; Bosnia and Herzegovina have passed into Austrian hands; Bulgaria, whose Czars carried

---

[1] It would perhaps be more correct to say, "confirming in 1848 what he had written in 1818," before Servia had secured her autonomy. See his "Middle Ages," twelfth edition," p. 135, and dates of prefaces to the first and twelfth editions of his works, twelfth edition, pp. vi. and xi.

[2] During the present century Turkey has lost Greece (1829); Wallachia and Moldavia (1856); Servia (1829-78); Bulgaria, Montenegro, Bosnia, Herzegovina, Cyprus, the Dobrudscha, and territory in Asia Minor (1878); a great part of Thessaly and Epirus (1881); Eastern Roumelia (1878-85); and practically Egypt and its dependencies (1840-1885).

their victorious arms to the walls of Constantinople long before the period of which Hallam writes, is practically freed from Turkish rule, and has carried off with her another rich province of the empire, Eastern Roumelia; whilst the cement that still holds Macedonia is fast cracking in pieces. In the East, the armies of the Muscovite are inundating Asia Minor, and are steadily making their approaches to the ancient city, the "keystone" on the Bosphorus; and in Africa, Great Britain has the whole of Egypt and her dependencies in pawn for debts owing to her usurers!

But there is another and even a more remarkable contrast between the downfall of the Greek and Ottoman Empires; it is this: When the followers of Mahomet were extending their arms over the east of Europe, the Christian nations of the west, and of Europe generally, presented a united front against their advance. Now, the disunion and rivalries of the Christian Powers are not only the salvation of the remnants of Turkish rule in Europe, but they are actually necessary to protect the threatened liberties of those young Christian States which have been saved from the general wreck. It is to what Dr. Holland, with unconscious humour and irony, has called "the European concert on the Eastern Question" that Bulgaria, and probably the whole of the Balkan Peninsula, owes the retention of its recently acquired liberties. Was there ever a "concert" so void of harmony as this international performance? Let us for a few moments regard the "motives" and the instruments of the leading players, beginning with one more metaphor, and then bidding adieu to allegory.

The animal which Russia has adopted as her national device is said, not inaptly, to typify her national policy. The hug of the Russian bear is fatal to those whom she embraces, but that policy is, I think, better represented by the octopus. By turns she extends her arms in every direction in search of prey: now it is eastward, a little nearer to the Himalayas, and when she has laid fast hold of some new tract of country, she appears to be content and preaches peace; but soon another tentacle glides round into Asia Minor and fixes its suckers there; and should she put out one of her feelers too boldly or hastily into any of her neighbour's territories, and meet with an uncomfortable reception, she quickly withdraws it, says it was a mistake, and bides her time for another attempt: that is what she is doing all round at the present moment.

It is generally supposed that the will of the Czar is supreme in Russia, and that, for the present at least, he favours the policy of peace. That he should not be eager to go to war is only natural. What has he or his dynasty to gain by war, or by an extension of his already vast and unmanageable Empire? His grandfather went to war, was beaten, and—died suddenly; his father went to war, and on his return home was assassinated. As for himself, what are the conditions of his existence in time of peace? What would they be in time of war—of aggressive war, I mean—for so far no one has threatened "the integrity of the Russian Empire?" As the head of the State, his appearance in public should be more cordially welcomed than that of any of his subjects; but supposing only one half be true that reaches us through the sealed and guarded portals of his realm, he never goes from home without a whole army to protect him from the hostility of his own subjects; this in time of peace. But every class of society is more or less in revolt against the system which he represents, including even the army and the surroundings of the court; for who has not some near relative or friend pining away his life in Siberia? And if it be unsafe for him to move about in time of peace, still more dangerous would it be if his armies were engaged in aggressive warfare in some far distant land; that would indeed be the opportunity of Nihilism!

But admitting for the present his pacific tendencies, is he really the all-powerful autocrat the world believes him to be? There is a strong war party in Russia, the members of which, whilst they profess to desire the liberation of the Slave races, really aim at reducing them to slavery, and there are military adventurers anxious and ready to fight anyone and anywhere. It is immaterial to them whether their enemy be English, German, Bulgarian, or Turk (for the moment they are full of affection for the nation whose armies visited them at Moscow in 1813, at Sebastopol in 1855); for those men occupation must be found, and the "Autocrat of all the Russias" must find it. Well would it be for him if he could carry out the obligations imposed upon him by the venerated memory of his father, as he telegraphed to Prince Alexander—"the interests of Russia and the peace of the East." At present he sits with the sword of Damocles above, and a case of dynamite beneath his throne. Truly has it been said of him that "he represents the Nemesis of despotism!"

People sometimes ask, Why does not Russia "occupy" Bulgaria? The answer is not difficult to find. Some reasons have already been given. Her society is riddled with Nihilism, and at any time we may hear of a "1789." Again, she may be feared by some of the Powers, but not all stand in dread of her, and what might appear to be a simple operation at starting, would soon become too complex and formidable even for her army (vast and powerful as it undoubtedly is), when the extent of her frontier is borne in mind. And, moreover, although they occasionally make gross mistakes, her counsellors are shrewd and reflecting men. She did practically occupy Roumania, a province immediately bordering on her vast empire; but where is her influence in that country now? If she were permitted to overrun Bulgaria, which is highly improbable, what would be her position there? Servia in the west, backed up by Austria and Hungary; Roumania in the north, supported by Germany; Turkey in the south—all knowing full well that her occupation of Bulgaria would mean a standing threat to their existence as independent nations—all would be anxious to drive her out; and the Bulgarians themselves, who once welcomed her as a deliverer, would be burning for an opportunity to expel her as a conquering oppressor. These are a few of the reasons why Russia is not at present attempting to gain her ambitions ends by brute force. She now prefers "diplomacy." That is to say, trading upon the fears or on the corruption or ambition of other States. In order the better to understand how that is managed, we must turn for a moment to the condition and attitude of those nations as they regard the Eastern question.

Her greatest enemy, Turkey, through her unfortunate financial position and her habitual want of energy, is a fit object for Russian pressure and intrigue. She owes Russia a large sum of money which she cannot pay: Russia can at any moment threaten her with foreclosure. Turkey has not the same hold upon Bulgaria, which owes her a large annual sum as interest upon her proportion of the national debt; for the Bulgarians say, "Comply with the spirit of the Treaty of Berlin; leave us the free choice of our ruler, and we are prepared to pay you." Here again Russia steps in and says, "If you recognise the Prince, who is not acceptable to me" (no Prince excepting a "Prince of Mingrelia" would be acceptable to her), "I shall consider that you have violated the Treaty of Berlin, and my army in Asia Minor shall move westward" (not logical; but the wolf was not logical in its famous argument with the lamb).

On the other hand, Russia says, "If you like to take back Eastern Roumelia, of which those ungrateful Bulgarians have robbed you, I will back you up and will otherwise befriend you. In return, you must help to restore my 'just influence' in Bulgaria." Not being in the secrets of diplomatists, I don't know what cogent reasoning our able representative, Sir William White, has used to prevent the Sultan and his Ministers from accepting such tempting proposals; perhaps he has found a brief reference to the past relations between Russia and Turkey a sufficient warning. But there is another little-known circumstance, to which reference has already been made, that has an all-powerful influence on the councils of the Porte. The Macedonians are ripe for revolt, and, excepting in those districts which abut upon Greek and Austrian territory, they are eager to become part of Bulgaria. My frontispiece is significant of the relations between them. An attack upon South Bulgaria would mean a rising in Macedonia in the north-west, and, most probably, an aggressive movement on the part of Greece in the south. These complications would suit Russia admirably, for they would weaken Turkey, and, in some degree, justify her own interference in the affairs of the Balkan Peninsula. The policy of self-preservation on the part of Turkey is undoubtedly to strengthen, not to weaken, the Balkan States, for they present the last

European barrier against the inimical operations of her deadliest foe. As I have shown, Mussulmans and Christians live together in amity in Bulgaria; why not conclude a friendly alliance with that State, instead of helping Russia to keep open a permanent sore for the accomplishment of her designs on Constantinople?

The Greeks are at present the quasi-friends of Russia. They delude themselves with the notion that, somehow or other, they will be permitted to creep along the eastern shore of the Balkan Peninsula to found another Greek empire in Constantinople; or, failing that, that they would at least be considerable gainers by the partition of Turkey. So they are inimical to the Bulgarians, whom they regard as rivals for the possession of Constantinople, and, moreover, dislike as schismatics, and they would not object to see Russia in possession. If, however, Turkey should fall a prey to the great Northern Power, and Constantinople become her southern capital, there is little doubt that the Acropolis, with its sad records of ancient Hellenic grandeur, would soon be guarded by Cossack sentinels.

In Servia, where Russian intrigues have been active in high places, Muscovite influence will probably not be of long duration; and, so far as the feelings of the Servians themselves are concerned, these are likely to improve in friendliness towards the Bulgarians. After the abduction of Prince Alexander, and whilst they were still smarting under the defeat at Slivnitza, the disposition of the Servians towards their neighbours was at least doubtful; and it was well defined by a telegram which was sent to our Foreign Office by Mr. Barrington, our Minister at Belgrade:—

"Servian Government have been taken by surprise by Bulgarian revolution, and, frontier being strictly closed, little is known of its actual course. Journey of King, who was to have left Servia to-morrow, is abandoned. His Majesty's intentions appear, at any rate for the present, to be quiescent. Moreover, want of money makes any immediate action difficult"[1]

---

[1] Blue Book (Turkey), No. 1. 1887, Dispatch No. 152, p. 85.

The last two sentences are very significant. However, from my own observations during a short stay at Belgrade, I feel convinced that the more thoughtful of the Servian leaders are anxious to let bygones be bygones, to promote a close alliance with Bulgaria, and to found a confederation of the Danubian States.

Roumania, for the present, at least, considers herself safe from aggression, and prefers to mind her own business. In the recent speech from the throne,[1] the King announced that she had kept outside of all conflicts, and was friendly with all the Powers, notwithstanding the troubles arising from events which had occurred near the frontier during the last few years. But Roumania knows Russia well, and she must be aware that the occupation of Bulgaria would mean the possession of the whole Balkan Peninsula; in which case no consideration, not even consideration for her friend and ally of Grivitza, would admit of a small independent State in the heart of her empire. The "events of the last few years near her frontier" have been more momentous for Roumania than the words would imply, for her independence is intimately linked with that of Bulgaria; and no country would derive greater security than she would from a Danubian Confederation. If Bulgaria tides over her present difficulties, her position will, in my humble opinion, be far safer than that of Roumania, which the Russians would never for an instant hesitate to absorb (just as they snatched Bessarabia from her, in order to secure a better hold upon the Black Sea), and to make the Danube their southern boundary. In the present condition of European politics, an alliance, offensive and defensive, between Roumania and Bulgaria (even if no other State joined in it) would give to both complete immunity from external danger. Some unexpected event may possibly hasten such an alliance.

Austria-Hungary is very favourable to the maintenance of the independence of Bulgaria; and the sympathies of the latter State are so warmly enlisted in her favour, that if an open attack were made upon her either by Russia or Turkey, the

---

[1] November 27, 1887.

Imperial Government would probably be compelled to strike a blow in her defence. I was told at Sofia that Austria has of late relaxed her efforts to obtain possession of Salonika; that may be owing to the task she has on hand in Servia, or in Bosnia and Herzegovina, or it may be due to some other cause; but be that as it may, recent events have shown pretty plainly that neither Austria-Hungary nor Italy would look on complacently whilst Russia advanced another step in the direction of the Ægean Sea. From what I learned in Budapest, I am convinced that the sympathy of Hungary for Bulgaria is thoroughly real and disinterested; there they are watching events at Sofia very closely, admiring greatly the statesmanship of the young Bulgarian leaders; and I am persuaded that in any action on the Eastern question the cue would be given by the "King of Hungary" rather than by the "Emperor of Austria."

"Germany is not primarily interested in the events passing in Bulgaria, and its efforts will be reserved for the preservation of the peace."[1] Those were the words of the German Chancellor, and until recently they appear to have formed the basis of his action, even when, as it seems to me, he injudiciously interfered in the affair of the Bulgarian traitors and helped to drive Prince Alexander out of the country. Lately, however, in consequence of the unnatural Franco-Russian alliance, formed for purposes of revenge on the one side and of aggression on the other, the German Chancellor deemed it necessary to *kotoû* to Russia; for the threat to send ironclads to Varna in consequence of some petty slight which had been offered to one of her Consuls and the publication of an offensive paragraph in a Bulgarian paper, can have had no other signification.[2] The confusion which has arisen in French home politics has, however, changed the whole aspect of affairs, and although it is impossible to predict what will be the relations of France and Germany or of Germany and Russia six months hence, the

---

[1] Turkey, No. 1, 1887, Dispatch No. 232, p. 110.

[2] The whole thing was highly amusing, and that it should for a moment have been taken *au sérieux* by the smart statesmen at Sofia (as it certainly was) surpasses all belief. Germany asking permission of the Porte to allow her to send ironclads through the Dardanelles to chastise one of her vassals!

probabilities are that common sense and prudence will prevail ; that there will be no serious collision between any of the great Continental Powers ; and that, in case of threatened complications in the south-east of Europe, Prince Bismarck will still be able to assume the rôle of pacificator or arbitrator.

France is too completely absorbed in her own affairs to extend to Bulgaria the same generous aid and sympathy which she formerly gave to Roumania in her struggle for independence.

And as for Great Britain, she too, like Germany, "is not primarily interested in the events passing in Bulgaria." If those events had occurred before Cyprus was ceded to her, or before she had planted her foot in Egypt, we should have been busy seeking anti-Russian alliances; our press would have been bubbling over with denunciations of the "Colossus of the North;" India would have been in danger; the liberties of Europe threatened by a Tartar invasion; and the spirit of the whole nation would have been aroused. Having satisfied what appear to be our national requirements, we are consoling ourselves with the idea that we have learned wisdom from past experience, and that it is better that we should mind our own business, and let our love for liberty in future be platonic. I have sought to do justice to our statesmen of both parties and to our representatives abroad; but observation has shown me that even our moral influence has of late greatly fallen in European estimation, although we are still credited, as a nation, with a desire to foster liberty and afford relief to the oppressed. But people on the Continent with whom I discussed political questions fail to see upon what principle we have taken Cyprus and Burmah and occupied Egypt. Why, they asked, are we continually adding this or that colony to our vast empire, and are yet ready to fire up as soon as any neighbouring State seeks to extend the blessings of its civilisation to some distant barbarous tribe ? And they expressed still greater astonishment to see our wealthy and powerful country standing in such dread of Ireland ; to read of statesmen of the highest rank, even those professing to belong to the same side in politics, branding each other as traitors and abusing one another like pickpockets because they cannot agree as to the policy of granting autonomy to a sister kingdom which we ourselves admit has been suffering under centuries of wrong;[1] and all this after denouncing the spoliation of Poland, fighting for the "integrity of the Ottoman Empire," for the liberties of Greece and Roumania, after applauding the revolution in Italy and in Hungary, holding up to execration the Turkish atrocities in Bulgaria—in fact, after standing forth during this whole century as the champions of freedom in every part of the habitable globe. If any of my readers imagines that I am guilty of exaggeration in thus expounding European opinion concerning us, I would advise him to take a trip abroad and hear for himself. To despots and reactionary Governments this state of things is, of course, highly gratifying; but to those who are interested in constitutional government and popular liberty, the recent changes in our policy are looked upon with apprehension and regret. There is no need for war, nor even threats of war; but if, as I firmly believe, our Government and people desire to see the liberties of the Balkan States firmly established, our course is plain and straightforward. Has Prince Ferdinand been "freely elected by the population," according to the terms of the Treaty of Berlin? None but the Russians deny that he has been so chosen. Then why not at least express our readiness openly in the face of Europe to acknowledge his authority? Why treat with the Ministers who represent the people, and refuse to approach the Prince, who equally represents them? Is it out of deference for the helpless Sultan, whose unfortunate position prevents him from doing what is right and proper? or is it to conciliate Russia, who regards us as her bitterest foe, thwarting her designs, and meeting her face to face in every quarter of the globe?

This appears to me to be the "European concert on the Eastern question;" and whatever mistakes I may, through ignorance, have made in the endeavour to explain the policy and attitude of the "Powers," the reader may rest assured that, with

---

[1] When I was abroad, we had not yet begun to incarcerate our Lord Mayors and Members of Parliament.

their superior information, they are no better able than he or I to solve the problem. They are simply waiters upon Providence, each looking anxiously for the next move of his neighbour, and most of them guided largely by considerations of self, and, I regret to say, *not* largely by the dictates of international justice and human liberty. May this policy and attitude towards the young Principality soon give place to one more worthy of civilised Europe!

In conclusion, I should like to add a few remarks for the consideration of those who hold the reins in Bulgaria. They know better than I can tell them that disunion amongst themselves would be fatal to their liberties, and that their only hope is in loyalty and cohesion. I think, too, that they are finding out that wherever it is possible to leave traitors and intriguers to the judgment of public opinion, such a course is preferable to State prosecution. There is no disguising the fact that Russia is their great and only enemy, and the antidote to her enmity is that they should ally themselves as closely as possible with all or any of the neighbouring States, and conquer the goodwill of Europe by moderation; to cultivate the peaceful arts; to facilitate access to their country, especially from the Western States of Europe, and to show their fitness for self-government, as they have hitherto done with such marked success. Of course vigilance and forethought are equally necessary where secret agencies are constantly at work to undermine the liberties of the country. There is just one other consideration. Europe has so far declined to acknowledge their *Prince;* when it is prepared to do so, would it not be equally ready to acknowledge him as *King?* Would Alexander have been abducted if he had worn a crown? A wiser man than I has said—

> "There's such divinity doth hedge a king,
> That treason can but peep to what it would."[1]

Many persons think that Bulgaria would have acted more wisely if she had declared herself a Republic after the abdication of

---

[1] "Hamlet," Act iv., sc. u. 5.

Prince Alexander. That is too wide a subject to be discussed in these pages. But having elected so far to abide by the Treaty of Berlin, it seems to me that it might now be politic to give the highest possible status to her elected Prince.

"May God protect Bulgaria!"

APPENDICES.

APPENDIX I.

Estimated Budget of United Bulgaria for 1887.

Revenue.

Direct Taxes.

		Francs.
1.	Dimes (tithes on agricultural products, commuted)	16,200,000
2.	Land and house tax	4,500,000
3.	Licenses	2,000,000
4.	Taxes on sheep and goats	4,800,000
5.	Taxes on pigs	250,000
6.	Taxes on rents of houses and buildings	200,000
7.	Road-tax	1,857,508
	Total direct,	29,807,508

Indirect Taxes.

1.	Tobacco, excise and import	3,298,000
2.	Spirits	900,000
3.	Customs duties on imports	4,900,000
4.	Customs duties on exports	530,000
5.	Customs, sundries	1,078,000
6.	Revenue from woods and forests	680,000
7.	Government buildings (stores, &c.)	113,000
8.	Lignite mines	45,000
9.	Fisheries, &c.	300,000
10.	Government printing-offices	396,000
11.	Revenue from law tribunals	977,980
12.	Post and telegraphs	1,687,400
13.	Salt monopoly	1,500,000
14.	Sundries	360,018
15.	Occasional revenue	1,245,360
	Total revenue,	47,218,266
	Deficit balance,	219,168
		47,437,434
	or, roughly estimated,	£1,890,000

Expenditure.

	Ministries of—	Francs.
1.	*War*	18,207,349
2.	*Public Instruction*	2,314,335
3.	*Foreign Affairs* (including Public Worship, Post and Telegraphs)	3,768,862
4.	*Justice*	3,486,742
5.	*Interior*	6,742,480
6.	*Finance and Public Works*	9,148,676
7.	*Interest on public debt*	2,239,898
8.	Crown and National Representatives	1,529,092
	Total expenditure,	47,437,434

APPENDIX II.

THE MOST IMPORTANT DECREES OF THE CONSTITUTION OF BULGARIA.

Concerning the Principality: that its boundaries shall only be changed by the Great Sobranje (National Assembly); that it shall be divided into Prefectures, Sub-Prefectures, and Communes, of which the last named shall be autonomous (cap. i.).

Concerning the Prince: he shall be hereditary in the male line; his person is sacred and inviolate; in him vests the legislative power, conjointly with the National Assembly, the command of the national forces, the sanction and, jointly with the Ministers, the promulgation of the laws, the executive power, the right to pardon and commute the sentences of criminals (except Ministers violating the Constitution), the representation of the nation with Foreign Powers (cap. ii.). It fixes his salary (Civil List) at 600,000 francs (cap. viii.); recites the oath to be taken by him to preserve the Constitution (cap. vii.); decrees that every Prince after the first must belong to the State Church, which is the Oriental Church subject to the Synod (cap. ix.); and it provides for a Regency in case the Prince is a minor (cap. vi.).[1]

Concerning freedom of Worship: every religious denomination may be professed without disabilities (cap. ix.).

Concerning the Laws: decrees that all laws must be voted by the Assembly, or, should emergency necessitate the promulgation of a law by the Council of Ministers, then its confirmation by the Assembly.

Concerning Citizenship, Naturalisation, &c.: defines the conditions of both; abolishes class distinctions, titles of nobility, &c.; forbids slavery in any form, torture, domiciliary visits; makes military service compulsory; declares letters to be inviolate, primary education gratuitous, the press free, press offences subject to the courts, the right of assembly and association unrestricted, if in conformity with law and order; gives the right of petition (cap. xii.).

Concerning the National Representation: decrees two National Assemblies (Sobranjes), the Ordinary, and the Great or Extraordinary Parliament. The *Ordinary Assembly* consists of deputies of thirty years and over, able to read and write, one to be chosen from every 10,000 inhabitants of both sexes, for a term of three years, by citizens of twenty-one years and over, possessing civil rights. It is presided over by a President and Vice-Presidents, who, along with Ministers, may participate in its deliberations. Contains instructions as to convocation, procedure, powers and privileges of members, the Budget, State loans, &c. (cap. xiii.–xix.). The *Great or Extraordinary Assembly*[2] must be convoked to consider questions of territorial changes, revision of the Constitution, election of Regents, or of a new Prince, in case the reigning one dies without issue. It is composed of deputies, two for every 10,000 inhabitants, and may not consider the ordinary affairs of State (cap. xx.).

The Council of Ministers: its powers, duties, and responsibilities are defined by cap. xxi., and the *Revision of the Constitution* by cap. xxii.

The "Constitution" contains decrees on many other subjects of lesser importance, such as the residence of the Prince; the arms and colours of the Principality; State property; taxes; regulations for the introduction of laws, &c.; and the whole occupies 169 clauses. It was passed at Tirnova on the 16th–28th April 1879, the Assembly of Notables comprising 213 persons, by whose signatures it is attested.

---

[1] There does not appear to be a provision in any part of the Constitution for a Regency, or for any kind of Government in case of the abdication of the Prince.

[2] The Ordinary Assembly meets at Sofia, the Great one at Tirnova.

APPENDIX III.

Bibliography of Bulgaria.

Allard, C. "Souvenirs d'Orient : La Bulgarie Orientale." Paris, 1863.

Anonymous. " La Question Bulgare." Paris, 1861.

„ " La Vérité sur la Question Bulgare." Paris, 1861.

„ " Les Causes Occultes de la Question Bulgare." Paris, 1857.

Arril, Adolphe. " De la Bulgarie Chrétienne. Paris, 1863.

„ „ " Actes Relatifs a l'Eglise Bulgare." Paris, 1864.

Baker, Valentine. " War in Bulgaria." London, 1879.

Barkley, H. C. " Between the Danube and the Black Sea ; Five Years in Bulgaria." London, 1876.

„ „ " Bulgaria before the War." London, 1877.

Bath, Marquis of. " Observations on Bulgarian Affairs." London, 1880.

Blanqui, J. A. " Voyage en Bulgarie pendant l'Année 1841." Paris, 1843.

Bradaska. " Die Slaven in der Turkei." (Petermann's Mittheil., 1869, xii.).

Braybrooke, W. L. " Diary whilst in Bulgaria." London, 1855.

Browne, Ed. " Travels in Hungaria, Servia, Bulgaria," &c. London, 1885.

Chozko, Alex. " Études Bulgares." Paris, 1875.

" *Constitution de la Principauté de Bulgarie.*" Sofia, 1886.

Consular Reports: No. 1, 1886 (Bulgaria) ; No. 3, 1886 ; No. 70, 1886 (Turkey) ; No. 185, 1887 (Turkey). Eyre & Spottiswoode, &c. No. 237, 1887 (Bulgaria).

Czirbusz, G. " Die südungarischen Bulgaren." Wien, 1884.

Dozon, Auguste. " Les Chants Populaires Bulgares : Rapports sur une Mission Littéraire en Macédoine." Paris, 1874.

„ „ "Chansons Populaires Bulgares Inédites," publiées et traduites par A. D. Paris, 1875.

Drandar, A. G. " Cinq Ans de Règne de Prince Alexandre de Battenberg en Bulgarie." Paris, 1884.

Dumont, Alb. " Le Balkan et l'Adriatique : Les Bulgares et les Albanais." Paris, 1873.

Farley, J. L. " New Bulgaria." London, 1880.

APPENDIX III.

Fisch, M. M. "Co-operation de l'Armée Roumaine en Bulgarie." Bruxelles, 1879.

Forsyth, Wm. "The Slavonic Provinces South of the Danube." London, 1876.

Fresne, Charles du. "Historia Regnorum Dalmatiæ, Croatiæ, Serviæ, Bulgariæ, &c." Pasonii, 1746.

Gladstone, W. E. "Bulgarian Horrors." London, 1876.

Gopčević, S. "Die Ursachen der serbisch-bulgarischen Erhebung." Wien, 1878.

„ „ "Bulgarien und Ostrumelien, mit besonderer Berücksichtigung des Zeitraumes von 1878–1886, nebst militärischer Würdegung des Serbo-Bulgarischen Krieges." Leipzig, 1886.

Hammer-Purgstall. "Geschichte des Osmanischen Reiches." Hartleben: Pesth, 1834–36.

Hinze, H. "Gurko und Suleiman Pascha: Die Operationen in Bulgarien." Berlin, 1880.

Holland. "The European Concert on the Eastern Question." Oxford: Clarendon Press, 1885.

Huhn, A. von. "The Struggle of the Bulgarians for National Independence under Prince Alexander." Translated from the German. London, 1886.

„ „ "The Kidnapping of Prince Alexander of Pattenberg." 1887.

Hungerbuehler, H. "Die schweizerische Militarmission nach dem Serbisch-bulgarischen Kriegsschauplatze: Aus dem Berichte an den schweizerischen Bundesrat." Frauenfeld, 1886.

Jackson, J. "Journey from India towards England in the Year 1797, by a Route Overland through Bulgaria, Wallachia, &c." London, 1799.

Jireček, C. J. "Geschichte der Bulgaren." Prag, 1876. Von Tempsky.

"Journey into the Balkan in 1847." (Journal of the Royal Geographical Society, 1854.)

Kanitz, F. "Donau-Bulgarien und der Balkan." Leipzig, 1875.

Kiss, K. "Hunyadi János Utolsó Hadjárata Bolgár és Szerborszaghban 1454." Pest, 1857.

Koch, Adolf. "Fürst Alexander von Bulgarien. Mittheilungen aus seinem Leben und seiner Regierung nach persönlichen Erinnerungen." Darmstadt, 1887.

Kohn-Abrest, F. "Zig-zags en Bulgarie." Paris, 1879.

Krek. "Einleitung in die Slavische Literaturgeschichte." Graz, 1887. Leuschner & Lubensky.

"Krieg, der serbisch-bulgarische v. 1885: Eine militarische Studie von einem deutschen Offizier." Darmstadt, 1887.

Laveleye, Emile de. "La Peninsule des Balkans." Tom. ii. Bruxelles, 1886.

Leach, H. "A Bit of Bulgaria." London, 1877.
Leger, Louis. "La Bulgarie à la Fin du xviiie Siècle." Paris, 1883.
Leger, Louis. "La Save, le Danube, et le Balkan." Paris, 1884.
„   „   "La Bulgarie." Paris, 1885.
Lejean. "Ethnographie de la Turquie d'Europe." 1861.
Lescœur, R. P. "Du Retour des Bulgares au Catholicisme." Paris, 1860.
Lonlay, D. de. "En Bulgarie, 1877–1878." Paris, 1883.
Mantegazza, Vico. "Due mesi in Bulgaria, Ottobre e Novembre 1886." Milano, 1887.
Minchin, J. G. C. "Bulgaria since the War in 1879." London, 1880.
„   „   "The Growth of Freedom in the Balkan Peninsula." London, 1886.
Moltke, Baron von. "The Russians in Bulgaria in 1828–29." London, 1854.
More, R. J. "Under the Balkans." London, 1877.
Paton, A. A. "Bulgarian, Turk, and German." London, 1855.
Poyet, C. F. "La Bulgarie dans le Présent et l'Avenir." Paris, 1860.
Safarik. "Gesammelte Werke." (Böhmen.)
St. Clair and *Brophy*. "A Residence in Bulgaria." London, 1869.
„   „   "Twelve Years' Study of the Eastern Question in Bulgaria." London, 1877.
Sax, E. "Skizze von Bulgarien." Wien, 1869.
Spencer, E. "Travels through Bulgaria." London, 1851.
"*Statistique de la Principauté de Bulgarie*." Sofia, 1884 and 1887.
Toula, F. "Geology of the Balkans." (German.) Neues Jahrb., Heft i., pp. 44, 45.
Turgenev, Ivan. "Un Bulgare." 10th edit. Paris, 1886.
Turkey, No. 1, 1887 (Blue Book.)
Verkovitch. Et. J. "Le Vedu Slave: Chants Populaires des Bulgares." Paris, 1875.
Vretos, A. P. "La Bulgarie Ancienne et Moderne." Paris, 1856.
Zinkeisen. "Geschichte des Osmanischen Reiches."

APPENDIX IV.

Whilst the preceding pages are passing through the press, the author has received from Sir Thomas Sanderson (Foreign Office, to whom he is indebted for several printed reports, &c.),

CONSULAR REPORT No. 237, BULGARIA (1887),

by Mr. O'Connor (Mr. Hardinge, Second Secretary), Sofia, October 15, 1887, the following extracts from which will be interesting to British readers:—

"The accompanying tables, which have been supplied by the Bulgarian Government, showing the imports and exports of the Principality for the years 1885 and 1886, contain information of considerable interest, although, from the manner in which these statistics have of necessity been compiled, owing to the course of late political events, it would be difficult to base upon them with any precision considerations relating to the commercial prosperity of Bulgaria, and her commerce with other countries."

EXTRACT FROM TABLES.

	1885.	1886.
British imports	frs. 11,129,008 or £445,160	frs. 15,829,805 or £663,192
Total imports .	frs. 38,843,517 or £1,553,740	frs. 61,687,169 or £2,467,486
Percentage of total .	28·6	25·6

(The figures for 1886 include both Bulgarias (North and South), and for 1885, North Bulgaria, and South only to November.)

IMPORTS AND EXPORTS FROM AND TO AUSTRIA-HUNGARY AND GREAT BRITAIN.

	1885.		1886.	
	Imports.	Exports.	Imports.	Exports.
Austria .	£411,362	£36,614	£659,263	£97,380
Great Britain .	445,160	491,106	663,192	183,427

The most important on the list in 1886 is Turkey, from which country the imports in 1886 amounted to about £516,000; the exports to about £670,000; the exports to Great Britain in that year being exceptionally low. After Turkey, the figures rarely exceed £100,000 for any other country.

"The opening up of the country by the promised railways is one more reason for urging the establishment of depots in the different commercial centres. British manufactures, of superior quality to the Austrian wares now scattered broadcast throughout the country by Austrian commercial travellers, could then be retailed to purchasers who, by being able to see and handle the goods in the depot, would in a very short time learn to distinguish a good from an inferior article, and to recognise the advantage of buying goods of superior quality, even at slightly higher prices. Such a scheme, if properly carried out, would possess possibilities of immense extension, and might be the means of largely increasing British commerce in the Balkan Peninsula. To secure these results enterprise on a solid basis is necessary, coupled with good management and intelligent watching of the development of the needs of a population which, however backward, is now gradually awakening to Western ideas, and to the need of Western civilisation."

. . . .

"The principal British imports are metals in the rough, rough copper and tin, iron bars and girders, tin-plates, &c. In proportion as the country becomes opened up by increased facilities of communication, there will no doubt be a gradually increasing demand for articles pertaining to this industry, and especially for all implements and machinery connected with agriculture; this is a subject to which attention should be paid by the iron industry in Great Britain."

The above extracts, as the reader will notice, completely confirm the statements in the text, that little reliance can be placed at present on values and statistics, and the author's advice that wholesale houses in Great Britain should send out pioneers, and that agricultural implement makers and persons in the iron trades should be watchful of the course of events in Bulgaria.

INDEX.

INDEX.

A.

ABDUCTION of Prince Alexander, 91–101; a national disgrace, 94.
Adrian, Pope, sends an archbishop to the Bulgarians, 28.
Agricultural colleges, 163, 164.
Agriculture, state of, among the Slaves, 15; present state of, in Bulgaria, 170, 171; resources for, 195.
Aleko Pasha, first Governor-General of Eastern Roumelia, 8; ambition of, 80.
Alexander of Battenberg elected Prince of Bulgaria, 8; manifests an independent spirit, 8; in disfavour with and thwarted by Russia, 9; is nominated Governor-General of South Bulgaria by the Porte, 9; concentrates his army on the Turkish frontier, 9; reorganises his army and marches against the Servians, 10; defeats the Servians, 10; makes peace under Austrian influence, 10; is compelled to abdicate by certain traitors in the army, 11; summoned to return, 11; is welcomed back, 11; sends a submissive telegram to the Czar, 11; is apprised that he had better withdraw from Bulgaria, as he was personally obnoxious to the Czar, 12; he finally abdicates on assurance from Russia that she would not interfere with affairs of Bulgaria, 12; the hero of a hundred biographies, 76; summary of his achievements as a ruler, 76; his antecedents and relationships, 76; election and accession of, to the throne of Bulgaria, 77; demands and obtains new powers from the Sobranje, 78; is compelled by Russia to relinquish them and adhere to the constitution, 78; attempt to kidnap, 79; and the revolt in Eastern Roumelia, 81; boycotted by the Great Powers, 83; reorganises the army, 83; in command of army against Servia, 86; bravery of, 87; successes of, against Servia, 87–89; compelled by Austria to stay his arms against Servia, 89; ignored by Russia, 92; abduction of, 92, 93; confiding character of, 94; manner of his enforcement, 95, 96; is forced to sign his abdication, 96; is delivered over to the Russians and set free, 97; is recalled by the nation, 97; confers with his brother Louis, 98; arrives at Rustchuk on his return, 100; sends a humiliating telegram to the Czar, 100; his return a triumph, and its course, 101; finds the disaffection of military too formidable and the traitors protected by Russia, 101; is admonished by Russian agents that his presence in Bulgaria is undesirable, 102; he abdicates on condition that liberty be granted to the Bulgarians to manage their own affairs, 102; nominates a Ministry, 102; issues a proclamation and departs, 102; returns to private life, 162; what he did for Bulgaria, 102; influence of, at present, in Bulgaria, 202; author's meeting with, 207; his personal attractions, 207; his frankness, 207; confirms the author's account of events, 207; his discretion, 208; political relations, 207; his modesty, self-denial, and generosity, 209; author's appreciation of the interview, 209.
Alexander II. of Russia, liberator of Bulgaria, 9, 65; desire to free the Sclavonic races of Turkey, 67; his respectful treatment of Bulgaria, 78.

Alexander III. of Russia, disaffection towards, in Bulgaria, 9; withdraws the Russian officers from the Bulgarian army, 9; hostility to Prince Alexander, 78, 92; his pledge to the Porte, 93; his reply to the telegram of Prince Alexander, 100; his peace policy, 213; his critical position, 213, 214.
Alexius III., 43.
Alexius Comnenos persecutes the Bogomiles, 32.
"Alliance, Kalojan's," 45.
Almanack, Whitaker's, referred to, 198.
Alphabet, the Kyrillic, 27.
Amsel. *See* Kosovo pole.
Amusements, 131.
Animals, domestic, 166, 167.
Aprilov, patriotism of, 63; the founder of the gymnasium at Gabrovo, 162, 163.
Arabas described, 167.
Arcadian experience, 153.
Arches, triumphal, 168.
Art, architectural, under Simeon, 36; at Tirnova, 179-182.
Asen, the brothers, uncertainty regarding their number and names, 6, 42; the two most famous, 41; visit Constantinople and are insulted, 41.
Asen I., founder of Asenide dynasty, 6; chosen leader against the Greeks and proclaimed "Czar of the Bulgarians and Greeks," 42; various fortunes in his struggles with the Greeks, 42; defeats the Greek army, but is assassinated, 42.
Asen II., 6; his fame, 46; dethrones Boril and succeeds as Czar, 46; his reign, 47; testimony to, of a Bulgarian monk, 48; reintroduces the Greek faith, 48; his capital, 48; constantly making and breaking alliances, 52; contributes to fall of Frankish rule in Constantinople, 52; his death, 52; effects of his reign, 52; possessions of, melt away, 53.
Asparich, a chief of the Bulgari, 23.
Athanasoff, Professor, 123.
Atrocities, Bulgarian, the exposure of, 7; extent and object of, 66; the English press and, 66; avenged, 66.
Austria instigates Servia to attack Bulgaria, and compels Bulgaria to a peace, 10, 89; trade of, with Bulgaria, 193.
Austria-Hungary, trade of, with Bulgaria, 192; and Bulgaria, 217; favourable to Bulgarian independence, 217.

B.

BAJAZET I., his victory at Kosovo pole, 55; celebrates it at Adrianople, 55; is repulsed from Wallachia, 55.
Baldwin of Flanders, Emperor of the Franks, 45; defeated and captured at Adrianople, 46; uncertain fate of, 46.
Baldwin's Tower, 34, 46, 49, 177.
Balkan Peninsula, early dominant races in, 4; invaded by the Turks, 7.
Balkans, the, as formerly and now, and the plains adjoining, 14, 111; aspect of, 112; slopes of, scenery and roads, trees and fruits, 165, 166.
Barrington, Mr., telegram from, to Foreign Office, 216.
Basilius II., the Greek Emperor, conquers and annexes Bulgaria, 5; his character and habits, 38; persistency and final success, 39; his cruelty, 39; celebrates the conquest of Bulgaria, 39.
Basilius, the Bogomile martyr, 32.
Begs, the Turkish, in Bulgaria, tyranny and cruelty of, 58.
Belogradčik, Grad at, 17.
Bendereff, Captain, 87.
Bendereff and Grueff, leaders of a plot against Prince Alexander, 10; their crime condoned at the instance of Germany, Austria, and Russia, 11, 101, 207; arrest of, 98.

INDEX.

Berlin, Treaty of, 7 ; stipulations of, as regards Bulgaria, 71, 72.
Besika Bay, our fleet at, 66.
Bessarabia given up by Roumania to Russia, 69.
Bibliography of Bulgaria, 227–229.
Bismarck, Prince, his remark on the reign of Prince Alexander, 102 ; his policy, 218, 219.
Bogomiles, the, a heretical sect, origin and name matter of uncertainty, 30 ; character of their doctrines, 30 ; influence with the masses, 30 ; articles of faith, 31 ; their leading tenet dualistic, 31 ; their religious practices, 31 ; degrees of sanctity among, 32 ; persecution of, by the orthodox, 32.
Boris I., 24, 26 ; his conversion to Christianity, 27 ; examination of his motives, 27 ; assumes the name of Michael on his baptism, after that of the Greek Emperor, Michael III., his godfather, 27, 28 ; his reward and consequent zeal, 28 ; the Boyards rebel against, and are crushed, 28 ; seeks alliance with the Pope, 28 ; evil effects of his oscillations between Greece and Rome, 30 ; abdicates and becomes a monk, 33 ; leaves his monastery to crown Simeon, and returns to his retreat, 33.
Boris II., defeated and captured by Sviatoslav, 5 ; compelled to abdicate and become a magnate at Byzantine Court, 38 ; references to him by Pope Innocent III., 44 ; Kalojan imitates his policy, 45.
Boril, the usurper, 46.
Bourgas, rising at, 103, 104 ; trade at, 191.
Bouza, a drink, 144.
Boyards, the, 50.
Bresnik taken by Captain Panoff, 88.
"Brigand Brigade," 89.
Brigandage, 137, 138, 185.
Bucharest, 187.
Budget, the last, 198 ; of United Bulgaria, 225.
Bulgari, the, origin and first appearance of, in the Balkan Peninsula, 4 ; political ascendancy, 5 ; origin uncertain, but distinct from that of the Slaves, 23 ; mythical tradition regarding ancestry of, 23 ; a warlike tribe of nomads, 24 ; their food, 24 ; shave their heads, 25 ; their standards, 25 ; military rules and practices, 25 ; ratification of treaties, 25 ; cruel customs, 25 ; treatment of criminals, 25 ; polygamists, 26 ; absolute power of the chief, 26.
Bulgaria (geographically), its area, 111 ; its divisions, 111 ; mountain ranges and their aspects, 111, 112 ; sudden transition from plain to mountain, 112 ; great part at one time under sea, 112 ; peculiarity of the plains, 113 ; soil, 113 ; rivers, 114 ; bridges, 114 ; towns, 114, 115 ; roads, 114 ; railways, 115.
Bulgaria (historically), present population, 4 ; early attempts to conquer, 5 ; first Russian invasion, 5 ; part of the Greek empire, 6 ; revolt under the brothers Asen, 6 ; under Servian domination, 6 ; tributary to Turkey, 7 ; completely subject to Turkey after battle of Kosovo pole, 7 ; after Crimean war, 7 ; delivered by Russia, 7 ; under Treaty of Berlin, 8 ; accepts Alexander of Battenberg as its first hereditary prince, 8 ; receives a constitution, 8 ; a crisis in her history, 10 ; hardly any mendicants in. 19 ; gets Bibles and other sacred books, 30 ; two faiths in, the Mohammedan and the Christian, 32, 33 ; annexed to the Greek empire by Zimisces and Basilius II., 38 ; the inhabitants of, 40 ; under Greek rule, 40, 41 ; inroads of barbarians, 41 ; under Asen II., 49, 50 ; in the succeeding reigns, 52 ; falls under Servian rule, 53 ; under Mussulman rule, 55–58 ; for three centuries and a half afterwards has no history, 57 ; records of, destroyed and name changed, 57 ; a Turkish province, 57 ; under Turkish rulers, 57 ; condition after Crimean war, 63 ; allowed to have an Exarch of her own choosing, 63 ; regarded as schismatic by the Greeks, 63 ; aids the Russians against the Turks, 69, 70 ; during Russo-Turkish war, 70 ; under treaties of San Stefano and Berlin, 71, 72 ; limits, and rights as regards Prince defined, 71, 72 ; is to have a constitution and religious equality among citizens, 72 ; humiliating treatment of, by Russia after Russo-Turkish war, 77 ; different

treatment of, by the late and the present Czars of Russia, 78 ; concludes a peace with Servia, 97 ; anti-Russian feeling in, 104 ; good feeling of, towards Servia, 107 ; the present Czar's opinion of, 128 ; agricultural, 188, 194.

Bulgarian army, organisation of, under Russian control, 73 ; reorganisation and strength under Prince Alexander, 84 ; present strength and cost of, 200.

Bulgarian billiards, 131.

Bulgarian history, its records under Greek and Turkish rule, 7.

Bulgarian Legion at Eski Zagra and the Shipka Pass, 70.

Bulgarian peasantry during Russo-Turkish war, 69.

Bulgarians throw off the Greek yoke, 6 ; bravely defend themselves against the Turks, 7 ; succumb to the Turks, 7 ; mostly Slaves, 21 ; question the Pope, 28 ; the masses under Simeon, 37 ; elect Peter Asen Czar, 42 ; achieve their independence with difficulty, 42 ; defeat and rout the Greek army under Isaac, 42 ; indebtedness to the Roumanians for their freedom, 68 ; retaliatory act of, on Turks, 70 ; treated as rebels by the Turks during Russo-Turkish war, 70 ; enthusiasm of, against Servia, 85, 86.

Bulgarias, the two, union of, 81, 82 ; union facilitated by Great Britain, 82 ; union consummated, 90.

"Bulgar-slayer," the, 39.

C.

Captives in war, ancient cruel treatment of, 39.

Caravans, 167.

Chadourne, M., obligations to, 132.

Charles, Prince, of Roumania, 68.

Christianity in Bulgaria persecuted by Omortag, 24.

Christians, defeat by the Turks at Kosovo pole, 55 ; at Nicopolis, 56 ; friendly relations of, with Mohammedans in Bulgaria, 64, 178, 216.

Church, desire for a national, 63.

Clement, Bishop, 11.

Clergy, the Bulgarian, 60, 61.

Concert, European, a discord, 212.

Confederation, a Danubian, desirableness of, 217.

Conference at Constantinople, 82 ; advice of, to the Porte to occupy Eastern Roumelia, 82.

Conspirators, the conduct of, in the case of Prince Alexander, 95, 96 ; denounced as traitors, 97 ; are arrested, 98.

Constantine and his brother Methodios, 26 ; becomes missionary first to the tribes on the Don and Dnieper, and then to the Slaves, 26 ; his labours appreciated, 26 ; adopts the name Kyril, 26 ; translates the Gospels, &c., into the Slave language, 27 ; dies at forty-two, 27 ; Methodios and his works, 27.

Constitution, Bulgarian, its democratic character, 76 ; framed by Russia, 76, 77 ; decrees of, 226.

Constitution, the Tirnova, office of, attacked, 134.

Consuls in Bulgaria, 50 ; murder of German and French, at Salonica, 66.

Cotton-planting, 195.

Court, the, in the time of John Asen, 51.

Crimean war, effects of, on Roumania and Bulgaria, 7, 68.

Criminals, their treatment, 119, 120.

Crops, rotation of, 170.

Crusade, Fourth, Crusaders of, Kalojan seeks alliance with, 45.

Couza, Prince of Roumania, his deposition a model to Prince Alexander's conspirators, 96.

Czar, the. *See* Alexander III.

Czarinas of Bulgaria, 51.

D.

DACIA, Roman and Greek rule in, 4; overrun by Goths and Huns, 4.
Daily News war-correspondence referred to, 69, 70.
Dandolo takes Constantinople, 45.
Danube regiment, daring and successful assault by, on the Servians, 87.
Danube, the beautiful, 187.
Debt, national, 201.
Demetrius, St., Church of, at Tirnova, 41; political meeting in, 41, 42; described, 181.
"Demonstration," a political, 131-134.
Derjavnii Vestnik, the, 135.
Despot, the, 51.
Dimitrieff, Captain, 95.
Diplomatists, European, 220, 221.
Dispatches referred to, 93, 94, 95, 96, 97, 98, 99, 101, 102, 103, 104, 105, 107, 216, 218.
"Djumi-Maritza," the, 87.
Dobrudscha, the, given up to Roumania, 69; a barrier between Russia and Bulgaria, 69.
Docetism, 31.
Dolgorouki, Prince, projected mission to Bulgaria, 100.
Dondukoff-Korsakoff, Prince, gives Bulgaria a constitution, 77; his popularity in Bulgaria, 77.
Drenovo, description of, 165; its khan, 165; its butter, 165.
Drigalsky Pasha, arrest and subsequent liberation of, 80.
Dualism in religious belief among the Bulgarians, 31.
Dushan, the Servian, 6; his name invoked by the Servians, 6; extends his realm, 53; assumes title of "Czar and Autocrat," 53; prosperity of Servia under, 53.

E.

EAGLE, the newspaper, 135.
Eagles in Bulgaria, 159, 196.
"Ecole Technique" at Kniajevo, 122; its superintendent and teaching staff, 123; its appurtenances, 123; cost of the institution, 123.
Education, revival of national, in Bulgaria, 63; a first effort, 63; technical, 122; as witnessed at Gabrovo, 162; agricultural, theological, and other, 163, 164; compulsory, 164; a good foundation laid, 200; expenditure on, 200.
Ehrnroth, General, mission of, 12; forces Roumania to yield, 69.
English traders and manufacturers, advice to, 193.
Eski Zagra, 70, 71.
Etapes, Turkish, 141, 142.
Euthemius, the Patriarch, stays the fury of the Turks, 55; driven from Tirnova, 55.
Exarch, the highest ecclesiastic, 35; choice of an, by the Bulgarians themselves, 63.
Expenditure compared with Great Britain, 199, 200, 225.
Exports, 189, 190, 230.

F.

FAUCHER'S, Julius, "Systems of Land-Tenure," referred to, 16.
Ferdinand, Prince, and Russia, 12; is elected to succeed and succeeds Alexander, 12, 105; election not yet assented to by the Porte and ratified by the Powers, 12, 105; addresses a mob, 134; how regarded, 202; favours the author with an interview, 203; his palace at Sofia and the audience-chamber, 203; his appearance and manner, 204; a vassal of the Sultan, 205; his opinion of the people, 205; his preference for the French language, 205; author's estimate of, 206.

Fish and fishing, 196, 197.
France engrossed at present in her own affairs, 219.

G.

GABROVO, its population, 160 ; its bridges, 160 ; streets and houses, 160 ; spinning women, 160 ; visit to its gymnasium, 160 ; ignorance of candidates for admission to it, 161 ; second visit to it, 161, 162 ; education at it representative, 162 ; report regarding gymnasium, 163 ; departure from the town, 164.
Game and love of the chase in Bulgaria, 195 197.
Gavril Pasha, 8 ; ignominious deposition of, 80.
Gens-d'armes, mounted, 185, 186.
Germany seeks to preserve peace, 218.
Giers, M. de, representative of Russia, 81.
Gipsies in the East, 19, 185.
Girls, treatment of, by Turkish officials, 58.
Gladstone, Mr., exposes the Bulgarian atrocities, 7 ; effects of his pamphlet, 65–67 ; demands autonomy for Bulgaria, 66 ; his advice, 67 ; his motive as regards Bulgaria, 106.
Gourko, General, assisted by a Bulgarian legion, 70 ; retreat of, 71.
"Government, Provisional," dissolved, 11 ; arranged by Zankoff, 88 ; collapse of, formed by the conspirators against Prince Alexander, 97.
Grad, the, or fortified home, 16 ; an appellation of places, 17 ; usual site of, 17 ; examples of, 17.
Graves, Turkish, 141.
Great Britain, facilitates the union of the two Bulgarias, 82 ; and the cause of freedom in Bulgaria, 98, 99 ; sympathy with Bulgaria, 99 ; part played by, in recent Bulgarian troubles, 105 107 ; holds Egypt in pawn, 212 ; her love for liberty platonic, 219 ; Continental opinion of, 219 ; her duty, 106, 220.
Greek Empire, decline of power of, 39 ; its restoration, 52.
Greeks in Bulgaria, 49 ; the present quasi-friends of Russia and their motives, 216.
Grueff holds a revolver at Prince Alexander's face, 96 ; his conduct afterwards, 97. *See* Bendereff.
Gutscheff, Captain, 87.

H.

HAIDUTS, band of, as executioners of justice, 61.
Hallam referred to, 45, 47, 52, 54, 211.
"Hissar," hill of the, in Tirnova, 55, 176, 178.
Holland's "European Concert" referred to, 8, 71, 169.
Hospitals, 129, 130.
Hotel bills, two, 140.
Huhn, Von, his account of Drigalsky Pasha's arrest, 80 ; defence of Prince Alexander, 81 ; on reorganisation of Bulgarian army, 84 ; on battle of Slivnitza 86–88.
Hungary, sympathy of, with Bulgaria, 218.

I.

IDDESLEIGH's, Earl of, dispatch, 92 ; telegram from, urging the Porte to recall Prince Alexander, 98 ; his motive in his action towards Bulgaria, 106 ; his reply to M. de Staal, 107.
Imports, 189 ; from Austria-Hungary, 191 ; from Great Britain, 191.
Innocent III., Pope, requires the submission of Kalojan, 43 ; reminds him of his obligations, 44 ; sends a Nuncio with powers, 44 ; admonishes the Bulgarians of their past infidelity to the Church, 44.

Inns, roadside, 138, 139.
Insolence, case of Turkish, 58, 59.
Insurance in Bulgaria, 195.
Isaac, the Greek Emperor, attempts to attack Bulgaria, but is defeated, and is glad to escape with his life, 42.
Isker, the, 114.
Italians referred to, 50, 130, 211.
Ivajlo, career of, 53.
Ivanko, the murderer of Peter Asen, 42, 43 ; takes refuge among the Kumani, 43.

J.

JANTRA, the river, 114.
Jews in Bulgaria, 47 ; Spanish, in Sofia, and their unfair treatment, 124 ; engaged in trade, and extortionate, 124 ; Austrian, as traders, 192.
Jireček referred to, 16, 30, 39, 42, 45, 54.
Johannitz. *See* Kalojan.
John of Ryl, patron saint of Bulgaria, 36.
Jones, Captain, his advice on the side of loyalty and freedom, 106 ; his trade reports, 192.
Judges, the, 121.

K.

KALIMAN II., the last of the Asenidæ, 53.
Kaliman, Asen II.'s son, 52.
Kalofer, visit to, 155, 156.
Kalojan wages a successful war against Alexius III., 43 ; the two most important events of his reign, 43 ; extends the boundaries of the Bulgarian realm, 43 ; seeks the sanction of the Pope, 43 ; is thwarted, 43 ; receives a Papal envoy, who claims his subjection to the Papal Chair, 43 ; expresses his loyalty to the Church and requests the Pope to send him a crown, 44 ; receives spiritual benefit, but no crown, 44 ; seeks in vain alliance of Fourth Crusaders, 45 ; submits to the Apostolic Chair, 45 ; his motives in doing so, 45 ; now receives a crown, 45 ; troubles himself little further with the Pope, 48 ; allies himself with the Greeks against Baldwin, 46 ; routs the Franks under the Count of Blois, 46 ; assassination, 46.
Kanitz, the archæologist, referred to, 37, 45.
Karaveloff, one of the Regents, 12, 102 ; a leading Minister of Prince Alexander, 78, 79, 101 ; represents Russia in Bulgaria, 127 ; demonstration against, 132 ; characterises Prince Ferdinand as a usurper, 132 ; indignation meeting against, 133 ; his house and printing-offices wrecked, 134.
Kaulbars, General, his tour through Bulgaria, 12 ; his mission announced in the *Journal de St. Petersburg*, 99 ; sent to advise the Bulgarians, 103 ; his demands and their enforcement, 103 ; cannot prevent the elections, 103 ; encourages rioting, 103 ; stumps the country, 103 ; his tour a failure, 103 ; is recalled, 104 ; makes charges against the Bulgarians which he declines to substantiate, 104.
Kezanlik occupied by the Russians, 71 ; manufactures at, 114 ; roses and otto of roses, 156.
Khans, the, 138, 139 ; one at Biela, 139.
Kosovo pole, the battle of, 7, 55.
Krek referred to, 5, 6, 39.
Krum, chief of the Bulgari, captures and kills Nicephoros, the Greek Emperor, 23 ; defeats Michael, his successor, and makes him pay tribute, 23 ; career cut short by apoplexy, 24.
Kumani, the, 41, 42.
Kuvrat, ancient conquering chief of the Bulgari, 23.
Kyrill. *See* Constantine.

INDEX.

Kyriak, St., the monastery of, situation and surroundings, 149; aspect of, 150, 151; the building itself and conveniences, 151; a sanatorium, 151, 152; an incident at, 152; arrival of a pilgrimage at, 152, 153.

L.

LAND-tenure among the Slaves, 16; in Bulgaria, 168, 169.
Lascelles, Mr., supports Prince Alexander, 10; his interest in Bulgaria, 106; refuses to acknowledge the military leadership of Grueff, 106.
Latin Emperors of Constantinople, 17 (note).
Leo, Cardinal, bears a crown to Kalojan, 45.
Leo, the Greek Emperor, invades Bulgaria, 24; makes peace with Omortag, 24; calls in the Magyars against Simeon, 35.
List, civil, 200.

M.

MACEDONIA threatens to rise in revolt, 215.
Magyars, the, lay waste Bulgaria, 35; are pursued and decimated by Simeon, 35.
Manuel, Bishop of Adrianople, martyred by Omortag, 24.
Manufactures, state of, 188; imports of British, in Bulgaria, 193.
Marinoff, Lieutenant, draws his sword in defence of Prince Alexander, 79.
Maritza, the, 114.
Marriages, court, under Asen II., 51.
Martyrs, Church of the Forty, 47; memorial of Asen II. in, 47, 179; history of, 178.
Matincheff, Dr., his devotion to the Jews in Sofia, 124.
Medical men in Bulgaria, 129; staff, 129; council in Sofia, 129.
Mendicancy, absence of, in Bulgaria, 19.
"Mera," the, among the Slaves, 16; among the Bulgarians, 168, 169.
Methodios translates Old Testament into the Slave language, 21; his influence and that of his brother, 27. *See* Constantine.
Michael, Asen II.'s son, 52.
Michael of Bydn, career of, 53.
Michael Palaeologos, 52.
Milan, King, refuses to negotiate with Bulgaria, 83; invades Bulgaria, 85; proposes an armistice with a view to peace, 89.
Minchin, J. A. C., "Growth of Freedom in Balkan Peninsula" referred to, 79.
Mineral wealth, state of, 188.
Mingrelia, Prince of, proposed candidature of, its failure, 12, 105.
Mircea, Voivode, repels Bajazet I., 55, 56.
Moesia, 3.
Monasteries under Asen II., 51.
Monks, the, keep alive the religious spirit in Bulgaria, 36.
Montenegrins, armed, 103.
Morier, Sir Robert, telegram from, to Earl of Iddesleigh, 99; represents to Russia the feelings of Great Britain in regard to Bulgaria, 106.
Mountaineers, the, their independence and brigandage, 61; Robin Hood life, 61.
Mountains in Bulgaria, 111.
Murad I., Sultan, subjugates Bulgaria, 7, 55.
Mussulman faith and rule established in Bulgaria, 55.
Mutkuroff, Lieutenant-Colonel, disarms the traitorous soldiers, 11; nominated one of three Regents after Alexander's abdication, 12, 94; heads a movement for Prince Alexander's recall, 97; marches into Sofia and arrests the conspirators, 98; notice of, 126.

N.

NAMES of places in Bulgaria, both Roman and Sclavonic, 20.
Narodne Sosnanje, the, 135.

Natchevitch, 94; sketch of, 126.
Nationalities on the Danube, 40.
Neander's "Church History" referred to, 28, 29, 30.
Nekludow, M., electioneering ardour of, 103.
Neofyt Rylski, educational zeal of, 162; his directorate of school at Gabrovo, 63.
Newspapers, 135.
Nicholas I., Pope, promises to send bishops to the Bulgarians, 28; is questioned by the Bulgarians, 28; sends answers, 28, 29.
Nicopolis, battle of, 56.
Nikeforoff, Captain, Prince Alexander's Minister of War, 83; appointed to Regency, 102.
Nikephoros Phokas, the Greek Emperor, attempts to conquer Bulgaria, 5; is slain by Krum of the Bulgari, and his skull made into a goblet, 23.
Nikolaieff, Major, agitates for union with Bulgaria, 79; deposes and arrests Gavril Pasha, 80; 94.
Nobleman, young, his brutality and its punishment, 61.
Novichan, 141, 142.

O.

OFFICER, young Russian, his insolent treatment of the Bulgarians, 78.
Officials, court, and their titles, under Asen II., 51.
Omortag, chief of the Bulgari, makes peace with the Emperor Leo, developes the resources of the country, persecutes the Christians, and builds palaces, 24.
Osman Pasha, defence of Plevna, 71; capitulation, 71.
Osman Pasvanoglu, career of, 61, 62.
Ottoman power, the occupation by, of Bulgaria, how achieved and its duration, 7; its appearance in Bulgaria, 53; decline of, 211; Hallam's reflections on, 211; present condition of, 211; its dismemberment, 211, 212.
Oxen, draught, 168.

P.

PAISIUS, effect of his history in fostering a national spirit, 63.
Palaces, ruins of, under first and second empires, 36, 37, 177, 178.
"Pandora's Box," a, 77.
Panitza, Captain, exploits of, 89.
Panoff, Captain, 87; takes Bresnik, 88; 94.
Paprika, 166.
Passports, 137.
Patriarch, a, desired by the Bulgarians, but refused, 28, 30; still refused, 35; independent election of, 42.
Peasant proprietary, establishment of, 169.
Peasantry, Bulgarian, 167, 170; migrations of, 169.
Perfecti, or perfect ones, among the Bogomiles, 32.
Peter, Czar, 36, 38.
Phaeton, a, 136.
Phanar, 59.
Phanariote clerics, their fanaticism, 7; their standing, and moral and general character, 59, 60; unscrupulousness, immorality, and tyranny, 60; fate of, sealed, 63.
Philippopolis taken by Sviatoslav, 5; falls to the Turkish arms, 7; hospitality at, 18; scene of a successful revolt without bloodshed, 81; excitement in, on advance of the Servians, 85; its situation, 114; its situation and population, 142; streets and houses, 142, 143; market, 143; hotels, 143; food industries, 144; various costumes, 144; Turkish women in, 144, 145; absence of beggars, 145; places of interest in, 145; the Prefecture, its garden and produce, 145; gymnasium for boys, 145; the instruction, apparatus, library, museum, coins, 145, 146; the girls' Lycée, 147, 148.

Pirot, 10; taken by the Bulgarians, 89.
Plevna, siege of, 7, 68, 71.
Plovdiv, the, 135.
Popoff, Major, marches into Sofia, 97.
Porte, the, the policy and action of, which provoked war with Russia, 68; inaction in regard to Eastern Roumelia, 82.
Powers, the, and the union of North and South Bulgaria, 9–10; and the election of Prince Ferdinand, 12; and the risings of 1875–77, 65; boycott Alexander and Ferdinand, 85; their present attitude, 212–221.
Preslava, Great, palace at, 36.
Prints, wall, and their political lesson, 183.

Q.

QUESTIONS, one hundred and six, sent by the Bulgarians to the Pope, and the Pope's answers, 28, 29.

R.

RACES fusion of, on both sides of Danube, 40.
Radoslavoff, M., account of, 127.
Ragusa, trade with, 50; merchants of, 50.
Railways in Bulgaria, 115.
Regency, the, 102–107; its firmness, moderation, and good sense, 104.
Religious rites among the Slaves, 20.
Reports, consular, 189, 231.
Revenue, 225.
Richards, Vice-Consul, on English imports, 193.
Risings in 1875–77, and the Powers of Europe, 65.
Rivers of Bulgaria, 114.
Roman, brother of Boris II., emasculated, 38.
Roumania, more under Russian than under Turkish rule, 62; joins Russia against the Porte, 68; her present position, 217.
"Roumania," references to, 5, 22, 28, 35, 39, 51, 55, 59, 62, 68, 96, 169, 196, 208.
Roumanians, the origin of, 40.
Roumelia, Eastern, under Treaty of Berlin, 8, 73; unites to Bulgaria under the name of South Bulgaria, 9; its boundaries defined, 73; movement in, for union with Bulgaria, 79; the agitation for union breaks into a revolt, 79; liberated from Turkish rule by success of the revolt, 81.
Roumelia, its governors, 57.
Russia comes to the relief of Bulgaria, 7; seeks to create a "Great Bulgaria," 9; tampers with the North Bulgarian army, 9; opposes the union of North and South Bulgaria, and the nomination of Prince Alexander as Governor-General of latter, 9; instigates a conspiracy against Prince Alexander, 10; purpose of, in 1875, 66; policy of, not always visible, 67; general opinion of her affection for Bulgaria and the Bulgarians, 67; declares war against the Porte, 1877, 68; blunders of, in its treatment of the Bulgarian people after their liberation, 78; recalls her officers in the Bulgarian army, and the impolicy of this, 83; refuses to allow Prince Alexander's name to appear in the union treaty, 90; plots to get rid of Prince Alexander, 92; approaches of, 212; policy of, likened to an octopus, 212; war party in, 213; present policy of, 214.
Russian invasion, first, its supposed results, 5.
Russo-Turkish war, events of, 71; result to Bulgaria, 71.
Rustchuk, journey to, passing notice of, 187.
Ryl, the monastery of, 36.

S.

"Sage femme," the, 129.
Samuel Shishman, his collision with Basilius II., 38; heroism and temporary success of, 38; dies of a broken heart, 39.
Sanitation, 130.
San Stefano, Treaty of, 7, 9, 68; important stipulation of, 71.
Saxons in Bulgaria, 49.
Schuyler, Mr., and Bulgarian atrocities, 66.
Schumla, 114.
School, first Bulgarian, opened, 63.
Sclavonians. *See* Slaves.
Sects, introduction of, into Bulgaria, 30; their chief opponents, 36.
Serfs in Bulgaria, 50.
Servia under Dushan, sovereign in the Peninsula, 6; declares war against and attacks Bulgaria, 9; is defeated and courts alliance, 10; unsuccessful attack on, by Michael of Bydn, 53; war of, with Turkey, 66; declares war against Bulgaria, 83; army of, enters Bulgaria, 85; concludes a peace with Bulgaria, 89; good feeling of, towards Bulgaria, 107.
Servians, the, bravery of, at Slivnitza, 87; first defeat of, 87, 88; defeat at Vidin, 89; defeat by Captain Panitza, 89; driven back into their territory, 89; present feelings of, 216–217.
Sevastocrator, the, 51.
Shipka Pass, defence of, 7; Bulgarian peasant boys at, 69, 70; walk over, 156, 157; memorials of the fight, 157; imposing obelisk, 157, 158; view from, 159; summit and descent, 159.
Shishman, Czar John, surrenders to Turkey, 7.
Sigismund of Hungary, defeat of, by the Turks, 56; his escape, 57.
Simeon, Czar, 5, 33; one of the heroes of the Bulgarians, 34; military exploits of, 35; cruel treatment of his Greek captives, 35; pursues and decimates the Magyars, 35; makes peace with Leo, 35; extends the limits of Bulgaria, assuming the title of "Czar of the Bulgarians and Autocrat of Greece," 35; appoints a "Patriarch" of his own, 35; prosperity of the country under him, 36; his residence, its magnificence, 36.
Sismans, the, 38.
Slaves or Sclavonians, their settlement in North Bulgaria and its historical importance, 4; their ethnological relations, 15; first settlements, 15; first appearance in the West, 15; originally pastoral, afterwards agricultural, 15; their objects of culture and manner of cultivation, 15, 16; their domestic animals, clothing, fabrics, and ornaments, 16; communism among, as regards land-tenure, 16; social polity, 16; aristocracy of, 17; National Council of, 17; underground treasures, 18; physical and moral character, 18; hospitality, 18; reckon poverty a disgrace, 19; women among, 19; conduct of, in war, 19; subaqueous retreats, 19; humanity in war, 20; medium of exchange among, 20; religion of, 20; constitute the majority of the inhabitants of Bulgaria, 21.
Slaves in Bulgaria, 50.
Sliven or Slivno, manufactures of, 114.
Slivnitza, 71; march of Bulgarian army to, 86; battle of, 86, 89.
Slivovitza, courage-inspiring, 186.
Sobranje, the, elects Ferdinand of Saxe-Coburg to succeed Alexander, 12; consent to Prince Alexander's demand for new power, 78; hall of, at Tirnova, 175; its members paid, 200.
Sofia, panics in, on the Servian invasion, 85–88; its situation, 114–116; population of and divisions, 117; new city, 117; old town and its features, 117, 118; chief interest of the inhabitants, 118; places of interest, 118; the prison and the criminals, 118–120; police in, 121; the courts, 121; the judges, 121; printing-offices, 124; the people of, 124; working classes in, 130; house-rent and living in, 130; working hours, 131; amusements in, 131.

Stambouloff, Premier of Bulgaria, 11 ; one of the Regents, 12, 94, 102 ; heads a movement for Alexander's recall, 97 ; sketch of, 125, 126 ; harangues a mob, 134.
Stanimaka, a Greek town, 153.
Statesmen, living Bulgarian, account of the, 125–128 ; peculiarity of, 128 ; a few words to, 221.
Stephen Uros, the Servian, 53.
Stoiloff, 94 ; sketch of, 126.
Stoyanoff, 94.
Stranski, Dr., agitator for union of Eastern Roumelia with Bulgaria, 79 ; account of, 127.
"Strategus," the, under the Greek rule, 41.
Struma regiment, the, 94 ; conduct of, 95.
Suleiman Pasha at the Shipka Pass, 71.
Sviatoslav, the Northman, overruns Bulgaria, 5 ; his victories and fate, 5.
Svoboda, or *La Liberté*, official journal of the Government, 135.

T.

TARTARS appear on the Danube and are resisted, 53.
Taxes in Bulgaria under Turkish rule, 57 ; at present, and the levying of, 199.
Thrace, its extent, 3 ; early inhabitants and conquest, 3.
Tirnova, grad at, 17 ; hospitality at, 18 ; seat of government, 37 ; under reign of Asen II., 48 ; its ruins, 49 ; siege and sack of, by the Turks, 55 ; banishment of its chief citizens, 55 ; occupied by the Russians, 71 ; its situation, 114 ; first glimpse of, 172 ; situation and aspect, 173 ; the town itself disappointing, 174 ; courtesy of the Prefect, M. Bondareff, and Professor Guincholf, 174 ; the "Bella Bona" and other hotels, 174, 175, 184 ; the hall of the Sobranje, 175 ; its irregular plan, 175, 176 ; the Trapezitz and Hissar, 176, 178 ; the Rocher Coupé, 176, 177 ; Baldwin's Tower, 177 ; traces of palaces, 177 ; Church of the Forty Martyrs, 178, 179 ; Roman column with inscription by Asen II., 179 ; metropolitan church and its antiquities, 179, 181 ; Church of St. Demeter, 181, 182 ; Sunday in, 184.
Tory Government and risings in 1875, 66 ; policy, 67.
Towns, rise of, 50.
Trade, inland, under Asen II., 49, 50 ; present state of, 188–197 ; carrying, 191, 192.
Trapezitz, the hill of, in Tirnova, 155, 176, 178.
Travelling, 136–141 ; cost of, 138.
Treaty with Michael Asen, 50.
Tumuli or burial-mounds, 113.
Turkish rule in Bulgaria, 54–61 ; after Crimean war, 63.
Turkey, her present dependent state and perplexities, 215 ; threatened and tempted by Russia, 215 ; threatened revolt against, of Macedonia, 215.
Turks, the, subjugate Bulgaria, 7 ; their cruelties to the Bulgarian Christians, 7 ; invited into Europe by the Greeks, 54 ; settle near Constantinople, 54 ; take Adrianople, 54 ; overrun and subdue most of Bulgaria, Albania, and Thrace, 55 ; defeat the Christians at Kosovo pole and Nicopolis, 55, 56 ; rule firmly established, 57.

V.

VANDALISM of the Phanariotes, 7, 180, 181.
Varna, Russian war-vessels at, 103 ; their recall, 104 ; trade of, 191.
Venetians, the, 50.
Vitosch, Mount, 116.
Vodina, the Greek village of, its miraculous spring and distillation, 150 ; suspicious character of the population, 150.

W.

WAGES, 130.
Waldemar, Prince, declines the crown of Bulgaria, 105.
Wallachia, once incorporated with Bulgaria, 6; its divisions as known to Greek writers, 40.
Wallacho-Bulgarian Empire, 6.
Wallachs, the, 40; in Bulgaria, 49.
Wedding, a Bulgarian, 181.
White, Sir William, supports Prince Alexander, 10, 82; interest in Bulgaria, 106, 215.
Women among the Slaves in Bulgaria, 19; Turkish, 144, 145.
Working-classes, 130-132.

Z.

ZALLONY, Marc, referred to, 198.
Zankoff, Dragan, 11; a leading Minister of Prince Alexander, 78; overhasty dispositions, 88; an exile in Constantinople, 127.
Zimisces, the Greek usurper, 5; annexes Bulgaria to the Greek Empire, 38.
Zinkeisen, referred to, 60.
Zivkoff, 94; account of, 126.
Zupa, the, among the Slaves, 16; chiefs of, 17.